UNKNOWN MONGOLIA

A Record of travel and Exploration in North-West Mongolia and Dzungaria

UNKNOWN MONGOLIA

A Record of travel and Exploration in North-West Mongolia and Dzungaria

BY

DOUGLAS CARRUTHERS

GOLD MEDALLIST OF THE ROYAL GEOGRAPHICAL SOCIETY

WITH THREE CHAPTERS ON SPORT BY

J. H. MILLER, F.Z.S.

AND A FOREWORD BY THE RIGHT HON. EARL CURZON OF KEDLESTON G.C.S.I. ETC.

WITH 168 ILLUSTRATIONS, PANORAMAS AND DIAGRAMS, AND 6 MAPS

VOL. I.

SECOND EDITION

GYAN

Published by

Gyan Publishing House
5, Ansari Road
Daryaganj, New Delhi-110002
Phone: 011-47034999, 9811692060
E-mail: books@gyanbooks.com

Distribution Network
gyanbooks.com
India, USA, Canada, UK, Australia, France

ISBN : 978-81-212-4634-7 (Set)
ISBN : 978-81-212-5019-1 (PB)
First Published, 1914

2nd Impression 2020

Printed at: Gyan Press, Delhi.

The book at your disposal is the edition of an old book originally published long back. The Text quality of this book may not be at par as compared to our other books but many readers approached us to reprint this important book so that it could satiate their hunger. We request all the readers of this book to help us to improve its quality by providing the necessary text of those pages which are not properly visible. Your valuable support in this case will be highly appreciated and acknowledged and our future readers will be benefitted immensely.

UNKNOWN MONGOLIA

A Record of Travel and Exploration in North-West Mongolia and Dzungaria

BY

DOUGLAS CARRUTHERS

GOLD MEDALLIST OF THE ROYAL GEOGRAPHICAL SOCIETY

WITH THREE CHAPTERS ON SPORT

BY

J. H. MILLER, F.Z.S.

AND A FOREWORD BY

THE RIGHT HON. EARL CURZON OF KEDLESTON
G.C.S.I., Etc.

WITH 168 ILLUSTRATIONS, PANORAMAS AND DIAGRAMS, AND 6 MAPS

VOL. I.

SECOND EDITION.

LONDON

HUTCHINSON & CO.

PATERNOSTER ROW

1914

AN URIANKHAI OF THE UPPER YENISEI BASIN.

FOREWORD

THE writer of this book, turning aside from the more familiar pathways of recent travel and reverting to the taste of an earlier generation, has selected a little-known portion of Central Asia as the scene of the explorations herein described. If a point be taken on or about the 45th parallel of latitude midway between the Caspian and the Sea of Japan, we shall approximately strike the region which he traversed, surveyed, and mapped, with the patience and thoroughness of the true geographer, during the years 1910 and 1911.

The regions in question are bounded by the Siberian dominions of Russia on the north; they include the little-known basin of the Upper Yenisei River, which our author explored and describes with genuine enthusiasm; they embrace successively the habitat of the Western Mongolian tribes and the plains of Dzungaria, and they are closed on the south by the long palisade of Tian Shan or Celestial Mountains. On the east they are shut off from the world and from the rest of China by the vast blank of the Gobi desert; on the west are the settled conquests of Russian Turkestan.

The great interest of the regions thus bordered lies in the fact that they constitute the Marches between rival races, creeds, and political powers. Here we see the Russian colonist, eager and competitive, pushing forward from Siberia into a land rich with minerals, fish, and furs, and serenely conscious that the future is his. We see the Mongolian tribesmen, heirs of a mighty past, long withered under the blighting influence of degenerate Lamaism, but now turning to the risen Sun of Russia to find a warmth and a protection which Chinese suzerainty has failed to give them. We see, on the plains of Dzungaria, the easternmost outposts of Islam, Turki tribes that still turn towards Mecca, and present a romantic and virile picture, not unlike that which in many a tract of Central Asia must have greeted the eyes of Marco Polo. We see China, at once, in movement and in decay, exhibiting in the provinces, known as the New Dominion, signs of considerable vigour and activity, elsewhere atrophied and effete. The question which Mr. Carruthers continuously poses and indeed lies in the background of all his investigation and reflections is: with whom does the future of these mysterious regions rest, which have played so great a part in the history of the world, and which seem once more destined to have a future? To those who read between the lines of this book, there will occur but one answer.

Our traveller is of the type of geographer which has been evolved by prolonged experience and research. He does *not* set forth in the spirit of dare-devil and unscientific adventure, with few resources but his own courage, to face unknown risks, and to survive incredible dangers—which was characteristic of the Central Asian explorer of the first half of the last century. Thoroughly familiar with the writings of all his European predecessors (and they have been but few) in the regions which he proposes to visit, a trained surveyor, accompanied by competent companions, equipped with the means of investigating and collecting the flora and fauna, the geology and zoology of the country, and marching at leisure with a carefully organized caravan, he sets before himself the ambition of making a definite and valuable contribution to the sum-total of human knowledge, and of writing a book that will long remain a classic on its subject. How well he has succeeded may be shown by the fact that in 1912 he received for these journeys and his account of them the Gold Medal of the Royal Geographical Society.

Those who depict Central Asia to themselves as a land of limitless desert, ribbed by occasional and mighty ranges, and characterized by general desolation, will perhaps be surprised, as they follow the writer, even within the compass of the explorations which he here records; at one time into a country of jungle and swamps, infested by insects, at others into primeval forests, again on to bowery meadows and grassy uplands, or again amid crags and glaciers and moraines. Sometimes he is floating in rafts or boats on the broad lakes, or paddling a canoe on clear rivers; he rides alternately the camel, pony, and ass, or is bumped about in a Chinese cart or a Russian tarantass; now we see him sleeping in grim and dirty caravanserais—the skeletons of an almost immemorial past; again he is the guest of nomad khans, hunting with golden eagles and falcons, and living in richly-embroidered huts of felt.

In the course of these varied experiences hardships are encountered, disappointments occur, and an inexhaustible patience is required. But our author is of the true fibre of the Asiatic traveller, and it may safely be wagered that this book describes the two happiest years of his life.

While these volumes present the broad picture and subserve the general purpose to which I have referred, there are chapters in them which merit special attention. Such, are the careful and scholarly account of the indigenous tribe of the Uriankhai, living in seclusion on the Siberian frontier with their herds of domesticated reindeer, which they drive and ride, and milk and occasionally eat; the chapter on the Mongols, which condenses in a succinct and picturesque form the history of that extraordinary people, who once planted sovereigns on the throne of Pekin, overran and nearly conquered Europe, created an amazing but ephemeral empire that stretched from France to Cathay, bequeathed to India the Mongol dynasty which has left so deep a mark on its architecture and history, and threw up the portentous figure of Jenghis Khan, who was probably responsible for more bloodshed than any human being that has ever lived, and is still appropriately revered as a deity among the Mongolian tribes; the very different picture of the Kirei Kirghiz, who also produced a medieval hero in the person of the semi-historical, semi-mythical Prester John, and who, while owning allegiance partly to Russia and partly to Pekin, still pay spiritual homage to Stamboul; the account of the little independent Mohammedan Khanate of Hami or Kumul on the western confines of the Gobi desert; and the description of an interesting tour of exploration in the Karlik Tagh. It may be added that Mr. Carruthers is the master of a very clear, agreeable, and scholarly style. His name is a worthy addition to the sparse list of English explorers in these parts of Central Asia that contains the names of

Younghusband, Ney Elias, and Stein, and even in the company of the illustrious Russians,—Prjevalsky, Kozloff, Potanin, Severtzoff, and others, whose pioneer labours, spread over a long term of years, have conferred such incomparable advantages upon their own country,—it will be held deserving of honour.

PREFACE

THE purpose of these volumes is to place on record an account of certain regions of Upper Asia, hitherto left undescribed. The narrative of the journey is interwoven with an account of geographical exploration, with a broad outline of the history, and with a description of the races and the physical features of the land as a whole. The scope of the work is set forth at length in the Introduction.

The difficulty of combining scientific observations, and a descriptive account of a particular region, with the story of our own experiences has led to the elimination of technicalities, except where absolutely necessary ; the scientific results of the expedition being published separately in journals especially devoted to such subjects.

It should be noted that this expedition was entirely a private undertaking, an original idea, carried out by individual effort. My own special thanks, and the thanks of all geographers, are due in the first place to my companions—Mr. J. H. Miller and Mr. M. P. Price, who liberally subscribed to the funds necessary for the carrying out of such an enterprise, and on whose never-failing energy and keenness the success of the expedition largely depended. My account of the expedition and its work has been supplemented by three chapters written by Miller, on the big-game hunting and the sport of the regions we visited ; while Price has published his impressions of the political and social conditions of the Siberian borderlands in a separate volume.[1]

To the Royal Geographical Society I owe a debt of gratitude for the support they gave me, in forming the

[1] "Siberia," M. P. Price. Methuen, 1912.

initial plans of the expedition, and for the loan of scientific instruments. I must also acknowledge the never-failing courtesy and help given me by the Librarian and his assistants, during research work which extended over many months; as well as the care taken by the cartographers during their preparation of the maps.

I have to thank Lord Curzon for his appreciation of my work, as shown in the Foreword, which he has written to introduce these volumes.

The illustrations are, with two exceptions, all from our own photographs, the authorship of those not taken by myself being acknowledged in the list. I have to thank Mr. J. D. Cobbold for the loan of the photograph reproduced opposite page 60, and Mr. T. P. Miller for that opposite page 334. To Mr. J. G. Millais we are indebted for the original picture of the wild sheep—*Ovis ammon*, which he was kind enough to paint in spite of the pressure entailed by his own work. The three coloured maps have been reproduced by kind permission of the Royal Geographical Society, under whose auspices they were compiled from my original surveys; they have already appeared in the Geographical Journals of June 1912 and April 1913.

I have also to acknowledge the great help in matters of antiquarian interest afforded me by M. Adrianoff of Tomsk University. To Capt. Ernest Rason I am grateful for help in connection with the translation of several Russian works. For many valuable literary suggestions and the reading over of the entire proofs I must thank Lady Owen-Mackenzie, and Mrs. Holden, whose respective advice in matters of arrangement and composition I find it difficult to sufficiently acknowledge.

D. CARRUTHERS.

LONDON, 1913.

CONTENTS

VOL I

LIST OF ILLUSTRATIONS

VOL. I

MAPS

INDEX TO IMPORTANT SUBJECTS IN THE ILLUSTRATIONS

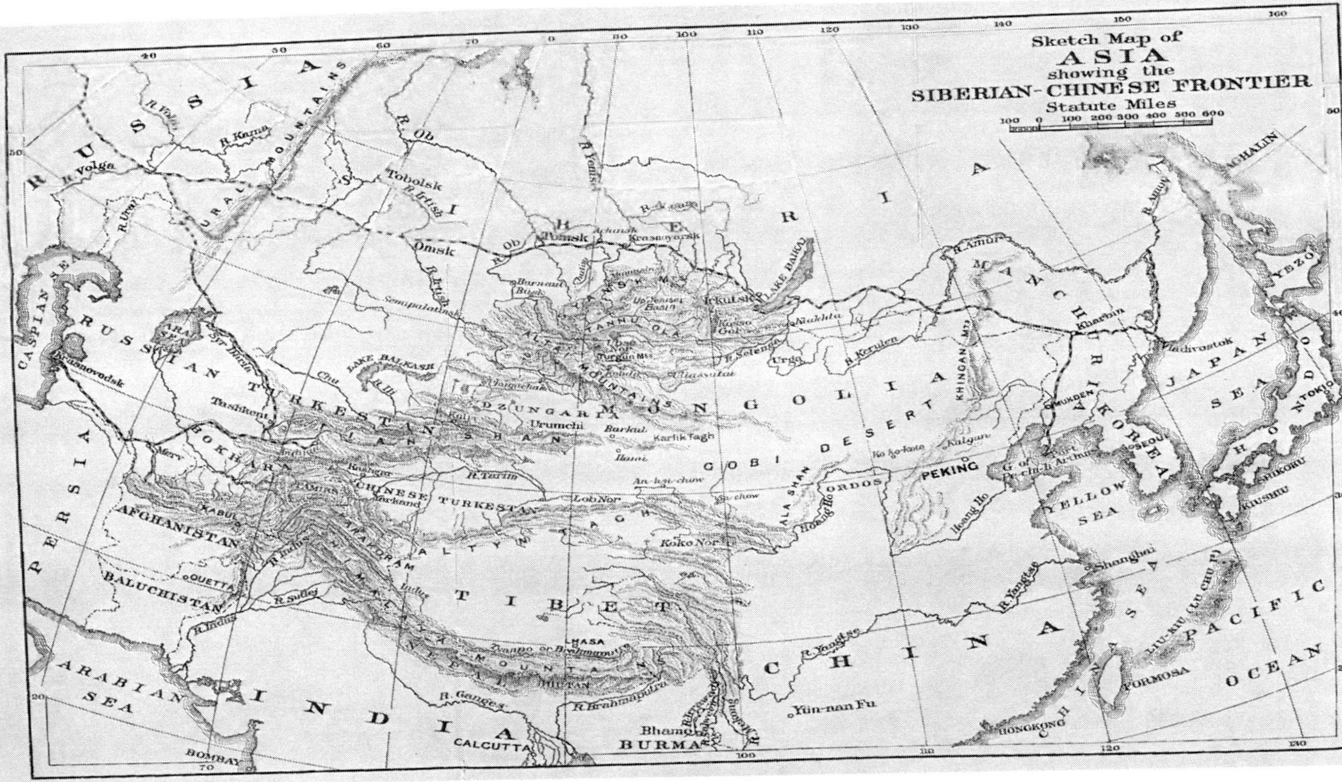
Sketch Map of
ASIA
showing the
SIBERIAN-CHINESE FRONTIER
Statute Miles
RUSSIA
SIBERIA
URAL MOUNTAINS
R. Volga
R. Kama
R. Ural
R. Ob
Tobolsk
R. Irtish
Omsk
Tomsk
Krasnoyarsk
R. Yenisei
Irkutsk
LAKE BAIKAL
CASPIAN SEA
Krasnovodsk
RUSSIAN TURKESTAN
ARAL SEA
Syr Daria
Tashkent
BOKHARA
Merv
LAKE BALKASH
R. Ili
Chu
Sempalatinsk
ALTAI MOUNTAINS
TANNU OLA
Turgun Mts
DZUNGARIA
Urumchi
Barkul
Karlik Tagh
THIAN SHAN
MONGOLIA
GOBI DESERT
Urga
R. Selenga
R. Kerulen
Kiakhta
KHINGAN Mts
Kalgan
PEKING
ALA SHAN
ORDOS
Hoang Ho
An-hsi-chow
Lob Nor
Koko Nor
R. Tarim
Kashgar
Yarkand
CHINESE TURKESTAN
ALTYN TAGH
KARAKORAM
TIBET
LHASA
HIMALAYA MOUNTAINS
BHUTAN
Tsanpo or Brahmaputra
R. Brahmaputra
R. Ganges
CALCUTTA
BOMBAY
INDIA
R. Indus
R. Sutlej
Indus
KABUL
AFGHANISTAN
QUETTA
BALUCHISTAN
PERSIA
ARABIAN SEA
BURMA
Bhamo
Yün-nan Fu
CHINA
R. Yangtse
Shanghai
HONGKONG
FORMOSA
CHINA SEA
LIU-KIU (LU CHU IS.)
PACIFIC OCEAN
YELLOW SEA
G. of Pe-chi-li
Port Arthur
MUKDEN
SEOUL
KOREA
MANCHURIA
Kharbin
R. Amur
Vladivostok
SEA OF JAPAN
SAGHALIN
YEZO
HONDO
TOKIO
SHIKOKU
KIUSHIU

UNKNOWN MONGOLIA

INTRODUCTION

FORMER experience in Central Asia, and a careful review of the labours of all previous travellers in the remote parts of this great continent, showed us that there was, at least, one region still worthy of examination.

In the exploration of the sources of the Yenisei River, of North-western Mongolia and Dzungaria, we have found a practically new field for original work in the study of geography, ethnology, and zoology.

This great tract of country, stretching across the heart of Asia, is one of those few regions in the exploration of which the British have had no part, it having been entirely monopolized by the Russians. For this reason, and since the labours of these Russian travellers are frequently left unrecorded, and, even when published, are unintelligible to investigators and scientists in other parts of the world—unless they chance to be well acquainted with the Russian language, it is our ambition to place on record a detailed description of these lands, which in many respects are quite unknown to English readers.

In these days the public expects something altogether new, some actual addition to knowledge, in a book of travel, and yet every year it becomes a harder task for the would-be explorer to find scope for his energy, the blank spaces on the maps being rapidly filled in, and pioneer work having almost become a thing of the past. We claim, however, that the countries we visited, namely, the Upper Yenisei basin, North-western Mongolia, and parts of Dzungaria, have been left almost untouched by previous travellers, and that our information is practically original. No apology, therefore, is needed for the writing of this book; it is, in no sense, an addition to the bibliography of a much-travelled-over land. The birthplace of one of Asia's greatest rivers, the region of the sources of the Yenisei, has hitherto escaped the discerning eye and eager foot of the traveller. The existing maps of this country are much at fault, certain regions have never even been mapped, and no attempt has been made to describe the wild stretches of dense forest and rugged ranges on the Siberian-Mongol frontier, or the strange tribes of shy, forest-dwelling Uriankhai inhabiting them.

Our aim was, primarily, to explore as thoroughly as possible the little-known sources of the Yenisei River, the upper waters of which, rise on the northern edge of the great Mongolian plateau. Here, in a mountain-girt basin, cut off alike from the plains of Siberia and the bleak uplands of Mongolia, protected from intrusion by a belt of the densest forest, and by the rugged heights of its border ranges, lies a region containing material of deep interest both to the geographer and to the naturalist. Here exists the last stronghold of the indigenous tribes of Southern Siberia—tribes that have been driven back into the far recesses of the forests, the Upper Yenisei basin being the resort of the Uriankhai—"the wild forest-dwellers"—who at the present day just hold their own against nature.

After penetrating into this region in the summer of 1910, and traversing the basin from the far north-east to the south-west, we passed out of it by crossing the Tannu-ola range—the watershed between Arctic drainage and the inland self-contained basins—and entered Mongolia. Through North-western Mongolia we continued our work, visiting that remarkable group of mountains—the Turgun or Kundelun—the headquarters of the Durbet tribe, and gaining an insight into the present-day conditions of the once-powerful Mongols.

A few Russian travellers had alone preceded us to the sources of the Yenisei, but travellers on the wide Mongolian plateau itself are more numerous. Atkinson, Ney Elias, and Younghusband represent the only British travellers; the Russians, however, form a considerable band of explorers amongst whom are the illustrious names of Prjevalsky, Kozloff, Potanin, Pievtzof, and Matussovski. We hope to add considerably to the information they have given us of the mountains, lakes, and pasturages, and of the wandering nomads of these wind-swept wastes. Our itinerary did not follow the same line as that of previous travellers, since a careful consideration of all their routes enabled us to steer a new course across the highlands of Mongolia.

Our route, then, led us in a westerly direction to the home of the Kirei—a nomad tribe of great importance, who, as the descendants of the people once under the direct chieftainship of that historical person, Prester John, present problems of considerable interest.

Dzungaria, a vague term used to include the whole

of the inter-Altai-Tian Shan region, also lacks any systematic or detailed description, and this occupied our attention after crossing Northern Mongolia. The information we gained during ten months spent on its border ranges and in crossing its inhospitable wastes, combined with the observations on the previous journeys of the great Russian pioneers, brings up to date the account of the ancient land of the Dzungars. We followed the Russian-Chinese frontier from the Altai to Kulja in the Ili Valley, at which point Price left us for further journeys in Russian Turkestan and the Caucasus, on his way to England, and Miller and I halted for several months. Beyond this, our plans at the outset were vaguely formed; the main idea being to turn eastwards, along the southern borders of Dzungaria to Urumchi and Kumul, thence to cross the Great Gobi to the Hoang Ho and so on to Pekin. The latter part of this programme was, however, given up, in order to track more thoroughly over Dzungaria. After carrying out a detailed survey of the Karlik Tagh group, to the north-east of Kumul, we turned back and again crossed Dzungaria. We included in our itinerary the Bogdo-ola sacred lake on the south, the Barlik Mountains on the north, the Borotala Valley on the west, and arrived again in Kulja in July of 1911; we then crossed the Tian Shan into Chinese Turkestan, and returned to England via Kashgar, Yarkand, and the Karakorum range, which led us to Leh, Kashmir, and Bombay.

The work was only accomplished with infinite trouble and patience. It was impossible to hurry across such a country. Slow plodding behind a crawling camel caravan across endless steppes, short stages in Chinese carts on still shorter winter days along the Chinese Imperial High Road, or five miles a day through dense forest on the Siberian frontier, prove that the journey was a laborious one, and that it was quickly accomplished in twenty months. Extremes of climate in Central Asia added to the difficulties of arranging an itinerary, for the winter months prohibited geographical work, and put collecting out of the question.

This narrative should be a counterpart of the regions we passed through,—varied in the Yenisei forests, monotonous in Mongolia and Dzungaria. The "feel and the smell" of the country should live in all we describe, whether it is sombre forest, misty plateau, racing river, or burning desert. It is the atmosphere of the country, the heart-throb of that great lone land, of which we wish to give an impression, not omitting, at the same time, exigencies of daily travel, the toils of survey work, or the joys of discovery. This is an account of a journey across 5,000 miles of Asia, between the railways of Siberia and India, accomplished by means of tarantass, canoe, boat, and raft, by ass, ox, camel, and pack-pony, through countries the mere mention of which must arouse a glow of enthusiasm in the most confirmed city-dwellers; a journey that led us through the ancient land of the Mongols, across the little-known deserts of Dzungaria. through sandy Turkestan—with its old-world, sleepy oases, and over the high-flung Himalayas.

Mongolia and Dzungaria are, to the average European, lands of romance and mystery. Lying off the track, midway between Siberia and Cathay, they do not possess the features of either of these wide lands, but form the most eastern portion of that great zone of waste-land which lies like a belt across the Old World, under the names of Turkestan and Transcaspia, Persia, Arabia, and the Sahara. The great trade-routes of Asia pass by Mongolia and Dzungaria without tapping them. The commerce and transport of the ancient world, which once connected east and west, passed far to the south, whilst the new line of communication passes across Siberia to the north; Mongolia and Dzungaria, lying isolated between the two, have remained untouched. The energetic exploiters of China's secrets have scarcely extended their labours farther than the boundaries of the Great Wall; the explorers of Chinese Turkestan have stopped short on reaching the bleak wastes of Mongolia, the Tian Shan Mountains being the most northern limit of their journeys. The true pioneers of travel in these regions have come from the north: the hardy colonists of Siberia, the scientists from her universities, and the soldiers from her garrisons, having supplied the units of the most daring and plodding band of adventurers into the Unknown, that ever honoured the annals of exploration.

With this intrusion of Europe into Asia came the best of the Russians, adventurers at heart and dauntless in spirit, eager to add to their area of Empire, to open up fresh spheres of trade, and to enrich their scientific collections. Came also the foremost of her soldiers, merchants, and scientists; Kozloff and Prjevalsky—the explorers, Severtzoff—the naturalist, Radloff and Adrianoff—the antiquarians, all having won their laurels on these lonely Asiatic frontiers. What yearnings for the "new" must they not have felt, when they saw the whole of Asia unroll before the foremost lines of their dusty columns! Little wonder that men grew ambitious when a whole continent lay spread out before them. Russia has overflowed into Siberia, and Siberia has absorbed every man she sent. China has, strangely enough, expanded into foreign lands,—into America and Australia, rather than tackle the problem of systematically colonizing her outlying provinces. For this reason these lands lie untilled and desolate, given over to the herds of wild-horses, to the shy, wild mountain-sheep, and to the roaming bands of nomads.

The call of Mongolia has remained almost unheeded throughout the ages. Men still look on that region as the birthplace of that greatest scourge the world ever experienced, the Mongol demi-god, Jenghis Khan. It is a wild land, a land of immense distance; one can travel continuously for a week, and still hold the same snowy peaks in view. The scenery is savage and the climate inhospitable, yet, in spite of the severity of winter, summer fills the land with song and flushes its plateaux with grass. Our Mongolia, of the Siberian frontier, is one which will surprise geographers, and tempt the would-be traveller to wander in wild but charming surroundings. Here, on the edge of China,—on the verge, as it were, of the Gobi Desert,—is a land of exceptional beauty; here are mountains, forests, lakes, and rivers, meadows of lush, long grass, a wealth of wild flowers, deep, shadowy forests of larch and pine, and racing streams of clearest water—in truth, a New Mongolia.

In this land of unique physical conditions is to be found the birthplace of many races now widely dispersed; the origin of so many breeds can be traced in this quarter of Asia, that men have lightly called it "the cradle of the human race." From these steppes and plateaux, in days gone by, emerged various migrating tribes and many world-wide movements had here their beginning, making the history of its inhabitants most difficult to follow. Here lies the ancient home of some of the greatest Asiatic races,—the Mongol and the Turk, the descendants of whom have ruled in Pekin and Stamboul. Such widely separated peoples as the Finns of Northern Europe, the Magyars of Hungary, and the Red Indians of America, not to mention the Samoyedes and the Eskimos, must be credited with having originated in these regions.

This strange land, which to-day is of little account, has profoundly influenced the history of the world. Here, countless ages ago, arose that Uigur Empire, the origin of which is shrouded in mystery and antiquity, its history extending so far into the dim distance that the most learned scholars have failed to unravel its problems. This is the land which has bred unrest from time immemorial; on these wind-swept plateaux wandered the Huns who eventually overran Europe; this was the home of the wild nomads who afterwards founded a dynasty in China,—which lasted until quite recently, who created an Empire in India, and who, by virtue of immense conquests in Asia, were actually in a position, for a time, to speak in dominating accents to Europe; here, too, was born that Mongol chieftain Jenghis Khan, whose name is still honoured by the Tartar tribesman, and whose personality has ever been invested with supernatural powers.

It is of special interest to study the great men-movements in these vast regions of Inner Asia,—on the marches of Siberia and China, to trace the manner in which aimless migration and stupendous military expeditions led to more systematic conquests by greater powers; and to note that the whole of that immense tract fell finally under the rule of two great peoples. An unusual combination of physical conditions adds further interest to this study of the Russo-Chinese border-lands. The opening up of Siberia is in itself a wonderful story; Siberia is the Canada of Asia, and its colonization has a great future. Mongolia, on the other hand, is a country with a past, capable of development, but presenting the serious drawback of being inhabited by an ancient and not very virile race. Dzungaria comes under the category of those lands which may be turned to good account, under favourable political conditions and a progressive and consecutive Government. Chinese Turkestan, on the other hand, is a paradox; it is the most fertile of all the lands here mentioned, and every available acre is taken up, the population is greater than the country can support, and it produces an inert, lethargic race, who, having enough, are content.

On to these lands are pressing the surplus population —the front ranks—of two peoples with a future; on the north and west are the Russians, and on the south and east are the Chinese. Who would dare to prophesy the future of the marches of Siberia and China?

If, as some think, it is "in Asia once again that will be decided the destinies of the world," then every portion of Asia claims notice, but more especially those parts where the Asia of the Asiatics borders upon the Asia under European rule—where the East and the West come face to face, and where doubt exists as to their respective futures. Since our return from Mongolia, that land, which yesterday was almost unknown, has, by a curious coincidence, leapt suddenly into prominence. The land of the Mongols has again appeared upon the world's stage, after having been for eight hundred years behind the scenes. China has been in the throes of revolution, Mongolia has seized the opportunity to throw off the Manchu yoke, and over a million square miles of Asia have come on the market. The importance of this cannot be overrated, for Mongolia is China's landward gate,—through Mongolia and Dzungaria run the roads from Cathay to Siberia and Western Asia. Between the Far East and the West the only line of communication, uninterrupted by natural difficulties, runs through Dzungaria. Some day, no doubt, the whistle of the locomotive will startle the wild-asses of the Dzungarian plains, and the slouching camel-caravan will no longer find employment; but for the present these lands lie quiet, and there is still an *unknown* Mongolia.

Our Forerunners

There are no means of going back as far as the *discovery* of Mongolia. Such a term is scarcely applicable to this part of Asia, which can never have been entirely unknown to the West. It is one of those lands which was known to Europe in the early ages; then it was forgotten,—for many centuries Mongolia disappeared off the world's stage,—only to be rediscovered once more during the latter half of last century.

We must retrace our steps as far as the fifth century, to find the first communications that passed between Mongolia and the West. Upper Asia—then called

Tartary—first came in contact with the outside world through the medium of Nestorian missionaries, who in those early days penetrated to the furthermost East, but by whose agency very little information respecting these far-off lands filtered through. In the fourth, fifth, and sixth centuries successive waves of Asiatic invaders poured westwards, namely, the Huns, those wild shepherd-warriors from the east, who materially altered the history of Europe.

It was not until the twelfth century that Tartary made the first real impression on the West. The earliest accounts of Mongolia and its people, which came through to us, were indeed romantic; Europe was then staggered by the reports which reached her of the triumphs and might of that semi-mythical personage "Prester John"—Khan of the Keraites—and of his supposed conversion to Christianity. Embassies went to and fro between the Courts of Europe and the Khan of the Keraites. High Asia loomed large in the imagination of the peoples of the West. Missions were sent out to brave the bleak steppes of Central Asia, in order to carry letters from the Pope, the King of France, and the Christian Emperor of Constantinople. Prester John managed to create an exaggerated excitement in Europe.

Then followed the Mongol invasions, and the Western world learnt only too well the character and nature of the Tartars, for the stupendous movements that originated in Mongolia, early in the thirteenth century, brought Europe into close relationship with the Mongols. It is a strange fact that we of the West never came in contact with these crude but successful warriors, until they visited us in Europe. All through the thirteenth century there was close intercourse between Europe and Tartary, chiefly, it is true, by reason of wars and invasions, but later also by means of intelligent missionaries, who were sent to convert the barbarians, and who gave us the first realistic account of Mongolia and the Mongols.

When the Mongols retired from Poland and Hungary, and the height of their lust for conquest was attained, there followed a period of more peaceful intercourse between Europe and Middle Asia. The rulers of Europe began to despatch emissaries to the Mongol Khans, and the Pope authorized missions to propagate religion and to encourage civilization amongst the barbarians, with the idea of changing the ferocious Tartars into mild and peace-loving people. Of these emissaries, two, John de Carpini and William of Rubruck, Franciscan monks, have given us excellent accounts of their impressions of the Mongols, and I repeatedly quote from the narratives of these two earliest Western travellers in Upper Asia. Carpini achieved the distinction of being the first Western traveller to make mention of the existence of the Mongol capital, Karakorum; and Rubruck was the first to actually visit it. Besides these, we have the story of Marco Polo, who includes in his wide-ranging descriptions allusions to parts of Northern Mongolia, and an account of its ancient capital.

After this, there followed a period during which we gained but little information; for the next three hundred years there was a blank in the history of intercourse between Mongolia and the West. The Mongol had already sunk from his high estate; his power was no longer a source of wonder and fear to the Western world. The centre of interest changed to Cathay, and affairs with cultivated China blocked out all thought of the wild Mongolian steppes and their barbaric nomads. Formerly the Tartars were only approached by the landward gates; it was by bravely facing the thousands of miles of barren Central Asia that the embassies and missions reached the Court of Karakorum; but now the depths of Tartary were forgotten, for men sailed in ships to the great ports of China. Thus, after the destruction of the Mongol power, and the retirement of the warrior-hordes to the innermost steppes, Tartary sank into oblivion, and for the time being all intercourse between it and the West discontinued. We hear very little of Tartary until the ever-pushing, insatiable ambition of a European Power found itself suddenly face to face with the desert frontiers of China, and the Russian Empire marched with Cathay along a vaguely delimitated border-land; then only did Mongolia begin to occupy a place in the minds of the scientist, the politician, and the trader.

As previously mentioned, it was men of Russian nationality who were chiefly responsible for the exploration of these regions. The great unknown that lay beyond the Siberian frontier, fifty years ago, was a "lode-star" to the Russian pioneers, who were for ever pushing on from the newly acquired territories into what they imagined might be richer lands. Slowly the great waves of European influence spread towards Inner Asia. Russia from the North, Great Britain through India, and in the east both these nations vied with other Great Powers for their share in a possible partition of China. With the quick flow of Russian colonization in Siberia, the

Russians were the first to reach the borders of Mongolia, and her territories there bordered on the ancient lines of the Chinese frontier.

It was early in the seventeenth century, that Russia began seriously to attempt to open up communication between her new Siberian possessions and China. All through this and the succeeding century there were repeated missions passing between the Courts of Pekin and Russia, but the intervening lands of Mongolia received only scanty attention at the hands of these early emissaries—China, not Mongolia, being their objective.

Mongolia was not such a land as would tempt a hasty exploration. Its trade was not such as would be an incentive to rapid penetration by merchants and traders, nor have strategical possibilities acted as an inducement to military occupation by a foreign Power; neither has popular enthusiasm in Europe helped on the exploration of Mongolia, as it has done with Africa or the Poles. There has been no great prize awaiting the traveller who has undertaken laborious journeys in this far land, and no great mystery has awaited solution. Only the historical fact of this being the home of the Mongols, the birthplace of the greatest scourge with which it has pleased Providence to punish the West, allows Mongolia to take a place amongst the most interesting regions of the world. To men of science, then, are we chiefly indebted for the rediscovery of Mongolia.[1]

[1] In treating of the early travellers to the region we visited, I use the term "Mongolia" in its widest sense—namely those wide, open lands which lie along the northern border-lands of the Chinese Empire, from Turkestan to Manchuria. In old days the term applied to this region was "Tartary," but that name was also extended to other parts of Central Asia which were then being overrun by the Mongols. In dealing with the more recent exploration I reserve Mongolia as the name for that region

In the middle of the nineteenth century the first scientific pioneers looked beyond this frontier, and, with the craving for the "unknown" which comes to all true men, set out to penetrate the wastes which lay between them and the Great Wall of China. The romance of exploration has no more enthralling chapter than the Russian penetration of Central Asia and Far Western China. It was a great undertaking, well suited to the Muscovite mind. The Russian does everything on a vast scale. His journeys are colossal undertakings. Prjevalsky, the pioneer, covered 19,500 miles of route, and spent nine years and four months in accomplishing it. Kozloff crossed the Great Gobi five times, and in three different directions!

The Russian exploration of inner Asia was a methodical undertaking, part of a great Plan organized by the Imperial Russian Geographical Society of St. Petersburg, under the able Vice-Presidency of A. M. Semenof. For the last forty years a small army of topographers has been mapping that vast country, and scientists have

which is ruled by the hereditary Mongol Khans—the true Mongolia. Dzungaria fulfils the duty of title of the western portion of this region; while the "Upper Yenisei basin" most suitably describes the enclosed sources of that great Siberian river. Of the whole area we traversed, this latter is the only one of which I can scarcely find mention in the old days. Apparently it remained undiscovered until 1860, when the modern traveller found it out. Raschid, who wrote a history of the tribes of Asia in the fourteenth century, made mention of certain reindeer-keepers of the Upper Yenisei, referring either to the Tunguses of Southern Siberia or actually the Uriankhai. His account certainly suits the latter, for he describes them as dressing in deer-skins, keeping neither oxen nor sheep, as living in birch-huts and using snow-shoes. Marco Polo shows a knowledge of certain reindeer-keeping people such as are the inhabitants of the Upper Yenisei basin, whom he describes as being "a very wild race," who "live by their cattle, the most of which are stags, and these stags," he assures us, "they used to ride upon." But these early references to the tribes of Southern Siberia are too vague to allow us to put them down as referring directly to those of the Upper Yenisei region.

been describing her wonders. All the energies of Russian travellers have been concentrated on this region. The great Empire which stretches for 3,500 consecutive miles across Asia might have had her work cut out in surveying her own lands without of necessity paying attention to those of others; yet she has found time during the last sixty years not only to explore her own territory, but to take the field against other nationalities in the colossal work of reducing areas equally as vast, such as Mongolia, Eastern Turkestan, Northern Tibet, and Western China, to the scale of a map. The Russian "40 versts to an inch"[1] survey is the standard map over some 8,761,000 square miles of Asia. It should, however, be noted that the whole area is contiguous, almost under the same physical conditions, and—a still more unique and important consideration—mostly united under one Government, which alone has made possible thorough investigation and research.

As the towns of Southern Siberia, namely, of the provinces of Semipalatinsk and the Yeniseisk, grew to be of importance, traders began to push farther southwards, and to make long expeditions into Mongolia in order to exploit the wealth of the country. These pioneers brought back the first information of the great plateau-land, of the wandering nomads, and their unlimited herds. It is noteworthy that, whereas our earliest information concerning Mongolia came through the medium of zealous missionaries in the thirteenth century, the pioneers of the nineteenth century who *re*discovered Mongolia were traders and scientists.

[1] Published by the Topographical Section of the Russian General Staff, St. Petersburg.

In this survey of previous exploration we can only deal with the work achieved in the region immediately under our notice. The majority of the travellers mentioned, covered far wider areas than those regions to which we draw attention. Many of them ran route-surveys across Mongolia on their way to Tibet and Turkestan, or mapped the Tian Shan ranges *en route* for China; in consequence we find little-known regions quite close to the Siberian frontier. These explorers, eager for greater prizes, neglected the lands that lay nearest to them and pushed ahead into the farther unknown.

Up to quite recent times, the maps showed a remarkable lack of knowledge, on the part of the map-makers, of the true topography of Mongolia and Dzungaria. This lack of knowledge accounts for their divergence from the truth. For instance, fantastic lakes were coloured blue where now dry steppe is proved to exist, and "Gobi" (desert) was then broadly written across unknown tracks, which now show pleasant hill-country where nomads camp and wild game find pasture. The map of the Upper Yenisei, the Syansk and Tannu-ola ranges, is still very poor in detail, chiefly on account of the impenetrable nature of those regions, where survey-work presents insuperable difficulties. Mongolia is an easier country to map, but even here there is a great want of really accurate work, especially in the mountains. In the Altai and in Eastern Tian Shan, the case is the same. The following résumé of exploration is intended to give an idea of the previous work carried out in this region, and by whom it was accomplished.

In spite of the fact that the Russians were first on the spot, and the monopoly of exploration was theirs, the earliest traveller of whom I can find record, to penetrate into those depths of Mongolia, was an Englishman. Thomas Whitlam Atkinson, an artist, traversed such an incredible distance over this part of Asia—at a most interesting period, between the years 1853–60[1]—that his accounts were at first received with incredulity. His reputation as a traveller was entirely based upon the extent of his wanderings (he claims to have covered 39,500 miles of country in the course of his seven years' wandering). His qualifications stop there; he made no addition to scientific knowledge, his unsatisfactory narratives are almost impossible to follow, and in the light of scientific research his achievements carry no weight. But there is little doubt that he actually accomplished the routes he describes. With travel in Siberia he included a ride across the heart of Dzungaria into North-west Mongolia, and back again to the Russian Altai; he claims to have been the first European to set eyes on the Tian Shan mountains and the basin of the Upper Yenisei, but to this later journey he pays no further attention than merely drawing his route on the map. His journeys cover the whole vast region between Kulja, in the Ili Valley, Omsk, Irkutsk, and Barkul.

The first true explorer was a Russian—Matussovski—who did magnificent pioneer work all through North-west Mongolia and Dzungaria. His labours began in

[1] That there had been scientific explorers on the frontiers before this date is shown by the volume published in 1845 by P. de Tchihatcheff, in which the writer describes a journey undertaken, by order of the Czar, to the "Eastern Altai and the adjacent regions on the frontier of China." No doubt there were others, but the literature on the subject is extremely difficult to get hold of, and as often as not the reports of the early travellers were not for public circulation.

1870, and extended over a period of five years. At first, under the leadership of Pavlinoff, he was in the Uliassutai country, and in the Upper Yenisei basin, being the first true explorer of whom I can find record to visit that region. Later, in 1872–3, with two companions, he penetrated as far as the eastern spurs of the Tian Shan, having crossed the desert from Uliassutai. This journey included a visit to Guchen and Barkul, and finished up with a fine bit of pioneer work along the course of the Urungu River from source to mouth in the Ulungur Lake, together with considerable tracking up and down the southern slopes of the Mongolian Altai. In 1875 Matussovski turned up again at Barkul, at the end of a long journey from China, having come this time from the south. Strenuous travels these, and for the most part composed of actual pioneer work. Matussovski was the first to probe the depths of Mongolia, and his energy shed a flood of light over this great lone land lying along the Russian frontier.

At the same time another pioneer was filling in large blanks on the map. Potanin—the Cossack officer—young, keen, and eager to throw himself into the romantic life of an explorer after he had suffered disappointment and exile on account of political intrigue. He made long and laborious route-surveys, marking, with red lines, his route over thousands of miles of unknown country; and, what is even more important, he gave us many bulky volumes describing in detail the regions he visited. Potanin still lives, a veteran of seventy-five years; he is the greatest living authority on the exploration of Mongolia, and is still capable of putting together the results of his journeys at his home in Omsk.

In 1876-7 Potanin covered the country between such widely separated places as Zaisan, Kobdo, Barkul, Uliassutai and Lake Kossogol. In 1879 he visited the Upper Yenisei basin and the Turgun Mountains. Some years later he made further long journeys, but in regions outside those which our descriptions embrace—such as in the Ordos, Koko Nor, and the central Gobi.

In 1872 a somewhat unusual expedition took place, which well illustrates the plodding and pioneering instincts of the Russians, whose remarkable exploits in Central Asia correspond to the great "treks" of the Boer traders in the early days of South Africa. A Russian merchant of Zaisan, on the Siberian frontier of Dzungaria, conceived the idea of outfitting and despatching a trading expedition into the remote corners of North Mongolia. The party was formed, and eventually trekked over some 1,700 miles of unknown country; they visited Kobdo, Uliassutai, Barkul, Guchen, before returning to Siberia. This expedition was carried out on the strength of the Russian commercial treaty with China, which opened up Mongolia and Dzungaria to Russian traders.

In the following year (1873) another Englishman appeared upon the scene—Ney Elias, who ran a route-survey from Pekin to the head-waters of the Ob River in Siberia, and, passing through North-west Mongolia on the way, left us the first accurate account of North Mongolia. Potanin, with his companions Rafailow, Matussovski, and Sosnovsky, together with Pievtzoff, who worked in the Altai, Eastern Dzungaria, and Mongolia, and Regel, the botanist,—these are responsible for the maps of this region up to the year 1879.

At this point comes in the renowned Prjevalsky, who has had a hand in every map of the Russian-Chinese border-land, and has achieved such a brilliant series of discoveries. His labours had hitherto lain mostly far to the south—on the Tibetan borders, and in the Southern Gobi; but in 1879, on his way to Tibet, he crossed the deserts of Dzungaria and visited the Eastern Tian Shan. Prjevalsky, with his unique training as soldier, geographer, and naturalist, has left us the most fascinating records of travel, containing mines of information and much detailed research.

In the eighties we have five travellers of note, who worked over widely different areas. In 1881 Adrianoff—who had already gained experience under Potanin on his second journey—visited the Kemchik region of the Upper Yenisei basin, and the Tannu-ola range and Kossogol. He has since written considerably on the antiquities of these regions.

Four years later Klementz also worked at the antiquities and the geology of North Mongolia, and his studies embraced a very large field; he made extensive journeys in North-western Mongolia between the years 1885–97, both on his own account and also under the leadership of Professor Radloff. Klementz covered very large areas of country; he was the first to explore the Kemchik sources of the Upper Yenisei, he also visited the sources of the Khua-Kem, and twice crossed the "divide" between the Upper Yenisei and Lake Kossogol. Later, being employed on the expedition sent out by the Academy of Sciences of St. Petersburg to investigate the ruins of ancient Karakorum, he was in a position to make extensive journeys on his own account over the whole area between Urga and the Altai, his routes crossed and recrossed the basins of Kobdo and Ubsa, they included traverses of the Tannu-ola and the Eastern Altai, and demonstrate the fact that he explored the sources of the Black Irtish, the Saksai, and Tsagan-gol sources of the Kobdo River, that he travelled round Achit Nor and the Turgun Mountains, not to mention far-reaching journeys towards the east, in regions which are outside the scope of our descriptions.

In 1887, two Englishmen visited the southern borders of our region—Captain (now Sir Francis) Younghusband and Colonel Mark Bell. The former traversed the Northern Gobi from Pekin to Hami, and eventually passed to Chinese Turkestan and India. The latter took the southern route through China to Hami, and went on to Barkul and Guchen. The accounts given us by these two travellers are the only ones in English up to date (excepting Dr. Stein's recently published work) of that out-of-the-way corner of Central Asia—the Hami and Barkul ranges. Another expedition of note passed through the same district two years later ; this was led by the brothers Grum Grjimailo—naturalists—who published their results in three fine volumes, in which they have a good deal to say on the subject of the far Eastern Tian Shan, where they worked for some time on their way to Western China.

In 1892, we have to record the visit of the botanist Kriloff to the region of the sources of the Upper Yenisei ; but his account does not amount to much beyond a laboriously kept diary. Pozdnyeff, a student of anthropology and archæology, carried on work at the same time in the countries between Urga and Kobdo.

The following year Kozloff, an explorer of great parts, came into the arena. When serving under Roborovsky, Kozloff surveyed in the Hami region on his way back from greater labours in Western China; a few years later he again took the field and put finishing-touches to the maps of the Eastern Altai ranges before crossing the central portion of the Great Gobi. These last journeys extended over the years 1899–1900; since then, in 1908–9, Kozloff has again worked in the central Gobi and in Southern Mongolia.

At about this date (1895), Borodaile, of the Indian Civil Service, the first Englishman to visit the site of the ancient Karakorum, proceeded from Pekin to Kobdo and gave us some account of that portion of Mongolia. In 1898–9, an account was published of the *Importance of the Uriankhai Country to Southern Siberia*, by Ostrovsky, containing the results of a research into the economic conditions of the Upper Yenisei basin. Another general description of this out-of-the-way region was published by Paikoff. The last visitor to these regions was M. Paul Chalon, who in 1904 rode from the Minnusinsk steppes to the Kemchik Valley in the western portion of the basin.

During the last eight years the work has been of a more concentrated type, the finishing-off in careful detail of roughly mapped areas. Obrucheff, after great achievements in the Southern Gobi and Ala Shan, set to work in 1905–6 to thoroughly explore the Northern border-ranges of Dzungaria, the Barlik and Sair groups; and in 1909 Sapoznikoff carried out surveys in the Altai, in the region of the sources of the Black Irtish and Kobdo Rivers.

The Altai Highlands have long attracted the attention of travellers, and of these perhaps the veteran is Prof. Sapoznikoff, who for fifteen years has made profound researches into the geology, botany, and physical geography of these alpine regions. Until 1905 his work lay in the true Russian Altai, but between 1905–1909 he investigated the long chain which he calls the Mongolian Altai (but which is generally misnamed on our maps the "Great Altai"), and which extends in a south-easterly direction into Chinese territory. The results of his journeys have recently been published at Tomsk, and this book includes so many different branches of science that it must take its place as the standard work on the Mongolian Altai. This range divides Mongolia from Dzungaria, and the story of its exploration affects our narrative in that, after hunting for some time on its north-eastern slopes, we crossed the heart of the main range into Dzungaria.

The antiquities of North-west Mongolia and of the Upper Yenisei basin received full attention from M. Granö in 1906. Since then specialists at the universities of Siberia have been busy working out the material collected on this subject by various travellers.

Apart from this, two journeys of importance have been accomplished in the northern parts of Mongolia—notably, by Major de Lacoste, who visited the interesting valley of the Tess whilst on his way from Urga to Kobdo, and by Dr. Paquet, who went, in 1908, from Kobdo to the Lake Kossogol. These were the most recent travellers in the northern portion of the region under discussion. During the last six years a few explorers have, however, touched on the southern edge of our region. Of these,

Dr. Aurel Stein and Mr. Clementi claim prior attention on account of the thoroughness of their work. At Hami and on the southern slopes of the Karlik Tagh, our surveys and descriptions overlap with Stein's work, as described in Chapter LXXXI. of his recent book, *Ruins of Desert Cathay.* Clementi's work only affects ours in that, at this point (Hami) his complete series of astronomical observations carried out systematically across the whole width of China from Kashgar to Kowloon (Hong-Kong), must be recognized as the most reliable.

In the winter of 1909 Lieut. Etherton rode along the north-western frontier of Dzungaria, between Kulja and the Altai, and during our own journey we came across Colonel Pereira, who was also traversing this region previous to carrying out further explorations in Western China. On the southern border-ranges—the Tian Shan and Bogdo-ola—we are dependent upon the detailed and most careful researches of Dr. Merzbacher, who explored the alpine region of the Eastern Tian Shan in 1909.

From this rough survey of previous exploration, it will be seen that the country has been visited by numerous travellers, the great majority of whom were Russian. A certain number of these travellers published accounts (the majority did not do so), and from these, many of them scanty and ill-written journals, we have to extract all information. Apart from this, our region remains untouched and undescribed. In order to make our account of the region as complete as possible, and to give a fair idea of these vast stretches of country, which are to all intents and purposes an unknown land to the English reader, I am trying to put on record all the information

I can possibly collect from our own carefully kept diaries and from those of previous travellers.

Our journey was accomplished and the greater part of this account written, before the proclaiming of an independent Mongolia. The conditions of the Upper Yenisei basin are here described as they were in 1910, but it will be noticed that a vague impression of coming change permeates the whole narrative. In the early part of this book I have made no reference to the new influences, but in the later chapters—especially Chapter X—I have supplemented our experiences by allusions to the new state of affairs. On the whole, this account must be taken as a study of the local conditions up to the year 1911.

CHAPTER I

ACROSS SIBERIA TO THE FRONTIERS OF MONGOLIA

"In Asia, where everything is immoderate, where a forest covers a kingdom, where a river deposits a country in a decade, and where man grows feeble from an abiding sense that Nature is too strong for him." No matter by which door Asia is entered, the truth of this forces itself upon us and we experience an overpowering sense of illimitable space, of nature built upon a colossal scale. Whether we catch our first glimpse of Asia from an Indian port and encounter the crowded millions of a delta, whether our introduction to the great continent is by the thousand-mile waterway of a Chinese river, or whether by way of the immeasurable steppes of Siberia or the sands of a Persian desert, the impression left upon us is always the same—one of inexpressible vastness.

Asia does everything in an exaggerated manner. She holds in certain localities the densest population per square mile in the world, and yet in others she shows illimitable expanses of poor lands entirely uninhabited. Asia can be discussed without mention even being made of China, yet the Celestial Empire, although representing only a corner of Asia, holds a third of the human race. It is difficult to believe that Persia, Japan, Mongolia, and Arabia are part of the same continent, such contradictions of race, climate, scenery, and religion do these lands possess. Who does not wonder at the close proximity and yet entire distinctiveness of the Aryan, Semitic, and Yellow races? In what way does the fearless believer in one God—the Arab of the sun-lit desert—compare with the timid Shammanist,—the nature-worshipper of the dark Siberian forests? Strange it is that this one continent should have given birth to a Christ, a Mohammed, a Gautama, and yet is able to produce the Ethics of Confucius, and the teaching of Zoroaster.

In this continent of paradox and surprise, men's minds have not only plunged into peculiar depths of thought, but have also shown a strange originality and a restless activity. The physical and ethnographical phenomena of the whole continent are on the same scale, and possess the same paradoxical quality, for a strange sense of proportion seems to pervade all Asia. Her calamities and catastrophes conform to her gigantic size, the very works of Nature run riot, and the so-called "acts of God" are here rehearsed with an unparalleled and relentless severity. Her wars and migrations, disasters and massacres have been on a scale at once so terrible and so overwhelming, that they would be scarcely credited in the West.

From all points of view her aspect is an exaggerated one, as is shown by the size of her rivers and mountains, by the multitude of her peoples, by the variety and strength of her religions, by her very joys and sorrows, which find no such parallel elsewhere. Asia is the continent of extremes—"no contrast is too great for her, no antithesis too profound"—the cold, bleak voids of Mongolia compare strangely with the steamy jungles of Burmah, and the sandy deserts of Transcaspia contrast with tropical India and fertile Siberia. The distribution of her peoples conforms to her peculiar physiography and gives rise to exceptional examples of racial dispersion. The same nomad tribe, for instance, is found in possession from the Caspian Sea to the Altai Mountains—a distance of half a continent,—and yet a different race may be met with in every other valley in Western China.

Asia also teems with exceptional studies and problems for the mind of the politician. China, the oldest nation, which is still a nation, stands as she has stood for three thousand years, and still holds her own against Western intrigue; while, on the other hand, the dismembered states of medieval India have been welded into a whole, and enrolled as part of a Western Empire. Greedy hands are stretching out from the West to seize any available territory, yet independent native States still exist, defiant and untouched.

The West has always eagerly devoured all available knowledge concerning Asia, her peculiar charm and unfathomable mystery possessing an unusual fascination for the prosaic European. Untouched fields of research still remain, and undescribed portions of Asia still await the appreciative traveller. One small portion of Asia in particular, Outer Mongolia, is far less known than the rest. This comparatively small area, it is true, occupies 650,000 square miles, and its scenery is composed of mountains and deserts, plateaux, forests, and sand-dunes; a land of infinite variety, of pleasing prospect and repellent monotony. It is this region which I intend to describe.

We first faced Asia from the watershed of the Ural

Mountains, which divides East from West. Here we entered a plain as big as Europe, which plain we traversed in a no more romantic manner than in the luxurious car of a Siberian express. This represented the first stage of our journey and the one by which we should most quickly reach the heart of the continent. We were on our way across Siberia, and, after leaving Riga, on the stormy Baltic, and experiencing five days' travelling over level plain-lands, we entered a rolling country of forested hills, an inviting land of pleasing aspect, and halted on the bank of the Great Yenisei.

We were anxiously awaiting our first glimpse of the great waterway, it being our intention to use it as a means of transport for some hundreds of miles farther up stream, but, alas! we found it to be still frozen solid. Even at this late date (April 23rd)—for the rivers of Siberia are generally open for traffic by mid-April—we found carts being driven across its frozen surface. We had expected to find Siberia a land bursting into spring after the long, relentless winter; but we were disappointed in our hope. When we had left England the may-trees were showing leaf in the London squares, when crossing Russia we were conscious of no throw-back into winter, but here in the heart of the continent, far away from the mellowing influence of the sea, the land was still held in the iron grasp of winter.

On April 23rd, when standing on the banks of the Yenisei watching the traffic crossing and recrossing the ice, the river-steamers which we had hoped to use as far as the town of Minnusinsk, 250 miles up-stream, showed us as yet no sign of summer-work. They lay ice-bound beside the quays awaiting the break-up of the ice. To the north stretched open and almost snowless steppes,

CROSSING THE FROZEN YENISEI.

to the south rose a hill-country where the snow still lay in patches amongst the open forest. Under these changed conditions it became necessary to transport ourselves and our kit, by road, over these hills to the plain of Minnusinsk beyond.

In our endeavours to obtain information as to the most feasible route from Siberia to the Uriankhai country at the sources of the Upper Yenisei, we had found it advisable to examine the whole of the region between the Russian Altai and Lake Baikal. Along this region extends a line of mountainous country—the northern edge of the Mongolian plateau, which abuts on the plain of Southern Siberia. This mountainous country stretches in a south-westerly direction and is fairly continuous all the way from Manchuria to the Tian Shan Mountains of Turkestan. Between the Altai and Lake Baikal the country is somewhat difficult and unknown. The outer border-range, which represents the first step up to the plateau, is composed of the Syansk Mountains; beyond these mountains lies the secluded basin where issue the sources of the Yenisei, and beyond this again is the second step, the Tannu-ola range, which leads up on to the true plateau of Mongolia proper. This mountain-girt basin, lying between the Syansk and Tannu-ola, we call the Uriankhai country, after the name of the only indigenous tribe inhabiting it.

In two places only do the Siberian plains connect with the Uriankhai country so as to give more or less easy access to that difficult and remote region, where the three main sources of the Great Yenisei have their birth. The traveller who wishes to reach the highest sources of the Yenisei has the choice of two routes. It appeared, from information which we gathered, that we might attempt our goal by way of Irkutsk on the east, or from Minnusinsk on the north. The Irkutsk route is the most difficult and the one most seldom used; this track leads over very rough country by way of Lake Kossogol to the uppermost sources of the Khua-kem and Bei-kem—main heads of the Yenisei waters. From Minnusinsk, on the other hand, we had the option of three tracks which lead southwards across the Syansk Mountains. This choice of routes led us to determine on Minnusinsk as a starting-point, and consequently, being baulked in our efforts to reach it by way of the Yenisei, we were forced to retrace our steps to Achinsk, some ninety miles to the west, from which town a post-road runs southwards towards the Mongol frontier.

A glance here at the romantic story of the Russian penetration of Siberia is not out of place. Geography is the handmaid of history; these sister sciences are so closely bound up, they divulge each other in so marked a degree, that it is almost impossible to speak of the one without touching on the other. When Yermak and his unruly followers burst into the great Siberian unknown, they found it inhabited by fiercer and more worthy foes than the present indigenous races. Side by side with the poor, cowardly Ostiaks and other tribes, were the progressive and valiant Tartars; for this reason, the Russian conquest of Siberia was not so easy as it might have appeared to be, under the present state of affairs. Siberia was not won without much cost. Doughty deeds were wrought by the first pioneers of her wilds, for the Tartars and Tunguses were worthy foes, and the stories of their battles against the Russians are crowded with adventure of the most exciting kind.

We read, with a glow of savage pleasure, of their

forays and their lines of block-houses, and of the treasure-hunting parties of independent Cossacks; how loyally the stout Tunguses and Buriats held out against the waves of invasion and kept their independence, for between twenty and thirty years, before being absorbed by the Russian Empire. Tempted by wealth of furs, many an independent expedition set out to explore and to trade through the bleak northern wastes. Many a tragedy must have been witnessed, many atrocities have been committed, yet, in spite of much suffering, borne with stubborn valour, in spite of disease and death, these hardy freebooters were not turned back, and eventually they won the crowning reward of Empire.

Yermak in a few years subdued vast areas of Siberia. In 1556 the Irtish and Altai districts were settled with bands of soldier-colonists, and in 1620 the Russian advance held the Yenisei. Then began, slowly but surely, the great and methodical Russianization of the nameless but limitless territory lying to the north of the present railway, and eventually the richer portions lying to the south became filled with the ever-advancing bands of colonists and exiles. By 1728—less than 150 years after the first crossing of the Ural Mountains, the Russians had accomplished their first experimental exploration of Asia, and with characteristic insatiability were starting afresh upon North America.

The open nature of Northern Asia, the vast extent of plain-lands without mountain barriers, rendered it suitable to quick and certain colonization by a great and virile people. With amazing rapidity the Russian penetrated to the farthest corners of Siberia and Central Asia, with the result that he is now as much at home in fertile, semi-tropical Turkestan, amongst the ruined civilization of Tamerlane, as he is in Kamchatka or at Verkhoyansk, the coldest spot in the world. Many advantages aid him in his success in colonization. For instance, the same language is spoken from Moscow to the Pacific; one religion binds him—this same creed is slowly absorbing the pagan tribes he has conquered; and *one* government holds its fatherly hand equally over all. The accessibility of Siberia has caused it to be over-run by the first new-comers, and has accounted for the slow but sure absorption of the indigenous tribes. Except for the northern tundra, which preserves the remnant of the Samoyede races, there are no mountain refuges or desert retreats to protect the native races from a complete Russianization. The mountains to the south, however, the plateaux of Mongolia, the forests of the inter-Altai-Baikal region, with their corresponding varied scenery and climate—these will be the last home of those tribes which manage to survive the inroads of Russia from the north and of China from the south.

Siberia in these days presents the spectacle of a country in the throes of a slow re-birth. The Russian is now established in the remotest corners of Northern Asia; he has connected up the whole region between the Urals and the Pacific with a net-work of post-roads, he has cut through the great continent by means of one long railway, he has placed steamboats on all the navigable rivers, created many towns of considerable importance—although somewhat far-removed from each other—and caused immense tracts of country to become populated and cultivated. But even so, vast areas remain untouched, pregnant lands await the hand of the agriculturist, and mineral wealth patiently awaits development. In spite of the fact that Russia possesses the most prolific race in Europe, and the population, it is said, doubles itself in sixty years, Siberia succeeds in tempting only a comparatively small number of the people from the home-land. Russia is not yet over-crowded, but can still provide room for her surplus population without resorting to Siberia as a colony.

Some of the finest and most promising districts of Siberia are situated along the frontier of China, where the almost continuous mountain-barrier stretches from the Pamirs to Manchuria. The northern slopes of these ranges are particularly favourable to colonization, and the immigrants have established themselves in snug settlements extending the whole length of the frontier. On the Chinese side, the Celestials are not absent, in spite of the natural conditions being very much poorer.

We experienced the worst of roads and seasons on our drive from Achinsk to Minnusinsk. I remember tracks of slush, mud, and melting snow, tedious stages at a snail's-pace, and numerous river-crossings, extremely unsafe in character. By April 27th the rivers at this latitude were beginning to break. The Chulim, for example, which we crossed twice, was especially dangerous, a flooded bank and an ice-laden main-channel making it difficult to embark our kit into the two flimsy canoes, which ferried it across the tide in relays.

On leaving Achinsk, we passed for the first stage through hills and forests ; the country then became more monotonous—a land of rolling steppe and occasional birch-groves. This continued the whole way up to the Upper Chulim, where we entered a more barren and truer steppe. In this locality forests were absent, with the exception of a few straggling pines and birches on the hill-tops, the type of scenery assuming a more "Central Asiatic" and a more arid appearance. The presence of herds of horses and cattle seemed to point to a nomadic condition of life. Here, for the first time, we saw signs of an ancient race which had lived, multiplied, and eventually passed away, leaving nothing behind beyond innumerable proofs of its distribution, in the shape of gigantic grave-mounds, or "tumuli."

The open nature of this country was a remarkable feature; with the exception of a few belts of pines, which had been planted by the colonists round about the larger villages, we saw no forests. Yet, at the back of the steppe conditions, prevalent at the present day, we discovered the existence of an ancient forest, the remnant of which remained in isolated and sorry clumps clinging to the hill-tops. This steppe-zone extends right up to the foot-hills of the Syansk Mountains, where, on account of its proximity to rain-producing area, it becomes more fertile and more productive of a heavier vegetation, until finally it merges into dense pine-forests of vast extent.

Our route led us southwards over rolling hill-country, and it was not until we reached the summit of that narrow ridge, which separates the Yenisei from the Chulim River—that short six miles which divides the two great river-systems, the Yenisei and the Ob-Irtish,—that we came within view of the plain of Minnusinsk. For this well-favoured and historical region is a hill-girt basin, cut off from the open Siberian plain-lands. From a grassy slope we looked across foot-hills dotted with innumerable tumuli, to the white, curving line of the Yenisei River, which meandered through a wide and fertile plain; far away at the back we could just discern

ON THE ROAD TO MINNUSINSK.

the faint outline of the Syansk Mountains, with dark-forested slopes, and glistening, snow-patched summits.

The impression we gained on entering the vale of Minnusinsk would have been the same, had we come by water instead of by land from Krasnoyarsk. Immediately upon leaving Krasnoyarsk the traveller passes, up-stream, through frowning gorges and fine rock-scenery; anon, the country widens out, the river winds in majestic sweeps, receiving giant affluents from the east; and later, upon reaching the plain of Minnusinsk, the traveller by boat finds the Yenisei to be of lake-like appearance, dotted with sand-banks and islets. Farther than Minnusinsk the Yenisei is not used for navigation. Fifty miles southwards, the foothills of the Syansk Mountains close in and the river passes through deep-cut, frowning gorges. Here, its course is broken by a series of rapids, which forbid navigation up-stream, and only allow the bold Siberian fishermen to come down in record time by raft from the quiet upper reaches, that lie at the back of that forbidding wall of crag and precipice.

The Yenisei, close to the town of Minnusinsk, where we crossed it, was a fine river in one great channel of four hundred yards in width. At that date, the 1st of May, it had a most interesting appearance, and our experience in crossing it shows the peculiar nature of these immense Siberian waterways, which rise in China and flow out to the Arctic Ocean. We found it to be sufficiently broken and free of ice to allow the passage of canoes from bank to bank, except for a narrow margin of ice on either side. But the shingly banks were piled high with gigantic blocks of ice, and broken floes were drifting down the current in such a manner, as to make it necessary for the boatmen to choose the right moment when to pole their flimsy, dug-out canoes, without mishap, across the flood, and to dodge the large and dangerous drift-ice. At that season the water was very low, and the banks showed that the river would measure another twenty-five yards across, at average water-level.

It appears that the Siberian rivers begin to break at their most southerly points. Even at Krasnoyarsk, 250 miles farther north, the river would not be open for navigation for another two weeks. Farther north still, the date of breaking becomes later, and the actual mouths of these rivers, which feed the Arctic Ocean, are only free from ice for about three months out of the twelve. It must indeed be a wonderful sight when the accumulated mass of ice, covering the whole length of some thousands of miles of frozen waterway, collects and jams at the mouth, until immense pressure bursts the barrier. Seebohm, who watched this "revolution of the ice" at a point on the river within the Arctic Circle, describes it graphically as "the battle of the Yenisei." At the point mentioned the great river did not begin to break until the very end of May, and it took two weeks of warfare between the ice-barrier and the floes from the upper reaches, before the river cleared itself to the ocean. This means that the Yenisei is in a state of siege for some two months before its waters run free from the grasp of the ice.

During the first week in June, Seebohm and his valiant companion, Captain Wiggin, who was the first to make the northern passage from Europe to the heart of Siberia, watched the Yenisei rising and falling in accord with the respective jams and bursts of the accumulating ice. Where islands or sharp bends in the river's course served as obstacles, mountains of huge ice-blocks collected and piled themselves up as the water rose. Eventually the main river reached such a height that it actually began to flow *back* up its own affluents, following the line of least resistance. Pressure from behind forced this wonderful flood of pack-ice and floes up the stream of the tributaries at the rate of five to six miles an hour. The ice dammed up the water behind it until the pressure was sufficiently great, then the barrier broke and the level of the water fell. Seebohm reckoned that some 50,000 acres of ice passed him during that week, and remarks that "some idea of what the pressure must have been may be realized by the fact that a part of the river, a thousand miles long, beginning with a width of two miles and ending with a width of six miles, covered over with ice three feet thick, upon which was lying six feet of snow, was broken up at the rate of a hundred miles a day." This battle of the Yenisei raged for two weeks, and during that period the season changed from midwinter to midsummer.

The Yenisei claims respect on account of its size. From the limit of its farthest source to its entrance into the Arctic Ocean, the river attains a length of close on four thousand miles; it has a drainage area only exceeded in Asia by the Ob-Irtish system, and vies with the Nile, the Amazon, and the Mississippi for the proud distinction of being the longest river in the world. At Krasnoyarsk, which is 1,700 miles from the sea, where we first saw the Yenisei, its banks are a thousand yards apart; farther north the river widens to over a mile, and eventually broadens, at its mouth, to the amazing width of one hundred miles.[1] Unfortunately its use is not in proportion to its size, for climatic

[1] The name Yenisei is of Tunguse origin, and means "wide water."

conditions, and the peculiarity of the land-surface only allow some four thousand miles of its total water-area to be used for steam-navigation.

We achieved the crossing without mishap, in the space of three hours, and, once on the east bank of the Yenisei, made good pace to the chief town of the district, Minnusinsk, which lies on a back-water of the main river. Minnusinsk we found to be the chief mart of agriculture and the centre of trade of a large district, including the cultivated plains that surround the town and the almost untouched lands,—awaiting development, in the way of mineral wealth and commercial enterprise,—which extend to the south.

The chief asset to this region is its remarkably mild climate as compared with the severity of climate of the rest of Siberia. Here no great and sudden changes of temperature hinder the crops and kill off the herds, such as so often happens on the unprotected Siberian plain.[1] Gentle rains lessen the risk of summer drought, and cause the land to produce crops in abundance, without the use of manure. M. Chalon gives the temperatures I have quoted, and also states that the land yields

[1] According to Russian observations, the average temperatures at Minnusinsk are as follows:

Winter . .	6° Fahr. (January is the coldest month)
Spring . .	43° ,,
Summer . .	67° ,, (July the hottest month)
Autumn . .	22° ,,

The rainfall, from observations extending over eleven years, averages:

Winter . .	·86 in.
Spring . .	2·16 ,,
Summer . .	5·56 ,,
Autumn . .	2·64 ,,

The mean yearly rainfall is put at 11·3 in. in the neighbourhood of Minnusinsk, but this increases in a marked degree as we travel southwards or eastwards towards the mountains. Forty-three miles to the east of Minnusinsk the mean yearly rainfall increases to 21·2 in.

twenty-two hundredweight per two-and-a-half acres, which is about half the average yield for the United Kingdom. In fact, the prairie region of Minnusinsk is said to be the most attractive and fruitful in all Siberia, and we are inclined to believe this to be the case. The scenery is varied by lakes, mountains, rivers, and forests; the interesting and somewhat picturesque Tartars live side by side with the Siberian colonists; and the early history of this district still invites research.

This happy valley stretches over an area of about 15,000 square miles on either bank of the Yenisei River, and is enclosed on the south by the Syansk Mountains, and on the east, north, and west by ranges of lower altitude, but of a sufficiently protective nature. The floor of the basin averages about 800 ft. above sea-level—remarkably low for its place in the heart of the continent. Across this alluvial plain of recognized richness flows the drainage from the wide area of mountain-ranges to the south. The main Yenisei, which collects the entire drainage of the Upper Yenisei basin, together with the Abakan, and the giant Tuba; all unite to water the Minnusinsk steppe.

These conditions, no doubt, account for the high state of civilization attained in the old days by the ancient indigenous races of this valley. In these days the presence of a thriving town like Minnusinsk showed a prosperous colony, living in a pregnant land, full of future possibilities. We spent ten days in this town, collecting information, buying stores, and bargaining for horses. The markets were full—here could be purchased almost every article obtainable in the great towns of Siberia. It possessed a bank, a museum of note, a hospital, schools, and a library. There was an atmosphere of development about Minnusinsk, as if she were well aware of what is in store for her in the future. Yet, in spite of her 10,000 inhabitants and the diligence with which we tried to obtain knowledge, we gained but little information in regard to the region lying beyond the cultivated plains. The mountains to the south were apparently beyond the limits of the imagination of the people of Minnusinsk, except for fairy-tales of the gold-fields there, which they delighted to relate to us.

Beyond Minnusinsk, southwards, there are numerous prosperous villages, but only one settlement of importance—the frontier station of Usinsk. The position of this small town marks for the traveller the easiest track into the region beyond. Situated as it is beyond the plain, hidden in a narrow valley between the Aradansk range and the main Syansk, it owes its existence solely to the presence of gold-mines and to the fact that it lies on the only open road, which connects the province of Yeniseisk with the Upper Yenisei basin and Mongolia beyond. We had reason to study the land-features very minutely, in searching for the best way to reach those further regions. The Usinsk route seemed to be the only authorized one. All official dealings with the frontier were in the hands of the Russian "Natchalnik" in that town. All travellers and traders have need to pass through it, and to take their permits from that official. In point of fact, this line of communication is the most direct, but by no means the easiest.

From Minnusinsk a cart-track leads southwards for about eighty-three miles, as far as the village of Gregorievski (or Dzelome); from there a rough trail runs over the Aradansk range, an offshoot of the main Syansk, to Usinsk. From this town two routes lead to the

A SIBERIAN COLONIST.

SIBERIANS PACKING.

basin beyond the Syansk, one to the east which runs to the Uiuk Valley, and one to the south to Cha-kul. Both necessitate a crossing of the Syansk, and the tracks reach an altitude of 6,500 ft. above sea-level. The drawback to this route is that, in May, the snow is still lying deep in the forests, and, as the track runs through them for many miles, and crosses two ranges of mountains, it is no light undertaking.

The route which is earliest open is that which leads from Minnusinsk to the south-west, up the valley of the Abakan, and over the western Syansk range into the Kemchik portion of the Uriankhai country. One hundred and six miles of this track can be used for wheeled traffic, beyond this a much more open type of country, with less forest, renders it the most feasible in the early months. But neither of these routes attracted us. For one reason, they led to the wrong end of the basin—the western or lower portion, whereas our aim was to explore the uppermost regions far to the east and up-stream. In a country where transport was so difficult, it seemed impracticable for us to add to an already lengthy programme by involving ourselves in heart-breaking and laborious "packing" through dense forests, in preference to the easy river-transport down-stream.

We determined therefore to strike due east from Minnusinsk, and descend into the basin at its least known point, and then, on the completion of our work there, to utilize these fine water-ways and to glide down-stream to the central region. It was only after persistent questioning that we found a well-recognized route, leading in the direction suitable to us. Seventy miles of plain would take us to the last village—Kushabar, in the valley of the Amil; from there a track used by hunters and gold-miners ran up the Amil and over the Syansk range to our goal.

But, on deciding that this should be our route, we had yet to deal with the technicalities of Russian bureaucracy. "That is an absurd route to take," they said; "nobody goes that road. The track to Usinsk will be easy in a week or two; why take a difficult one?" The passports necessary for that region were only obtainable from the officials of Usinsk, and, as even the officials of Minnusinsk were not in a position to take the responsibility of allowing us to proceed and to leave Russian territory for China, the whole matter had to go before the Governor-General of the province of Yeniseisk at Krasnoyarsk. Eventually, however, we were permitted to make our way out of Siberia by the Amil route.

During this period of delay, we had occupied ourselves by preparing our kit and making inquiries about transport. In order to avoid putting up the price of horses by purchasing our caravan at one spot, we divided our demands between here and the villages on the Amil. Every day a mixed crowd of horse-dealers—Siberians and Tartars, gathered near our lodgings, and tried the usual tricks of the trade. The horses they brought for our inspection were of a good but mongrel type,—Siberian-Tartar and Mongol being characteristics which included a rather too heavy build for hill-work. Price, who is a well-known figure with the Ledbury hunt, tried their paces and tested their qualities down the main street of Minnusinsk, whilst the owners suggested that their horses were not accustomed to be so ridden! By degrees we got hold of twelve horses at an average cost of £4 each.

Here too, besides the purchase of numerous stores,

we had to draw all the money that was necessary for the cost of our journey during the next five or six months. Our next banking town would be Chuguchak on the frontier of Semipalatinsk, a distance of 1,500 miles away. The uncertainties of the road, and how far money would go, made it difficult to estimate the expenses; but, as luck would have it, we were destined to find a country where money was scarcely appreciated—in Mongolia men stared blankly at the Russian notes, and we came through well on the safe side. We carried a considerable amount in gold and silver, and the remainder in rouble notes.

Our journey onwards from Minnusinsk to the foothills of the Syansk Mountains much resembled the journey from the railway. We found thriving villages and colonies of Russians, for this eastern side of the basin is without that Tartar element which is predominant on the west in the Abakan steppe. The Abakan Tartars, by the way, are a good example of the ability, Russia shows in westernizing the Eastern. Here you may see Tartars of ancient race turned into devout members of the Orthodox Faith, dressed more or less in Russian costume, and living, many of them, in villages of Siberian aspect. Yet they hold to their old customs and mode of life. They still live by herding their immense droves of horses and cattle; some even still use the felt-yurt, or log-built reconstructions of the same.

Once in the Amil Valley, we got a clear view of the country that lay ahead of us, and were conscious of the marked change in the natural features of the Minnusinsk basin, which begins on its southern and eastern edges. After thousands of miles of steppe—endless, monotonous steppe—stretching interminably from the distant Baltic, across Russia and Siberia, the face of the land at last altered. The plains, heaving in great wave-like folds, led onwards to foot-hills, which finally rose to highlands and rugged mountain-tops. To the south and to the east a mountainous country barred the way, forming not only a refuge for strange tribes, but serving as a vague boundary to the Chinese Empire. This was the most northern wall of the great Mongolian Plateau.

We crossed the Amil River on May 15th, where there was a good ferry, across a somewhat turbid flood of a hundred yards in width. Close to the eastern bank began that solid, impenetrable zone of forest which limited both cultivation and human progress in this direction. The first view of the "taiga" is a wonderful and impressive sight—as amazing as is a first impression of tropical jungle or papyrus-swamp; something intangible, mysterious, inviting inspection, but unpleasant to experience. The blank wall of dense forest which rose up ahead of us held all the country east of the Amil in its grasp, with a strength that no other natural force could exhibit. For well-nigh three hundred miles it stretches eastwards to the neighbourhood of Lake Baikal. Rugged mountains and big rivers add to the difficulties of penetration. Uninhabited and foodless, this forest-zone presents a problem of strenuous work to the explorer or to the prospecter. Small wonder, then, that the country is unmapped, that the mountains are nameless. We soon learnt to respect its impenetrable fastness. The forest phalanx is so dense and so unbroken, its area so immense, that no astonishment arises at its power to hinder the advance of man.

Kushabar, the little village situated on its outer fringe, is an old settlement with a prosperous and increasing population; yet, during seventy years, it has not advanced one half-mile to the south towards the forest-region. The dark wall of pines rises in an unbroken line beyond the meadows and corn-land. It remains the same to-day as it was a thousand years ago. The villagers fell the timber on the outskirts for their own use, the hunters penetrate into its innermost depths in search of the valuable sable, but its borders are inviolate as yet from the rapid march of man across Siberia.

CHAPTER II

ANCIENT SIBERIA

THE whole of the black-soil region of Southern Siberia, was at one time particularly favourable for the growth of a dense population of primitive races. At the period when Western Siberia, Turkestan and the Dzungarian plains were one vast sheet of water, forming a great mid-continental sea, the climate would not have been of such extreme opposites as it is at the present day; warmer and damper conditions would have given a more abundant vegetation and a more congenial climatic condition, suitable to the well-being of primitive man. No such ice-age troubled mid-Siberia as retarded the advance of Western Europe, and on this account the rapidity of the progress of man was here probably far greater; the mammoth and rhinoceros roamed these lands until that great Asiatic Mediterranean disappeared, and further alteration in the climate—from temperate to excessive cold—brought about radical changes in the human and animal life of inner Siberia.

The Minnusinsk district, and the country bordering on the middle Yenisei seem to have been the headquarters of these early races. Although Southern Siberia was never the seat of an empire, yet it is so rich in the remains of prehistoric peoples that the region must have been exceptionally suitable to the rise of early man, and the development, later on, of civilized tribes. It was the home of a race which attained to a considerable height of intelligence, which learnt the use of metals and the art of agriculture, but which was eventually driven out by invaders from the south, who replaced it, and who, on account of a change in the climatic conditions, lived a nomadic life instead of the settled life required for practising agriculture. The first signs we came across of this ancient race were the tumuli, "Kurgans," or grave-mounds, which we encountered just north of our second crossing of the Chulim River,—at the point where the good, open, grazing country commenced. From here onwards to Minnusinsk, and even southwards for some forty miles beyond that town, we found the country full of historical remains.

Let us recall the past, and search far back down the dim vistas of time, in order to find out the origin of these tumuli and gain an insight into the history of ancient Siberia. Before the dawn of history Southern Siberia was evidently occupied by a dense population, who merged by slow and successive stages from the Stone Age to a knowledge of the working of bronze and iron, leaving us a veritable museum of their handiwork in the tombs and tumuli of the steppe. Who these earliest inhabitants were, how deeply their culture extended, and whether they were one and the same people with those who evolved from the bronze to the Iron Age, we know not and probably will never know. Students have classified these unknown people under the broad title of Yeniseians, or Tubas, whilst the less-learned colonists call them the "Chudes," or "strangers."

All we know of these people is at the stage when they were in an embryo state, emerging slowly from the neolithic age. They apparently acquired considerable knowledge of husbandry, and of workings in metals, and their rock-drawings testify that they herded reindeer, cattle, and camels. They used bronze implements, and could work in gold and silver; but they were ignorant of the use of iron, the knowledge of which came later with an influx of newcomers from the south. These were the people who raised the tumuli over their dead, and whose custom of burying personal belongings in the graves, left us valuable information as to the condition of culture they had reached. We know nothing as to the length of time this race held their own, nor through what stages of mingling with other races they passed. The knowledge of their existence is simply proved by the tumuli.

This was a period of great racial movement in Asia. North and south, east and west, the struggling tribes were seeking outlets for their increase, or refuges from their oppressors. Many wars, many migrations, and much contention for the best localities caused a disorder, which make it difficult for us now to trace even the main movements. Strivings for a place in the Upper Yenisei region were occupying the attention of the tribes of Far Eastern Asia, who were either tempted by the favourable climatic conditions of this country or who were being unwillingly pushed forward by other waves of emigration. The Upper Yenisei formed an important centre in those early days, as indeed it does now. For on soil and climate depend the rise of civilization, and no race can rise to any state of culture under unsuitable conditions. The condition of the Yenisei Valley allowed the rise of the old Tuba races, and their comparatively high state of culture. Later on these same favourable conditions tempted the rude nomads of less hospitable Mongolia to fall on the Yeniseians and to seize their land. Finally in the present day the Russians have themselves settled in this land of promise.

About the third century B.C. there emerged into prominence a people who were destined to leave their mark on the whole civilized world. Somewhere from the far south of Mongolia, perhaps from the borders of China—from the present-day provinces of Shensi and Kansu—came a wandering people, the Uigurs. The origin of the Uigurs is problematic, but as far back as this it can be traced with fair certainty. These tribes wandered northwards, and eventually settled in Mongolia. Here they increased and flourished, and eventually spread over the Yenisei regions as far north as the Chulim River, until, in the eighth century A.D., their kingdom reached over the whole of Northern Mongolia, from Lake Kossogol to the Black Irtish.

The greatest power of the Uigurs (according to Professor Adrianoff of Minnusinsk) "extended from the fourth to the eighth century, when they exercised considerable political ascendency in these districts. The Chinese annals described them as being a light-haired and blue-eyed people. They were probably, at this period, of a very mixed race, showing great variation in type, especially as regards the protraction of the eyelid." In the ancient Uigurs we have the origin of the Turkish race, who, later on, overflowed all Central Asia and made an Empire on the shore of the Bosphorus. The history of the Uigurs and the migrations of the Turki tribes are outside our story; it is only the influence these races had upon the people of the Yenisei region that affects us.

When the Uigurs conquered the whole of the Upper Yenisei basin, and the present-day Minnusinsk region, they mixed with the indigenous Yeniseians, and it is to these people of mingled origin that the title of "Ugro-Samoyede" has been given. As these stronger tribes came into the land, the weaker Yeniseians were pushed back or absorbed. Some fled into the depths of the forests, and there found seclusion from the invaders, whilst others followed the line of least resistance, to the north. It is to this period that we must look for the original estrangement from the Yeniseians of the present-day inhabitants of the Upper Yenisei basin—the Urian-khai. Into this region one branch of the Yeniseians retreated, where, to this day, they remain under the name of Tubas or Uriankhai, protected from destruction by the impenetrable nature of the country.

We can picture those dwellers in the pleasant vale of Minnusinsk, gradually being ousted by more intelligent races, retreating down the banks of the Yenisei River, journeying northwards into a great lone land. There, no doubt, they found game and fish in plenty and safety from invasion, but the conditions of life were so strenuous that they slowly but surely sank into a condition of decay, lost their knowledge of mining and agriculture, until, at the present day, we find that they have reverted to the state of the Stone Age. This is the origin of the Samoyedes—the uncouth nomads of the farthest north, who are doomed to wander, for their appointed time, in the lands of bleak, monotonous tundra within the Arctic Circle.

Now the Uigurs were of a higher stamp than the former inhabitants of the Yenisei steppes, and during the occupation of North-west Mongolia and the Upper

Yenisei they left traces which have come down to us, and which enable us to prove this fact. It is supposed that they also erected tumuli, for two distinct types are to be found, namely, those that are surrounded by upright stone slabs, and those that are not. Inside the former are to be found iron and copper objects, but rarely gold and silver objects, as in the case of the older Yeniseians. To the Uigurs are ascribed all the old Turkish inscriptions, which are to be found all through Mongolia, and which are easily distinguishable from the undecipherable writings of the older inhabitants.

With the Uigur period of influence we find another slowly growing power, also of Turki origin, which eventually asserted itself and finally, in the seventh century, overthrew the Uigur Empire. This was the Kirghiz or Hakas tribe, a branch of the original Uigurs, who rose to power in the Kemchik region of the Upper Yenisei basin, and later on held the Siberian slopes of the Altai and Syansk until the coming of the Russians. The Uigur or Turkish influence in the Upper Yenisei regions lasted until it was supplanted by the Mongols. With the growth of the Mongolian hordes into a recognized power the Turki tribes gave way, civilization disappeared from the regions of the Upper Yenisei, and a veil is drawn over the politics of the Siberian-Mongol frontier. The Mongol destroyers swept the open lands to the south, but did not overflow far into Siberia, which always remained outside the sphere of their influence.

We have record of Jenghis Khan sending an expedition against a turbulent tribe in the Upper Yenisei basin, when, doubtless, the Turki races residing there were driven farther northwards, where they took refuge in the Minnusinsk and Chulim steppes, and along the northern side of the Altai, until the coming of the Russians. Now the two dominant races—the Chinese and the Russians—face each other on the waters of the Upper Yenisei, that region which has been so long the scene of many changes between conflicting tribes and migrating hordes. The Turki tribes (Kirghiz, or Hakas) migrated from the country in the face of the Russian advance, and left a comparatively open field for Siberian expansion into the vale of Minnusinsk.

It was at the beginning of the seventeenth century, that the Russians first dealt with these regions, and since that date the growth of their influence has been sure and steady. The Russians arrived on the banks of the Yenisei in 1629, and in 1775 were collecting taxes from the weak tribes whom they found inhabiting the upper tributaries of that river. Adrianoff mentions that a tribe called Kamash, living on the Man River—right affluent of the Yenisei, some twenty miles above Krasnoyarsk, seem to be a remnant of the once strong Samoyedes, and are probably nearly related by language to the Uriankhai of the Upper Yenisei basin. "This tribe," he says, "like all tribes in the territory of the modern Minnusinsk district, until the arrival of the Russians, were the subjects of China, and at no very distant date were probably living farther south." A few Tartars also lived here, but, by reason of their rapid decrease in population and by emigration, the country is now deserted. Such, in brief, is the varied history of these lands, which have been favourable to human progress from the earliest ages. The battle has been between the weaker indigenous races and the stronger alien tribes. The Uigur ousted the Yeniseian, the Hakas drove out the Uigur; now the Russian has

STONE IMAGE,
"With folded arms grasping a vessel."

UNWROUGHT STONE SLABS.

established himself, and will no doubt absorb the remaining tribes.

With reference to the monuments and inscriptions which remain as a field for research into the ancient beliefs and customs of the various inhabitants of the Upper Yenisei region, the moment has now come to discuss them more fully. At various times during our journey we came across many monuments of antiquity. To understand more fully the present conditions of the remnant of the ancient Yeniseians—the Uriankhai—we must endeavour to understand the ancient beliefs and customs which caused those primitive inhabitants to set up these monuments. We shall thus be able to trace the close affinity existing between the inhabitants of the far Yenisei and the people of other primitive civilizations.

As to the origin of the rock-pictures, the monoliths and stone figures, we must retrace our steps and endeavour to discover the relations of the early Yeniseians, in regard to religious ideas and mythological beliefs. The association between art and religion has been so closely bound up, even from the earliest times, as to make it almost certain that the one is the outcome of the other. It is thought that the origin of all art—all representation, is based upon the old anthropomorphic idea of primitive man wanting to give a definite life to the things or persons of his imagination.

Primitive people were not satisfied with the spiritual alone, but depended upon a strong sense of anthropomorphism. "They had always ambition to give a definite existence and personality to their vague ideas, which their minds could hardly grasp without some external aid." This may be the origin of those first attempts of man to express himself, namely, the picture-writing and designs, which are to be found all over the world. They are generally the expression of vague ideas. Early man drew those objects which closely affected his existence; he depicted the domesticated animals, and the wild game on which he depended for food. Pastoral and hunting-scenes are common amongst the rock-drawings of the Yenisei. The Bactrian camel, the reindeer, the goats and cattle, the bear, ibex, and wapiti were all well known to him, as proved by the rock-pictures. One notable scene of herdsmen "rounding-up" camels and reindeer was depicted. Of interest, also, are the pictures of men mounted on reindeer; for although this is still the custom of the forest-dwelling Uriankhai, yet these pictures exist in a district where no reindeer are now found. The artists of the Upper Yenisei were occasionally independent-minded enough to put in what they did not see, but what they knew was there; for this reason we have the strange appearance of an ox, in profile, with a portion of his skeleton and internal organs drawn in their right positions—like some anatomical chart.

This same idea is clearly traced by Professor Ernest A. Gardner in his *Religion and Art in Ancient Greece.* I cannot do better than quote him: "The association of acts of worship with certain specially sacred objects or places lies at the basis of most religious art, although art has but little or nothing to do with such objects in a primitive stage of religious development. Stocks and stones, the latter often reputed to have fallen from heaven, or trees, were to be found at all the centres of religious cult. Such sacred stocks or stones were not regarded merely as symbols of certain deities, but were looked upon as having occult or magic qualities inherent in them, and as being in themselves potent for good or evil. The ceremonies used in their cult partook of the nature of magic rather than of religion as far as these consisted of anointing them with oil or with drink-offerings."

Unwrought stones all the world over, and from the earliest ages, have been deemed sacred, sacrificed to, and even anointed. To this day we find the simple natives of this region holding in veneration their crude monoliths and the more finished monuments of stone. The stones are subject to offerings; they paint them with bright colours and wrap them in draperies, thus implying that the same things please the deity as please his worshippers.

The same idea held good with the temples—the dwelling-places of the gods. The more attractive these temples were made the more surely the god would remain, otherwise the god was apt to change his abode. This idea was forcibly impressed upon us when watching the erection of a booth for the reception of a god, on a hill-top in the Upper Yenisei basin, and the careful attention paid by the Uriankhai to the attractiveness of the dwelling, and the care given to providing offerings of food and drink.

Although the Uriankhai and the Mongols will tell you nothing about these stone figures, for they are loth to talk about them, they hint that they were made by a strange race, about whom they have no knowledge. Nevertheless, they treat them as sacred and in most cases venerate them by hanging them with bits of cloth and ribbon, and even old clothes. We have seen these monuments presenting a most ridiculous appearance as they stood alone on the wide, open steppe, dressed up in old clothes like some scarecrow on an

English plough. The Uriankhai sometimes undress and bow before these idols, beating their foreheads with the palms of their hands. All are not considered equally holy, only certain ones appear to be worthy of a sacrifice, namely, those that are recognized as being able to bring good or evil to the natives.

In regions where the monoliths are found in the neighbourhood of cultivated lands the productiveness of the soil is put down to them ; and in this respect it is interesting to note that the monuments are especially numerous in the fertile lands, which were occupied long ago by the old races. The Mongol and Kirghiz races are more indifferent to these antiquities; it is the Uriankhai only who hold them in real superstition.

As a general rule, we find these stones in all places where there are other definite traces of an ancient civilization. In Siberia they are to be observed on the steppe and in the open valleys away from the forested areas, where there are traces of old cultivation. The figures could not have been erected by a people who *depended* upon agriculture, for we find them also on the open Mongolian plateau, where no race lived any other life but a nomadic one. They are to be seen as upright stones, rough-hewn or polished, plain or sculptured; in fact, in all stages from a crudely scratched to a finished representation of a human face, from a terminal bust to a complete, if somewhat crude, figure. We found stones with nothing but the simplest lines to denote the eyes, nose, and mouth, and others, we noticed, had the addition of the cheeks being just rounded off. Later the primitive sculptors managed to shape a complete bust, and even, in some cases, full-length figures.

Here we have a continuous picture of the progress of

their ideas of art, from the earliest "*herm*" to the more or less complete figure "in the round." The monoliths which surround the old tumuli represent the most primitive ideas of a monument; they correspond to the "*herms*" of Greek belief, and are examples of man's first attempt to impersonate natural objects with the character of the deity supposed to inhabit them. Originally they were used as boundary-stones, or as monuments to mark a grave. The *herm* merely marked the sanctity of a spot. Jacob of old was only doing what the Yeniseians did, when he set up a stone and anointed it with oil, finding himself to be on sacred ground.

By degrees, as men realized the existence of deities apart from sacred objects, the stones became mere symbols—a great advance in religious ideas. The stones were even transformed into human shape, so that not only might the stones see and hear, but also take the image and character of the deity whom they were supposed to represent. As in the case of other primitive races, who painted eyes on the prows of their ships to enable them to find the way, so the Yeniseians also carved the head, eyes, and ears out of the sacred stone, the idea being that such carved eyes and ears actually served to transmit impressions to the god.

In these monoliths with a rudely scratched face, and at a later period with a more or less well-defined head, we have the earliest idea of sculpture. These early monuments resemble nothing more than a column, square in form, having practically four distinct sides, with a roughly modelled head. Later the *herm* became of a peculiar shape; they "tapered downwards"—a copy of the human form, and, still later, this column became more rounded, the head had more care bestowed upon it, the limbs began to take shape, and, as in the case of the earliest Greek sculpture, the arms appeared closely held to the side.

Although the terminal figure grew to be a free statue, or "stele," yet the sculptors never made any further progress. The arms never became detached from the body, and a leg never advanced with bent knee, to give the indication of the knowledge of balance. We can trace the slow progress of the sculptures as they grew to perfection, or, rather, to their standard of perfection, for they never went further, and they never idealized. Their original idea was probably to give a definite existence to some one they wished to remember, an attempt to place the image of a dead man on an idol.

It is these effigies which are such a remarkable feature of a certain area of Central Asia. In the now silent and uninhabited steppe, the traveller may suddenly come across these images standing solitary, waist-deep in the dry, dusty soil. Silent witnesses they must have been of the various waves of migration and military expeditions that have passed and repassed across these great lone lands, and in them we may look for a likeness to their creators; in fact, they themselves are the only indication to us of what their makers were like. Generally of natural size, roughly hewn out of granite or sandstone blocks into the bold, free likeness of some departed warrior, they present to the mind an analogy of ideas between them and the effigy of some Crusader in an English Cathedral, or the painted likeness on the outer case of an Egyptian mummy. All the way from the banks of the Yenisei to Southern Russia we find, at intervals, these curious

A TYPICAL STONE EFFIGY IN MONGOLIA.

monuments, which appear to represent an ancient and primitive custom. We, on our journey, did not actually see a great number of these stone figures, but by a study of the characteristics and distribution of all that have been described by other travellers, I find that there is a certain amount of valuable information regarding them which is worthy of record.

We conclude that the effigies were sepulchral, and were set up as monuments to the departed. Friar Rubruck, the earliest recorder of these stone effigies, stated this as a fact. When describing the customs of the Comans, the ancient nomadic Turki inhabitants of Southern Russia (before the arrival of the Mongols), he says they "raise a tumulus over the dead, and set up a statue to him, its face to the east, and holding a cup in its hand at the height of the navel." On another occasion the same traveller found many idols in a temple in Mongolia, and, imagining them to be representatives of deities, questioned the priests concerning them. The Mongols, however, surprised him by saying,—"we do not make images to God, but, when some rich person among us dies, his son, or wife, or some one dear to him, has made an image of the deceased and puts it here, and we revere it in memory of him."

These ancient customs, all of which seem to point to a form of ancestor-worship, can be traced, at the present day, in certain crude idols which are to be found in the homes of some of the Shammanistic Siberian tribes. The Ostiaks, for instance, practise the custom of shaping a rude wooden image of a man who has died; to this effigy they present offerings, and the widow embraces and caresses it. At the end of three years these idols are generally buried, but sometimes they are set up permanently and treated as saints. Other tribes keep little effigies in representation of each member of the family, and the number is added to or diminished, as the case may be, by a newly born member or a death.

No doubt, in the case of the stone figures, only the great men had this honour bestowed upon them, and when we find a burial-mound with one of these images standing—waist deep in the soil—beside it, we may consider its features as a probable likeness of the hero, whose remains lie below the giant mound of earth. We certainly noticed some very remarkable effigies with most striking facial features. It was obviously intended that there should be a facial resemblance to the man whose memory the effigy was to immortalize. We often saw the strong features of the warrior—a type we amused ourselves by likening to a Colonel of the British Army, by reason of his well-groomed moustache and general military appearance. Adrianoff describes one particularly sacred effigy, which the Uriankhai very naturally named the Jenghis Khan. This image he describes as being very well carved, and gave the impression of a strong man of severe expression, with a round face and high cheek-bones, with a drooping moustache and a small "Imperial." He had a short plaited pig-tail, and his head was covered with a skull-cap.

With reference to the remark of Rubruck's about the statues holding a cup, I can supplement his careful observations by recording that almost invariably, in all cases which have come before me, or which have been recorded by others, these figures are represented with arms folded across the chest, holding vessels in their hands. Those writers who have remarked on this fact of the vessels make no further comment. I can find no theory advanced as to their use, or any reason for their presence. I may be seeking a somewhat trifling origin for a very far-reaching custom, but it seems obvious that these vessels are the snuff-bottles which are the life-companions of the Mongols. Snuff-taking is the most universal custom of the Mongols; it has a well-established social meaning, and the strictest etiquette envelopes its use. The wealth and standing of a Mongol may be judged by the kind of snuff-bottle he uses; it is the criterion of his social rank. Some Mongols spend (for them) fabulous sums on snuff-bottles of carved jade and transparent stone; they would sooner part with their wives or a favourite horse than their snuff-bottles. As a sign of their position, and also no doubt in order to prevent their being without snuff on the long journey to the next world, the monuments were erected with the favourite bottles tightly clasped in their hands.

No matter what race we make responsible for this peculiar custom of erecting these stone monuments, it is certain that the creators themselves of these stone figures, or their influence, spread all the way westwards from here to Southern Russia. There is one essential difference between the Mongolian and Russian figures, which is so constant and so remarkable that it is worthy of record. According to M. Vladimir Riedel, the stone figures, or "effigies," of Southern Russia are similar to those of Mongolia (they even hold snuff-bottles); they differ fundamentally, however, in that they are nearly always of female form.[1] This is a very noteworthy fact, as in Mongolia the vast majority of figures are of male form, although figures in female form are also to be found.

[1] The Russian peasants have only one name for the stone figures—"babi," *i.e.* women.

It has been suggested that those of Southern Russia represented goddesses; but, as a matter of fact, in the old Slavic faith there were no goddesses. Moreover, during recent researches in Asia Minor, a representation of a goddess has been found there, which belongs to so early a date that it was supposed to be the original from which arose the idea of the Virgin of the Christian faith. At that period the idea of female-worship, as such, was not known anywhere north of the Alps.

A more plausible theory is that put forward by M. Riedel, who thinks that the stone figures date from the introduction of Christianity into Russia. In those days many heathen customs survived, the most typical and revolting of which was that of burying the wife in the same grave as the husband. There are instances of the bones of men, women, and horses being found in the same grave. These latter were, no doubt, considered necessary for use in a future state. On the introduction of Christianity this barbaric custom would naturally be the first that the missionaries would endeavour to suppress. It is, therefore, thought probable that these stone figures were the earliest substitutes for the human being, an important change in their customs brought in by the Christian priests in order to do away with female sacrifice. The women were, on the death of their husbands, persuaded to erect a stone figure representing themselves, and these they placed over the graves. As a proof of their dating from a period after the introduction of Christianity it is significant to note that there have been found figures with a *cross* cut on the breast.

Apart from the stone figures, there are other indications, of even greater antiquity, of the customs of the ancient Yeniseians, namely, the tumuli. So amazing is the quantity of these grave-mounds in the Northern Minnusinsk region that a portion of the district has earned the name of the Azkiezkaia Steppe, or "The Plain of the Dead." These monuments are to be found distributed over a wide area from South Siberia along the Urals as far as the Volga. Their number in the Russian Altai, in Mongolia, and in the Uriankhai country is astounding. In the tumuli are hidden the secrets of ancient history, and of the progress of early man. These secrets would reveal to us the history of a nation, which reached a higher degree of culture than the people now occupying this land, a nation which has now disappeared, leaving as a record these tombs and figures in which are wrapt up the riddle of their life-history.

The tumuli, or "Kurgans," *i.e.* "strangers' graves," or graves of the "Chudes," or "aliens,"[1] form a study in themselves, and have occupied the attention of several learned Russian archæologists during the last few years. From what I can gather, the tumuli were not always of a sepulchral nature, *i.e.* mounds built over the graves, but held a deeper meaning, probably a mythological one, and played a definite part in the affairs of the tribes. Gigantic mounds, which might well be supposed to be monuments to great chieftains, have been excavated and found to contain nothing. These mounds were probably tribal meeting-places, where assemblies of the tribesmen were called together.

The shape of the mounds, their dimensions, their relative positions and details of construction, vary a great deal, but, according to Adrianoff, we may place

[1] The name Ostiak—a tribe of Southern Siberia—between whom and the Uriankhai there are some affinities, also means "stranger."

them in two groups, which are easily differentiated. Those of the Kemchik Valley, the Upper Yenisei, and the Russian Altai, he groups together and entirely separates those of the Abakan and Minnusinsk steppes. The first type have a cobbled surface, and are always surrounded by a circle of stones; the second type are earthen mounds surrounded by large stone-slabs, in the form of a square.

All the mounds we saw in the Chulim and Minnusinsk steppes were remarkable for the presence of monoliths, or upright stone-slabs, set up round the tumuli; this is, in fact, the characteristic feature of the mounds of this particular district, for although in the course of our subsequent journey we came across graves of a variety of types, and occasional isolated monoliths, we never again saw graves to resemble these. The slabs were placed in every conceivable combination of numbers, yet they were always alike in one respect, namely, in the orientation of the face of the stones. All slabs, without exception, faced north and south, with their narrow edges east and west. Their position was so exact in this respect, that we could always observe the points of the compass so long as we were in sight of a grave-mound.

As regards number and size, the stones varied considerably. Some measured above the ground 10 ft. in height by 3 ft. in breadth and 8 in. in thickness; some, indeed, reached to 13 ft. in height. Although the total number of stones surrounding a particular grave was generally even, the stones were placed without any apparent method; we counted six on the east side, and six on the west, three on the north side and three on the south,—a total of eighteen. Other examples gave

TUMULUS AND MONOLITHS ON THE CHULIM STEPPE.

twelve, and twenty, made up in like manner. It has been suggested by some writers that these rough stone slabs were supposed to represent the number of enemies killed in battle by the dead heroes. This may be a solution of the varying number of the slabs. The greatest number I can find record of are those which are placed by the tomb of Tomyukuk, a Turkish hero of the seventh century, near Urga. In this case there is a single straight line, not a circle, of three hundred monoliths ![1] From Chinese sources, also, we learn that it was "customary amongst the ancient Turks to place around a tomb as many upright stones as the deceased had killed persons in his life-time.[2]

The mounds were not placed on any particular site; sometimes they were on hill-tops singly, and at others in great profusion on the steppe. The very largest were generally placed singly or in couples, but the cemeteries of hundreds of tumuli were composed of mounds of a relatively small size. The actual location of the tumuli may perhaps largely have depended upon the necessity of their being situated in the vicinity of a stone-quarry. In the Kemchik Valley, for instance, they are more numerous and more thickly set on the hills near the stone-quarries than they are in the valleys. In the northern part of the Minnusinsk steppe, where we came across the first great cemetery of tumuli, a stone-quarry was conspicuous in the background, which had no doubt supplied those ancient people with all the material they needed; yet, on the other hand, they did achieve much in the way of transporting huge blocks of stone,

[1] See Mr. C. W. Campbell's report on *A Journey in Mongolia*, 1904.

[2] See *Chou Shu* (The Annals of the Chou Dynasty) as quoted by Rockhill in his translation of *Rubruck*, p. 82. Haklyut Society edition.

for we have seen giant monoliths far away from any quarry.

In Mongolia the choice of a site for burial depended largely on the superstitious ideas attached to certain localities. A feature of Mongolian scenery is the presence of peculiar uplifts of windworn granite, little isolated rock-ranges which stand up here and there as landmarks on the plateau. These throughout all time have been a source of wonder to the natives, and were considered sacred; in consequence, we find the burial-grounds concentrated there.

In the depths of the grave-mounds have been discovered a host of interesting relics, such as skulls, which show us the ethnographical type of man who lies buried there; death-masks of beaten gold, which indicate to us their exact facial features—features, by the way, which the authorities describe as being remarkably European; and besides this a harvest of stone, bone, bronze, gold, silver, and iron ornaments, trinkets, mining-tools and implements. The bones which have been taken out of the mounds afford much material for consideration and discussion. Care, however, must be taken in theorizing with the information at our disposal. Many graves apparently contain only one body, and the deductions are obvious; but succeeding inhabitants were inclined to bury their dead in the same mounds as constructed by their forerunners, and different generations are found in layers, under the same tumuli. These different layers may represent the different types of inhabitants which have held the Yenisei plain at various periods, and research work in connexion with the skulls which have been found, may result in a clearer understanding of who these ancient people were.

The fact that mounds are found in great numbers in certain localities, points to the possibility of their position having been the scene of some great conflict between warlike tribes, or between the indigenous races and the foreign invaders. Adrianoff remarks that, in this latter case, it might be of the greatest interest to excavate, with the view of unearthing two types of skulls and thereby gaining material for comparison, from which we might deduce the respective ethnographical characteristics of the natives and of the invaders. Mention has been made, by that same keen scientist, of one giant mound of from 20 to 30 ft. in height, which was found to contain between ten and fifteen bodies of men and horses, with other belongings.

The nature of the contents of the tumuli varies as much as their construction. On sinking a shaft down a mound in the Minnusinsk region, the excavators first came upon a rotten beam of timber; four or five yards deeper they found many bones in disorder, the skulls of five men and the bones of eleven, also the bones of sheep and six earthenware vases. Further, a horizontal shaft was found reaching to a vault, which was empty.

Amongst the wonderful collection of antiquities found in the mounds, or discovered by chance in the ground wherever the soil has been turned by the present-day colonists, there are a few items well worthy of consideration. For instance, from the tumuli have been taken certain metallic discs which were evidently used as looking-glasses. These mirrors chance to be identically the same as those still in use amongst the Buriats of Southern Siberia, and although it is claimed that the burying-places belong to a race wholly distinct from the present-day inhabitants of this part of Siberia, yet this fact would oblige us to hold the opinion that there must be some far-distant connexion.[1]

From contemporary history we learn that in the days of Herodotus (fifth century B.C.) these Yeniseians were in the Bronze Age, whilst four centuries later Strabo remarks that they used gold and bronze, a little iron, but no silver. The relative ages of culture as compared with those in Europe are of interest. The Tartars were in the Iron Age when visited by medieval travellers, yet the Tunguses of Siberia to this day use stone arrowheads. The influence of the Yeniseians may have been very far-reaching. According to tradition, the working of gold, silver, copper, and bronze was introduced into North America by foreigners; and the evidence that North America has received its population from Asia is fairly well established, on the strength of the physical, social, and linguistic characteristics of the aborigines, which are so closely allied to those of the Mongolian tribes in Siberia. May not the introducers of the art of metal-working have been these same skilled mineralogists from the banks of the Yenisei?

As to the extent of the practice of agriculture in these regions we have only, as data, the presence of old irrigation canals. It is mere conjecture as to which period these works can be ascribed, but, as the climate of the Minnusinsk basin was so favourable to human progress, we may look to the very earliest development of husbandry as taking place here. In some localities, at the present day, the modern settler has actually found it

[1] Some of the skulls found in the mounds are of the "dolicho-cephalic" type, which shows that the earliest builders of the mounds were probably men of the Stone Age, whilst the gradual influx of a foreign element is proved by the fact that the majority of the skulls belong to the "brachy-cephalic," or Mongolic type.

convenient to open up the old disused canals, and has proved that their engineering was in no way at fault. Obviously this country must have had attractions and conditions most suitable to the people of those days, otherwise why was this region so favourable to the production, growth, and advance of prehistoric man? Why, later on, did it arouse the greed of invaders from the south?

To carry the question further, why is this district, at the present day, the home of the most progressive Siberians, and why is the Upper Yenisei region calling forth the energies of the prospecter and the miner, and why are the regions beyond it the desire of the trader, when at length a commercial treaty allows him a free hand? It seems as if the land is coming back to its old prosperity. The necessities of more advanced civilization in the west, find need of the hidden and untouched riches of the east. Thus Minnusinsk holds out fair prospects to the farmer, the gold of the Upper Yenisei attracts the prospecter, and the scope for trade in wool, hides, and fur tempts the Russian trader into Far Mongolia. May not all this alter the colour of the map? may it not bring Russia into antagonism with China, or even into alliance with the independent Mongol chieftains? This last invasion is from the north and the west, but it corresponds in many ways to the old invasion from the south, when the Uigurs, in the earliest days, descended into these fair regions from the bleak plateaux of Mongolia.

Before leaving this region of ancient associations mention should be made of, and full credit given to, those Russian scientists who have been carrying on the work of excavation in their eager desire to search out the mysteries of these antiquities. As long ago as 1881, the first "Kurgans" were opened up in the neighbourhood of Minnusinsk, but systematic excavation did not take place until between 1892–1903. The result of this work has been published from time to time by the Imperial Russian Geographical Society, and by the Imperial Archæological Committee.

To Dr. N. Martianoff and latterly to Professor Adrianoff we are chiefly indebted for our knowledge of ancient Siberia; the wonderful results of their labour being shown by the collection exhibited in the Museums of Minnusinsk, Tomsk, St. Petersburg, and Moscow. In the Minnusinsk Museum can be seen an unrivalled array of stone, copper, bronze, and iron implements, prehistoric pottery, and a series of five hundred skulls from the Kurgans. Beside these, many stone monuments and inscribed pillars find here a resting-place, and have thus been preserved from destruction. The metallurgical finds are kept in the Historical Museum in Moscow, whilst the gold and silver ornaments are treasured in the "Eronitash" in St. Petersburg.

We had the pleasure of meeting Professor Adrianoff whilst in Minnusinsk, where we found him engrossed in his work of deciphering the old runic writings from the region of the Upper Yenisei. The results of his labours are at the present moment in the hands of the Imperial Archæological Committee, in preparation for publication, and we eagerly await the appearance of this work, for it should settle many questions of importance, and give us a knowledge of many things which are at present without explanation.

CHAPTER III

THE SIBERIAN BACKWOODS

THE country that lies at the foot of the Mongolian plateau, in which we outfitted for our journey, and where our first difficulties began, constitutes "the edge of cultivation," beyond which is a gloomy region of primeval forest and dismal fen. This whole region between the Altai Mountains and Lake Baikal, along the Russo-Chinese frontier, is a hill-country of a densely forested nature, holding a scanty population and possessing few ways of communication. Along the foot-hills of this mountain-region extend the settlements of Siberian colonists—settlements which represent the advance-guard of that great immigration which Asiatic Russia has been absorbing from Europe during the last fifty years. Here end the rich, open plains, and with them the advance of civilization, for beyond lies the unknown depth of forest backed by the Syansk border-range.

This is a happy, fruitful country of great capabilities and rich resources. The land is of the best, the climate is mellowed by the protecting ranges, and the great waterways give easy and quick transport. The Siberians, as good colonists as one could meet anywhere in the world, but lacking that "push" and originality which is indispensable to bring their country into the first rank, have slowly but surely advanced southwards towards the Mongol frontier. The border-ranges, which form the frontier, are in themselves no barrier to the further advance of the Siberians; it is the dense forests which clothe them that constitute the real hindrance to further colonization. At the edge of the forest-belt the Russian settlements stop entirely; into the forests it is only the most energetic of the traders, fur-hunters, and fishermen who venture to penetrate, with the idea of opening up a somewhat unsatisfactory trade with the indigenous tribes, and in the hope of benefiting by the great wealth that the "taiga" contains in the shape of minerals and furs. Beyond the forest-barrier, however, in the heart of the Yenisei basin, we found many small colonies where Siberian settlers had made isolated and secluded homes.

The impenetrability of this zone of forest and mountains, the little knowledge that men seemed to have of it, as well as the actual season of the year, caused the first obstacles in our advance southwards, and called for much resource to overcome. These peculiar physical conditions have kept the sources of the Yenisei a *terra incognita*; they have hindered the Russianization of a land which orographically belongs to Siberia, and they have helped to make it a refuge for the indigenous tribes.

The basin of the Upper Yenisei is neither truly Russian nor Chinese; its physical features give the appearance of being in a stage of transition between those of Siberia and Inner Asia. From this narrative it will be noticed that, in the course of our journey, we met with forests of spruce, Scotch pine, and larch as well as areas of arid steppe; that we encountered lush green meadows, damp forests, and a wealth of wild-flowers on one slope of a mountain-range, and the pale aridity of desiccation on the other side of the same range; that we saw the birch-bark "tepee," or wigwam, and the felt-covered yurt in close proximity, and in quite a small area we found such a variety of domesticated animals as reindeer, camels, horses, yaks, and cattle.

Kushabar, where we spent two weeks, outfitting for our plunge into the "wild," is a typical frontier village. Situated as it is, at the very foot of the most outlying spurs of the mountain, within half a mile of the edge of the forest-belt, and on the banks of the Amil River, it possesses all the characteristics of a prosperous colony. Here is land, fuel, and water-transport; here is shelter from the cold in winter, and sufficient rain in summer; the severe Siberian climate being mellowed on account of the proximity of the mountains.

Arriving here in the beginning of May, we soon discovered that considerable difficulties and delays were ahead of us; we had, however, during the following two weeks ample opportunities for enjoying this attractive and interesting season of the year in a region of contrasting climate, where a sudden plunge took place from depth of winter into brilliant summer. Although no snow lay, at this date, on the edge of the forest near by the village, yet it was said to be quite deep farther in. As no grass had been able to grow, we could not move with our horses—being dependent upon the country for fodder. Moreover, all tributaries of the Amil—insignificant little streams at other seasons—were swollen to a prodigious size and consequently unfordable. All these things united to make communication between Siberia and the regions of the Upper Yenisei exceedingly difficult, and hindered our advance. There are only two periods when travel can be said to be comparatively easy, namely, in autumn, when the rivers are low, and in mid-winter, when they are frozen solid; in both seasons use being made of the rivers, in autumn by canoe and in winter on the ice by sleigh.

Winter is the only season when the hunters can penetrate into the depths of the forest, namely, by following up the frozen water-ways, dragging with them light sleighs with provisions and traps, and using always the river as a base for further operations in the wilds. Winter is the time when the Siberian colonists have little to do, for the land is hard-frozen, and the stock only has to be fed. With the sudden summer, however, comes a rush of work and movement. The fishermen pole their canoes upstream, and net the chosen waters in the upper reaches; the gold-miners outfit with canoe and pack-horse, to prospect new country, or to do summer-work at a mine which has been shut down all winter; the traders move southward with their merchandise, and barter their goods with the forest-dwellers for furs, hides, and wool.

The Siberian spring is accompanied by somewhat unsettled weather. When the ice breaks on the Yenisei River the weather breaks also. Strong winds, sudden storms, and great changes in temperature occur. In Minnusinsk we even had a little snow, but in Kushabar, two weeks later, we read a maximum temperature of 86°, and the heat was quite oppressive until thunderstorms cleared the air. The latter part of May was hot and sunny; with magical rush spring swept past on its north-bound journey, leaving in a few days a carpet of fresh green grass and budding flowers on a ground which, a week before, had just escaped from the grasp of frost. In the forest flowers sprang up in profusion—marigolds, forget-me-nots, primroses, and anemones; the birches showed the first film of green. On the wings of spring

SPRUCE FOREST ON THE LOWER SLOPES OF THE SYANSK MOUNTAINS.

FORESTS OF SCOTCH PINE,
Near Kushabar.

came a million summer birds, and at once prepared to nest, instinct making them aware of the shortness of the time at their disposal in these their summer haunts.

On our arrival on May 16th there was no sign of green on the steppe or in the forest, but by the 26th the spring was so far advanced, and the grass was so abundant, that we were enabled to graze out our caravan-horses on the meadows. The birches and the poplars burst into full leaf during the same short period. Each day, as we rode out, we could notice the increased growth. Flowers appeared as if by magic, banks of forget-me-nots, yellow pansies, small irises, and anemones in the forest and great beds of orange ranunculus in the swamps. The grass in places where the ground was burnt by forest-fires sprang up in five days to as many inches. Price estimated the growth of plants during the eight days between May 19th and 27th to have been on this scale: ranunculus, 1 ft. 6 in.; forget-me-nots, 1 ft.; buttercups, 6 in.; grasses, 1 ft. 3 in. and 1 ft. 10 in.

In the forest we spent many days. Much "lumbering" had been going on along its edge, and, in consequence, the trees had been thinned out, this outer zone of forest being largely made up of magnificent Scotch pines. Price, who spent most of his time during our stay at Kushabar in studying forestry, noted the chief characteristics of the trees of this region. This part of the forest-belt is composed of pine, birch, and poplar, with a few spruce. The pine, Price observes, thrive best on the slopes facing south, south-east, or south-west, where there is plenty of light and sun; in fact, these slopes were more or less covered with Scotch pine only, whereas on the other aspects poplar, aspen, birch, and a few spruce alone found sustenance. He noted that the distribution of species of trees seemed in no way dependent on the underlying soil.

The pine-forests were in some parts closely grown and in others of an open character. The closer-grown trees attained a height of 120 to 140 ft., with a girth of 7 to 9 ft. These trees had evidently sprung up very close together when quite young, and had, later on, been considerably thinned out. In the more open forest the mature trees gave maximum heights of 90 to 120 ft., with girth of 10 to 12 ft. The thinning of the pine-forests appeared to be brought about by the fact that the trees in middle age, when crowded, automatically thinned themselves, the weaker becoming suffocated, and dying out. The deep soil enables the stronger trees to get their roots far down, and thus to draw water over a larger area during the time they are crowding the weaker out. The weaker trees thus either die, are blown down, or are burnt by grass-fires in the summer.

With a view to ascertaining the problematic changes by climate in this region, Price's notes on the regeneration of the Scotch pines are significant. He observed that there was very little generation going on at the present date. The shade of the older trees, the grass, which seemed to have encroached on the forest and swamped the seedlings, the grass-fires in spring and summer, and the absence of moss in the ground-flora, seemed to reduce pine generation to a minimum. Only a few isolated seedlings could be seen here and there. The chief regeneration was that of poplar, and birch, which, shooting up under the pines, could easily push their heads through the long grass. "It seems to me," Price goes on to state, "that the pine-area in the forest had evidently been formed under conditions far more favourable to pine growth and regeneration than at the present time; these conditions were, probably, absence of grass and presence of moss, accompanied, in former years, by greater rainfall and a colder climate."

After waiting impatiently for three weeks, we became anxious about our departure. Snow still lay in places in the forest, and, from all accounts, the ridges a few thousand feet higher were impracticable for the passage of a caravan, besides which, in the rapid rise of the Amil River we had sufficient proof of abundant snows in a melting condition. Hot, sunny weather continued, which melted the snows in the higher regions, and the river rose accordingly. Every evening we examined the flood; by May 26th it had overflowed the country for a considerable distance on either bank. Towards the east, where the river was more or less hemmed in by hills, there were 6 to 800 yards of water; towards the north, communication by road was cut off, and, taking everything into consideration, it seemed as if we might be delayed here indefinitely.

But on May 27th the water was stationary, and on the following days it fell in the proportion of 18 in., 2 ft., and 1 ft.; in fact, the water, owing chiefly to cold nights, fell in three days as much as it had risen in a week. On the flood came fishermen from the upper waters, using small rafts with great "sweeps" in front and behind; some of them stopped at Kushabar, and gave us news of the forest, others drifted past on their way to the Yenisei, with their cargo of barrels of salted fish.

These men reported much snow twenty or thirty miles in the forest; and another wanderer, who arrived from the Russian gold-mines in the mountains, warned us of six feet of soft snow on the passes. These notes are of interest with regard to the opening up of ways of communication in this region. Great, and almost inconceivable differences exist in the rain and snow-fall, and the possibility of utilizing the waterways in different localities. The north side of the Syansk is very different in this respect to the south; the forested routes of the Amil cannot be compared at all with those of the more open valleys of the Abakan. Surveyors of this region, searching for reasonable routes across the mountains, will have to consider carefully the different climatic conditions of each district.

We became quite accustomed to the quiet village life, and found the Siberian colonists most hospitable and entertaining. They were a type to be found anywhere on the outskirts of a new country,—the best type,—those who push on ahead of the others, and who are capable of handling nature, and fighting her complexities in a plain, stubborn manner. The same characteristic is found in the Canadian backwoods, or on the high veldt in South Africa. Kushabar has been a village for about seventy years; it consists of about two hundred log-houses, holding about twelve hundred inhabitants. The whole village seemed to us like one large family. Nothing was done without common consent and agreement. For instance, a deputation waited on us one day, and the spokesman informed us that it had been decided by the village council that, during our stay, we should pay a rouble per horse for the grazing-rights. The grazing-ground being shared by the whole village, the keep of horses was paid for in proportion to the number; it was only fair and natural that we strangers, with our dozen animals, should not be given free use of these special rights. The spokesman explained to us that

CAMP IN THE "TAIGA"

THE START FROM KUSHABAR.

travellers passing through would, in an ordinary way, be welcome to the use of the pastures, but we apparently had settled in the village indefinitely. The money was, of course, paid willingly, while at the same time we pointed out that *our* ambition was to continue our journey, as we had no intention of settling down in Kushabar.

By degrees we purchased more horses, until our caravan numbered twenty-four, twenty of which were intended for transport. The organization of this part of the journey was attended with the maximum amount of difficulty that could be experienced by any traveller. We were at the outset of an unusually long journey; all our kit, clothes, instruments, and outfit had to be "packed" on horses unaccustomed to baggage, by men unaccustomed to managing baggage-animals, and it had to be transported over a zone of country full of natural difficulties. These horses cost, on an average, forty to sixty-five roubles each; they were mostly in good condition, having grazed out on the steppe; but they were animals from the plains, rather large and heavy, and not exactly suitable for hill-work. We had to make the best of it, however, for we were, as a matter of fact, in the wrong locality for "fitting out" our expedition. We were on the north side of the ranges, and in consequence were hampered by the maximum amount of snow; we were amongst settled Russian peasants, instead of, as would have been to our advantage, amongst nomadic Kalmuks, or Kirghiz, where we should have had the pick of great herds of horses, and the choice of skilled horsemen to manage a caravan.

Saddles had to be bought and fitted, felt saddle-pads, halters, ropes, girths, etc., had to be procured before we were ready to trek. The village was very nearly self-supporting, and we could buy the greater number of things we needed, though others had to be sent for from the larger settlement of Kara-tuz, to the north. Home-spun material was found to be most useful and durable for making sacks and for covering the felts, etc. We bought our supply of flour, and filled up every available tin with cheap and good honey, and generally ransacked the village for anything that might be of use to us.

The food question was a difficult one. The expedition consisted of three Englishmen, our Georgian interpreter, Gregoireff Makandaroff, and seven Siberians of Kushabar whom we employed for the management of the caravan. Our party of eleven men had to be fed for an indefinite period, as the region ahead of us supplied fish only with certainty, while flour was only to be procured if our route happened to lead us into some Siberian traders' settlement. We guaranteed for these Siberians a daily allowance of tea, and of three pounds of "sukari," or toasted bread—a not excessive allowance to sustain largely built men, undergoing considerable physical exercise; but they appeared to be contented with it, as this is their usual fare when on journeys in the "taiga." We did not, however, quite know our Siberians; for there was plenty of trouble in store for us as regards the food allowance, and the demands they made for meat. Some days were spent in collecting a sufficient supply of sukari, which is the ordinary Russian bread chopped into small pieces, and baked quite hard. This is very light to carry, and, if preserved dry, keeps indefinitely. Four hundred pounds' weight was prepared for the journey; with this we carried 150 lbs. weight of flour for ourselves, and a reserve of another 150 lbs. of the same. Our food-supply, together with our kit, made up sufficient loads for twenty horses.

Finally, a long agreement with our men was drawn up in the presence of the village council and the parties concerned; this, after considerable haggling, was duly signed by the village elder and the men, some of whom, by the way, could not write, and had their names written for them.

On June 2nd we were ready to start. Never shall we forget our departure from that little Siberian village. The men were incapacitated by an all-night's carouse, the horses were unmanageable, the heavy loads were both awkward and difficult to pack! Besides all this, the fresh and untried horses, the new saddles and unstretched ropes, added to the difficulties of our work. The head-man was so intoxicated as to be quite fearless, and managed the wild Tartar horses most skilfully. Often we had to "rope up" a horse before the baggage could be put on, and when it was packed a mad fit of "bucking" as often as not necessitated a re-packing. It is a well-known fact that the first day of any journey with pack-animals is always the worst, but this particular one beat all our previous experiences.

At last the caravan was set in motion, the twenty pack-horses filed down the long village street, past the gaudily painted church, and out into the meadows. In the open the horses at once became still more trouble-some, for a slip of a pack or the catch of a rope would stampede the Tartar broncos unused to such work, and we had the pleasure of seeing our wild horses careering over the hill-sides dragging their loads behind them. This stampede would be followed by a "round up," a repacking of the loads, and yet another start. It took us some seven hours to get out of sight of the village, but, having once gained the narrow forest-path, we made better progress.

The foot-hills and the edge of the forest were spangled with many-coloured flowers; sheets of blue and gold indicated forget-me-nots and ranunculus, the birches showed up against dark pines in vistas of softest green, and under them were spread lawns of grass. The day was brilliant, the air was full of summer sounds, and, as the route unveiled itself before us, and the caravan tinkled through the forest, we realized that only natural difficulties and struggles with the elements were before us. The last link with civilization was broken. There was nothing beyond us but the mountains, the forests, and the great breezy plateaux. Later in the day, when the first camp was pitched, the birch-logs were burning, and our horses were grazing in the wealth of grass around the camp, we felt once again that strange contentment alone known and appreciated by the inveterate wanderer.

Eastwards and southwards, beyond Kushabar, the country changes in character. From the edge of the forest near the village, and from a slight elevation on the first foot-hills, the Syansk Range becomes clearly visible. Here, by a far-away glimpse of bare crags, lifting up above the endless stretches of dark forest, we obtain the first indication of the northern declivities of the Mongolian plateau. Although of no great altitude, the crags are impressive after the endless monotony of the Siberian plains. The sunny meadows beside the swirling Amil are a bright foreground to the vast stretches of pine forests seen in the middle distance, these allowing the eye to rest at length on white snow-fields and the jagged tops of the main ranges. The watershed of the range was about forty miles away, in a direct line; but those forty miles meant, even in the best season, four days' journey; under the present prospect of snow and of flooded rivers we did not anticipate reaching the summit under ten days of strenuous marching.

The Syansk Mountains extend under that name for a distance of between three and four hundred miles, along the whole northern side of the Yenisei basin. The range, as a barrier, is complete except at the one point where a narrow defile, called the Kemchik Bom, lets out on to the Siberian plains the pent-up waters of the main sources of the Yenisei. Although of no great altitude, the range is a remarkable physical feature. The long, continuous, and regular watershed, as shown on the maps, does not exist; it is made up of an uneven line of disconnected uplifts, which render the country awkward to negotiate, and also make it difficult for the surveyor to grasp the exact character of the ranges.

As before mentioned, the main ridge was about forty miles distant from Kushabar, the intervening space being filled up by the outlying spurs and offshoots of the mountains. These spurs occasionally attain an altitude equal to the main range. The Aradansk Range, for instance, rises to an altitude of 8,000 ft., and forms a double barrier to the traveller proceeding southwards from Minnusinsk, for he must cross this ridge before approaching the main watershed. On our route we made use of the valley of the Amil for the most part; but even in doing so we had to pass over several cross-ridges and to climb the outlying spur called Chokerok; then we dropped again into the Upper Amil Valley before finally starting to ascend the actual watershed of the

Syansk. Thus it will be seen that the ways which approach the Syansk from the north are rough and devious; the traveller must not count on the actual distance, but rather on the nature of the ground, when trying to estimate his marches. Our track, at the start, lay along the north side of the Amil River, as far as a place called Petropavlovsk, where a fisherman had built a log-hut and had named the place after himself. Thence our route lay along the south bank of the river, over a more hilly country, until we gained the upper reaches of the Amil, where the river flows parallel to, and close under, the Syansk Range. Crossing the river in its upper reaches, a tributary took us up to the crest of the Syansk.

The first days were the most trying; in fact, the first struggle with the taiga was the most exhausting encounter with nature that we had ever experienced. The exertion of manipulating the caravan, of keeping the men up to the work, of ensuring their contentment in order to avoid mutiny—all this had to be borne, as well as the physical fatigue of plunging through stifling jungle, wading through bogs, and battling with innumerable and most voracious mosquitoes. The first stage from Kushabar to Petropavlovsk was twenty-six miles, and we took five days to accomplish it! Into those twenty-six miles the most exasperating difficulties were crowded. We had frequently to start in the morning after a three or four hours' struggle with the horses and their packs; often indeed this struggle was preceded by a hunt through the surrounding jungles for horses which had strayed, and was followed by endless labour with pack and pack-horses, which continued throughout the day. The loads were off the horses as much as on them, a continuous march for any length of time with the full quota of

SLOW PROGRESS THROUGH DENSE "TAIGA."

horses rarely occurred, for some horses had always fallen out by the way. The steep climbs up the ridges and the scrambles down the other side, made the loads still more likely to shift, and, at its best, the track could only be described as having once been a horse-track.

During the second day's trek we met with rivers—small rivers, it is true, but of a sufficient depth to forbid fording. It was then we congratulated ourselves on having brought a folding-boat, and, in spite of the ridicule of the Siberian boatmen, who were incredulous as to a boat of canvas being really of any practical use, we succeeded in ferrying our kit across the Bogart River in a couple of hours without mishap. The horses swam over the flood, and we packed again rapidly in order to continue our trek until dark. The canvas boat, of the "Accordian" pattern, journeyed with us all the way to Kulja in Turkestan. Owing to lack of time and opportunity we did not make the use of it that we had intended. It was, however, of great use on a few special occasions; it made up into two packs which constituted a light horse load, and it could be put into working order in a few minutes. We were generally able to ferry no less than four packs across a river at a time, and, if carefully handled, the boat would carry three men; on account of being so lightly built it was unsafe to use in a very strong or turbid torrent.

Beyond the Bogart River we entered a forest of exceptional density, the virgin taiga of primeval character, where the trees were smaller and more closely grown together, while the ground was covered with a soft bed of moss and damp, sodden undergrowth. With a feeling of vague uncertainty, even of repulsion, we plunged almost blindly into this vast sea of choking vegetation, this turmoil of taiga, which hid from us all distance, and baulked all effort, which tied our hands and obstructed our feet, in apparently grim determination to force back the intruders. With us was the almost overpowering sense of Nature being too strong for us, and at times it seemed absolute folly to battle against her. The horses appeared out of place, the baggage unnecessary and cumbersome, and we ourselves were dwarfed by this giant world of forest. We were of those, however, who become encouraged rather than disheartened by the presence of great odds, and these first days' struggle with the taiga appealed strongly to our imagination, making us indifferent to everything but the desire to advance.

Nature here showed diabolical ingenuity in placing every conceivable obstacle in the way of the would-be explorer of her wilds. Human progress was hindered by vegetation, both alive and dead, by rushing streams in flood, by deep, stagnant lakes and treacherous bogs. These difficulties are expected, welcomed, and gladly faced by the real nature-worshipper. They represent the ordinary incidents of daily life when lived away from civilization. Travel without such experiences would be but a tame venture, scarcely worth the undertaking.

On reaching the Black River, a small affluent of the Amil, we were stopped on our course by the deep, swift flood which cut across our track. This forced us to turn aside and follow the bank through a forest of even greater entanglement. Up till now we had been travelling over successive ridges where the hilly nature of the country had encouraged drainage, and the ground had become more or less dry; but now we met the true taiga, or "swampy forest"—the real meaning of the

FLOODED FOREST.

word, as used in Siberia. Our struggling caravan made no more than a verst an hour, and the work was extremely exhausting. Soft ground bogged the pack-animals, fallen timber caused many a pack to be thrown, and the closely grown trees necessitated continual axe-work before the horses could pass.

It was a strange and weird experience. The endless forest, damp and dripping with the rot of ages, silent, sombre, and sodden, hemmed us in on every side. All that we saw was the tangle of growth, the young living forest springing up above the dead fallen timber which lay crosswise on the ground, trunk piled on trunk—three generations deep—all overgrown with moss, and treacherous to walk over. Around us hung the murky atmosphere of the jungle, above us festoons of lichen, showing hoary white against the dark pines, draped the trees and waved from the branches. We became more alive to the strange contrast of the living and the dead, when the deathlike silence was suddenly broken by the sound of the axe clearing the way for our advance, and by the cries of the men encouraging the horses, these sounds of life echoing through the lofty pines. A profound impression was made on me by these strenuous days—days when we pushed our caravan by sheer determination across nature's inviolate boundaries.

Anon we came to swampy bottoms, half-lake, half-forest, where growing trees stood foot-deep in stagnant water and fallen timber lay below the surface, rendering any advance most treacherous. These bogs looked so mysterious that if some prehistoric monster—some shiny-skinned amphibian, had suddenly raised its snaky head above the water to exchange glances with us—intruders, it would not have been surprising; we should have felt that its presence was entirely in keeping with its surroundings, and was, in fact, far more natural than our own.

The men worked well and silently during these trying treks. Their character as pioneers came strongly to the fore in the slow, plodding, indomitable spirit which plunges ahead, blindly and obstinately, in spite of all difficulties. I well remember one stretch of bad ground, 200 yards in length, which took us two hours to negotiate; as soon as one fallen horse gained its feet, and was reloaded, another went down, while the ropes had frequently to be cut in order to free the horses from their packs. I remember we used at dusk to throw ourselves down, exhausted, such a moment of slackness generally resulting in lost horses, and obliging an aggravating hunt for them in the morning, over miles of surrounding jungle. The nights were not too pleasant; we could not rest with any degree of comfort on account of the mosquitoes. Our camp used to present the hazy appearance of a pile of baggage and a tent or two surrounded by a dozen little camp-fires, and enveloped in smoke, caused by covering the fires with wet green grass. We were always in disagreement as to whether the prevention was better than the cure; we were divided into two parties—those who preferred smoke to mosquitoes, and those who preferred mosquitoes to smoke!

By superhuman axe-work on the part of Miller, as well as by the combined efforts of the whole party, the entire caravan—without loss or harm—was pushed through this trackless zone to the comparatively well-known settlement of Petropavlovsk. One day we suddenly found a well-cleared track; following this for a few miles, we were encouraged by the distant sounds of cocks crowing and of the lowing of cattle. At evening we came out of the forest on to the banks of the Amil, saw the familiar-looking log-huts, and received the kind welcome of some Siberian fishermen. With the aid of the local boatmen, the crossing of the Amil was accomplished the next day. The horses swam the flood and landed on the south bank a quarter of a mile downstream. The baggage was conveyed across the river in dug-out canoes, which the boatmen handled in an amazingly efficient way on the high flood. The transportation of the baggage took eight of these journeys, and it was not until evening that the whole of our expedition was encamped on the farther bank of the river. The Amil here was about 180 to 200 yards wide, and flowed in a single channel. From this point our track led us at a more rapid rate, those accustomed to use this route being here forced to travel by land instead of by water—it is on this account that this part of the trail has been kept fairly open.

The aspect of the surrounding country now changed considerably. The dense, unbroken expanse of forest was relieved by large areas of natural meadows. From points of vantage—for we were now again climbing and descending ridges—we saw nearly as much open country as forest. These patches were overgrown with fine grass and many flowers, and hemmed in by the dark belts of forest. We obtained some magnificent views from these open meadows. To the north rose a wild turmoil of hills leading up to some fairly high peaks, but clouds overhung the summits and we could only just see the snows. The sensation of climbing, of being gradually lifted out of the stifling forest, was most exhilarating. During the following days we reached a height of 2,000 ft., and finally passed over the ridge of Chokerok at an altitude of 3,200 ft. Here for the first time we found snow. It lay deep amongst the pines at the summit of the ridge, and some skill was needed in order to manœuvre the caravan across without mishap.

When we reached the Amil again we found that it had considerably decreased in size. It was now only 80 to 100 yards across, and the volume of water was quite inconsiderable. Only one tributary of any size joins the Amil between here and Petropavlovsk—the Kandat; I am inclined to think, on this account, that the latter river is really very much larger than it has been reported to be.

A few days of river-crossings and forest-travel brought us to the foot of the main ridge. We now began to realize the true character of the Syansk Range. At this point, at any rate, it was obvious that its topography was very different to what we had supposed it to be, and its physical features in no way corresponded to their representation on existing maps. Before us we noted a low, rounded, forested ridge possessing neither rugged summits nor "drifted snow and naked boulder," nor even ground above the tree-zone. We passed over the actual watershed at an altitude of 4,524 ft. above sea-level, the track lying over a small col (the Ahgiak Pass) situated between forested hills. For this reason no vast panorama of the isolated basin beyond awaited our eager eyes. The Syansk Range, nowhere composing a high uplift, has, in this particular part, a remarkable break in its chain, forming three or four passes, all of them at a low altitude. Far to the east and far to the west we noticed higher summits, sudden, broken uplifts, the special feature of the Syansk Mountains.

APPROACHING THE SYANSK RANGE.

In marked contrast with this sudden dip in the range in its central portion, a single isolated peak rose above the forest. We at once turned off the track into the tangled forest, and plunged blindly ahead in the direction of the snow-patched summit. Our hopes were concentrated on this peak; we dared hope our goal would here be in sight, and that at last, from its cold summit, we might gaze down into the mysterious basin of the Upper Yenisei—the region of our hearts' desire.

CHAPTER IV[1]

THE BASIN OF THE UPPER YENISEI

THE low altitude of the Syansk Range considerably minimized the glamour surrounding the secluded basin of the Upper Yenisei which lay ahead of us. The secret valley below could be reached without any clambering over sky-scraping ridges or difficult passes. The Syansk Range did not give the impression of being a great barrier; yet the seclusion of the basin is complete. This is owing more probably to the impenetrable and hostile forest-zone, which, even more than the mountain-ranges, is effective in preserving intact the mysteries of this region.

Sending the main caravan ahead to await our arrival on the banks of the Upper Sisti-Kem, Miller, Price, and I, with a couple of Russians, plunged blindly into the forest, and steered as direct a course as possible towards the summit, which we had marked out as being a possible point of vantage. When buried in the depths of the forest, however, it was no easy matter to find our way, and we had repeatedly to resort to the expedient of climbing some trees and felling others to get some idea of the position of our goal. When, on these occasions, we caught sight of the cool snows showing up behind the dark pines, we often found that we had been travelling

[1] This chapter, describing the physical features of the basin, is of interest to few save geographers, and can be omitted by the general reader.

IN THE SYANSK MOUNTAINS.
Looking north-east along the main ridge.

steadily in a wrong direction, and it was only after many false attempts that, late in the day, we emerged from the jungle on to upland meadows, knee-deep in marigolds, and covered with luxuriant bog-plants, and camped on the edge of the tree-line below the peak. The next day we climbed over banks covered with dwarf rhododendron, on to slopes of moss and lichen, which led up to rocky skrees culminating in a snow-patched summit.

We greatly appreciated the change when at length, after eleven days of toilsome jungle and curtailed views, we climbed triumphant to the summit above the forests and gazed down for the first time into the romantic region beyond. The form of the mountain was that of a table, and its flat top was composed of a jumble of granite boulders; moss, lichen, and dwarf rhododendron grew even at its highest altitude in places where there was sufficient soil, while a few patches of snow were still lying in deep drifts. Beyond and below us were long reaches of pleasant country, park-like meadows brilliant with wild-flowers, with depths of sombre forest to give contrast; here and there glistened a winding river, and far away were the rocky summits of distant ranges.

The scenery was a study in opposites, giving a wealth of beauty in detail, but a lack of beauty as a whole. Nothing could be more monotonous than the endless expanses of unbroken forest, nothing more beautiful than the flower-spangled meadows, and nothing more striking than the upheavals of bare, jagged peaks that rise suddenly out of the forest. Overlooking the forests, the dreary monotony of the landscape brings a feeling of repulsion, as ridge after ridge of endless, sodden jungle opens up before one, and uninspiring vistas of forest stretch to the far horizon. A hundred miles of desolate sand-waste is not so repulsive. In a desert-land even, the scenery does not affect the traveller with a feeling of such hopeless uniformity. There, the eyes strain their gaze with searching; they are fascinated by and intoxicated with the sense of light, colour, and distance; the very mystery of the desert is inviting, and its air invigorating. But a view of the taiga—the swamp-forest of the north-land—chokes all such feelings. The whole impression given by the banks of pines, with their sorrowful downward-drooping lines, and the falling outlines of the scenery is one of depression. The eyes alone find rest and satisfaction when they alight on some jagged mass of snow-covered rock and crag, which has the appearance of being thrown up out of the forest towards the sky, where altitude defies the tree-growth and where naked rock holds sway.

For a long time we gazed, drinking in the essential features of the landscape. So fascinated were we by the mystery of the unexplored country ahead, that we almost forgot to take our bearings by prismatic compass on to the more prominent peaks that showed up towards the east, and to record the hypsometric readings for altitude. Far to the west rose the higher summits of the Aradansk and Usinsk groups; far to the east—after a gap of some miles—rose other summits, situated no doubt on the main-range of the Syansk. It was difficult, however, to understand the lie of the land; the line of the watershed could not easily be followed, the uplifts being exceedingly broken and disconnected, and out-lying spurs and ranges rose obviously to a higher altitude than the actual watershed. The snow-capped ranges to the east and north-east, which we could only just discern, attracted us strongly, knowing them to be the first glimpse of the

"New Land"; a region indeed where "the mountains are nameless and the rivers all run God knows where."

This first view of the Upper Yenisei basin left a new impression on me. I realized that this region, although within the limits of the Chinese Empire, is essentially Siberian in character. It is an integral part of Siberia, its drainage flows to Siberia and the Arctic, the conditions (at least so far as we could see in the northern part of it) as well as the climate, are Siberian rather than Mongolian. Orographically, it is naturally the first terrace of the Mongolian plateau, but, as the Syansk Mountains form no true boundary, the flora and fauna of Siberia have overflowed across the border-ranges and given the basin a northern character. Physically, politically, and economically the basin should belong to Russia, and not to Mongolia, and the inevitable absorption of this region by the Siberian element could easily be imagined. Nevertheless, at present the basin remains politically a part of Mongolia, thus showing how absolutely it is shut off and protected from Russian territory. As a result of certain topographical features this region comes more into contact with Mongolia than with Siberia; the influence of a western trade must, however, gradually overcome the natural difficulties of the barrier and eventually bring it into closer relationship with Siberia.

At this point of vantage—the summit of the Syansk—it would be advisable to call a halt, in order to reconsider and carefully note the physical features of this interesting and remote region. It is unnecessary that the order of presenting the information should coincide precisely with the itinerary of our journey. It is my wish to deal with the information we collected in sections, according to the subject under discussion, and to describe each as a whole instead of scattering them broadcast throughout the volume, as would naturally be the case if our experiences were given precisely as they chanced to occur on the line of march. These observations on the topography of the basin are the result of our journey, which occupied the following two months.

The basin of the Upper Yenisei comprises an area of about 64,000 sq. miles, and is watered by the two main heads of the Great Yenisei, namely, the Kemchik, and the Ulu-Kem, with its two sources the Khua-Kem and Bei-Kem. The entire drainage of the basin is caught by these rivers, and is let out through a narrow defile towards the Siberian plains. Topographically the basin is a mountain-girt region, shut off from the Siberian plains to the north, and in a lesser degree shut off from the Mongolian plateau to the south. Towards the west the mountain-wall merges into the Altai ranges, and towards the far east the encircling barriers divide this basin from the Baikal depression. So unique is the position of this basin, that a detailed description of its physical features is necessary in order to understand the curious position it holds; for the geography of such a region is the most potent factor in deciding the climate, fauna, and flora, as well as ethnological characteristics. The special characteristic of this region is its being an isolated basin, and it is in order to thoroughly appreciate the nature and conditions of the tribes inhabiting it, that we must first realize the unusual significance of its topography.

Broadly speaking, the basin of the Upper Yenisei constitutes a portion of the great plateau of Eastern Asia. It lies within the boundary limits of the plateau, as represented by the encircling border-ranges, yet, being of a

A FLAT-TOPPED SUMMIT OF THE SYANSK MOUNTAINS.

98]

slightly lower altitude than the true plateau, it represents rather the first step from the Siberian plain up to the Mongolian highland; it might, therefore, be described as a lower terrace of the latter. In altitude the floor of the basin, at its lowest level, is 1,656 ft. above sea-level, whereas the Siberian plain, at a distance of about 30 miles from the border-ranges, is but 900 ft. above sea-level. On this terrace rise the main sources of the Yenisei, just as the Selenga sources of the Angara tributary of the Yenisei rise a short distance away, and descend from the plateau in an opposite direction towards Lake Baikal. Caught and hemmed in as these rivers are by the surrounding ranges, they have joined forces and cut a deep trench which conducts the drainage from the plateau to the lowlands, by a more or less gentle gradient. This is the case with all the rivers which rise on the Mongolian plateau or its lower terraces, and which find their way through deep-cut gorges on to the plains below.

The border-ranges, however, present the most interesting study from an orographical point of view. Up to the present, the size of these ranges has been represented in proportion to the importance of the watershed. And yet it is a well-known fact that a divide between Arctic and Pacific waters is often scarcely noticeable in actual nature, although, as a parting line, for water destined to flow into such widely separated oceans, it might well be supposed to need intensification on the map. These giant watersheds have, as often as not, been created by the cartographers at home. A representation of the proportionate altitudes of the ranges enclosing the basin, and of North-western Mongolia, has never before been attempted. It would be difficult to get any idea of such ranges, except by continual ascents and by taking numerous readings for altitude. In the instance of the Syansk, as well as in other cases on the map of those regions we traversed during the course of our journey, we wished to obliterate the artificial lines of demarcation denoting the frontiers of Empire, in order to give greater strength to and a truer idea of the orography of the mountain-ranges. The frontier-lines cause regions to appear divided when no real division is there. We would depict the boundaries of Inner Asia from a geographical and not an empirical point of view. The map accompanying this volume is intended to give a true idea of the topography of the region.

The basin of the Upper Yenisei may be roughly described as of pear-shape formation, lying east and west, with the stem towards the west. On the north the Syansk Range encloses about half the basin. This range merges into the Altai system on the west, and on the east it is lost in the nameless ranges that form the divide between the basin of Lake Baikal and Lake Kossogol. On the south the Tannu-ola performs the same duty as the Syansk and corresponds to it. On the east alone the border-ranges are lacking in character. Here there is a fault in the nearly universal north-east to south-west trend of the border-ranges of the Asiatic plateau, and for a gap of 120 miles we have a broken and rather featureless divide lying in a north-west to south-east direction.

The Syansk Range extends for some 300 to 400 miles, and, from our own observation, it presents a complex chain of no uniformity, a series of disconnected uplifts. Want of symmetry in these uplifts, as well as a difference in the structure and texture of the rocks, has caused the chain to be of great irregularity. As an unbroken range the Syansk does not exist. The watershed forms great zigzags, and the upper waters of the rivers flowing off to the north and south are dovetailed into each other. The main direction of the chain is from south-west to north-east, but there are numerous offshoots,—subsidiary spurs,—which have a general trend from south-east to north-west, such as the Aradansk and Kandat, which form a portion of the border-ranges; and the Chapsa, Tastandi, and Ogarka-ola ranges, which stand isolated, inside the basin. The Syansk is merely one small section of the northern border-range of the great plateau of Eastern Asia, which is continuous right across Asia from the Caspian to the Sea of Okhotsk.

The southern border-range, as well as forming the southern wall hemming in the basin and making its isolation complete, stands as the second step up to the main plateau of Mongolia, and incidentally acts as the watershed between the Arctic and inland self-contained basins of Mongolia. This range—the Tannu-ola—runs nearly due east and west, has a length of about 350 miles, and is very evenly formed, with no especially high summits, or low cols, nor has it spurs or off-shoots of any note. In fact, the Tannu-ola is a range of remarkably soft outline. The summits are flat-topped, and the slopes descend in easy, terraced declines. On an average the summits rise to 8,000 ft., and the actual passes are 6,800 ft. The passes are flat-topped, and the gradients leading up to them are very easy. We only crossed the Tannu-ola in two places, and both of the crossings were in the western portion; but, from all accounts, this characteristic is preserved throughout its entire length. As will be seen from our description, the Tannu-ola differs from the Syansk, both as regards its formation and its climate, and on this account as regards its fauna and flora.

The two main walls of the basin meet on the west in the Sailugem Range, a portion of the Altai group. Here the barrier is even greater in magnitude, for the peaks that rise up at the far western end of the basin, at the sources of the Kemchik, reach an altitude of over 10,000 ft. Towards the east alone is the mountain-wall varied by a change in direction. Here for a considerable space the watershed runs in a line from south-east to north-west; nevertheless, the wall is complete, as this portion of the barrier attains to altitudes of 6,000 to 7,000 ft., and connects, without a break, the Syansk on the north with the Tannu-ola on the south.

These are the ramparts which have protected the basin from foreign intrusion, which have kept the hidden valleys inviolate, and which have formed a safe retreat for the tribes, who, recognizing their protective qualities, have made good use of their natural fastnesses. From the summits of the southern border-range, no doubt, the Mongol hordes, eager for conquest, gazed down enviously into the basin and realized that the land that lay before them was not for them. They looked at a region of frowning forests and rugged mountains, antagonistic, both of them, to mobility and to desert warfare, and then turned back again to the free steppes and boundless plateaux which for ever called them towards the west. The more enterprising Uigurs, indeed, penetrated into and finally passed through the basin, tempted by the rich plains which lay beyond. Their ephemeral empire existed outside the basin, and quite distinct from it.

In these present days the ambitions of a western

TYPICAL SCENERY IN THE UPPER YENISEI BASIN,
Overlooking the central basin.

Power halt before the same barrier, and the Upper Yenisei basin still remains intact, shunned alike by Chinaman and Russian. Natural conditions have created the political situation, and Geography has thus once more proved herself to be the basis of History. Now let us study the interior of the basin and note what potent effects this borderland of mountains has had upon the heart of the land.

Firstly, it must be noted that the floor of the basin between the border-ranges is not an even plain, but is broken by serrated ridges with a trend either east and west, or south-east and north-west. One main upheaval is especially noticeable, namely, that one which divides itself off from the Syansk at the head-waters of the Uss River, and extends across the basin towards the east until lost in the eastern border-range of Shargak-taiga. This uplift, under the names of Tashkil, Sin-taiga, Artcol, and Ogarka-ola, is continuous, but is broken in one place by a remarkable rift, where the Bei-Kem River cuts through the barrier in a deep-cut gorge.

The whole of the eastern portion of the basin, from the junction of the Bei-Kem and Khua-Kem, may be described as mountainous. There are wide flats beside the rivers, and there are some beautiful, open, rolling downlands in the upper Bei-Kem region, but, on the whole, the eastern portion gives the impression of being hill-country, for the traveller is never out of view of those ridges of naked rock which crown the summits of all highlands above the forest-line. The central portion, especially that part which lies to the south of the Ulu-Kem and the eastern Kemchik, represents the more open area, a region of steppe or rolling downs, without encumbering ranges. The far western portion, namely, the Upper Kemchik, is again a region of highlands, much the same in character as the far eastern side.

The orography of the interior of the basin decides the very important question of the floristic conditions. The basin is, in its own little area, a very marked transition zone—a zone which leads one from Siberia to Mongolia, from damp forests to arid steppe. Generally speaking, the steppe-lands lie on the southern borders of the basin, and in its central part. This is partly owing to altitude, for in such a region, where the steppe-land is obviously encroaching gradually upon the forest zone, the aridity producing such conditions has an initial effect on the land which lies at the lowest altitude.

Even in the upper basin we noticed little isolated bits of country in the process of becoming deforested, and drier; but they were always situated close along the river banks and nearly always at the mouths of tributaries which entered the main rivers from the north. This was especially noticeable at the mouths of the right affluents of the Bei-Kem, and there is a most pleasant bit of grass-land, devoid of heavy forest, in the Dora-Kem steppes of the upper Bei-Kem, which, although far removed from the arid zone, presents the features of the more desiccated region. Dry, grassy hills and larch groves extend in marked contrast to the damp, forest-ridden ranges which surround it on all sides. The central steppe extends some way up the Kemchik; but, farther west than the Chedan Valley, hill-country causes more forest and allows a smaller area of a suitable altitude for steppe-conditions. Nevertheless, the whole of the western portion of the basin is considerably drier than the east.

Looking at the basin as a whole, we are in a position to define certain main lines, which determine the limits of various kinds of vegetation; these, by their character, show the successive changes of the conditions from damp to dry. In proceeding southwards, a radical change is noticed; the damp forest area gradually gives way to a drier and more Central Asiatic type of country. Vegetation becomes scarcer, forests are restricted to the northern slopes of the hills, and true steppe-conditions hold the valleys, and gradually creep up the slopes which possess a southern aspect. The natives of the forest, who live in birch-bark tepees and exist on reindeer, are replaced by herdsmen of a more "arid" type, who utilize as dwellings those tents of felt which, in method of construction and use, may be said to stand as an emblem of a dry climate. Even methods of cultivation are practised, and, on account of greater ease in transport and communication, men seem to be less indolent. There are, indeed, many marked differences condensed within a narrow area.

It remains for us to enumerate the zones and their dividing lines. First we have the Syansk, as moist on the north as it is on the south, and producing the same flora on both its flanks. Farther south, at a point midway between the Algiak Pass and the mouth of the Sisti-Kem, begin the larch forests, which demonstrate a marked change in the conditions towards a drier and more sunny clime. Another line, which cuts across the basin on about parallel 52° N., delimitates the northern edge of the steppe-zone. Forests here begin to loose their hold of the southern slopes. The hills in the neighbourhood of the Uiuk Valley, for instance, show the typical Asiatic aspect of barren southern, and heavily forested northern, slopes. When we begin to climb the northern foot-hills of the southern border-range, after passing the low, dry, tree-less central zone, forests again appear, but they are neither in such profusion nor is their character the same as those of the Syansk. Larch predominates, the spruce mostly disappears. On reaching the summits of the Tannu-ola we see before us the endless vistas of barren Mongolia, to all appearances destitute of tree-growth. The watershed of the Tannu-ola makes a general dividing-line between Siberian and Mongolian flora; but it can be only taken as the boundary in a very broad sense, for the different zones overlap one another.

In ages gone by, this region was subject to the same extreme glacial conditions as Europe, but it is probable that the Ice Age here was not so severe as might be expected, owing to that vast inland sea, an Asiatic Mediterranean, which then covered half North-west Asia, and reached from the present Arctic Ocean to the heart of Asia, and which rendered the climate much milder than it would otherwise have been. The plateau-region, however, must have been subject to considerable glaciation, and, on the recession of the ice and the formation of innumerable lakes, the upper portion of the basin assumed the typical post-glacial appearance of an Asiatic upland. The plateau of Tibet has had the same history and shows the same present-day conditions. The eastern or upper part of the basin is consequently a lake-land, and innumerable sheets of water of various sizes drain the uppermost sources towards the Bei-Kem and Khua-Kem waterways. This lake-dotted region is one of the features of the basin, and is of surpassing beauty. Of its scenery, its inhabitants, and its wonderful fisheries we shall have more to say anon.

Along the western slopes of the semicircle of ranges, formed by the bends of the Tannu-ola and the Syansk inwards towards the Ergik and Shargak Taiga ranges, rise the three main sources of the Great Yenisei. From a thousand streamlets, and innumerable marshes, start the many-headed tributaries of the Bei-Kem, the Kamsara, and Khua-Kem. Gathering many an affluent from the Syansk and Tannu-ola, these rivers flow westwards at an average altitude of 2,800 ft. until they meet and form the Ulu-Kem. From their respective sizes at the point of juncture, it appeared to us that the Khua-Kem was very much the smaller of the two rivers. As the rivers here flowed in single channels over a flat country, and at an even speed, it was fairly easy to judge their proportionate sizes. It is difficult to decide which river can claim to be the true source of the Yenisei. The Khua-Kem rises farthest east, but the Bei-Kem is by far the larger stream. Of the two heads of the latter, the Kamsara and the main Bei-Kem, there is little doubt that the Kamsara carries the larger volume, and is the main source of the water-supply which goes to form the Upper Yenisei. The difference in the volume of the Bei-Kem and Khua-Kem rivers is entirely dependent upon the rainfall of the respective areas they flow through. Thus, from the greater size of the rivers in the north of the basin as compared with those of the south, it will be noticed what a difference in rainfall there is over a comparatively small area.

The Ulu-Kem continues its way due westwards down the central basin as far as Cha-Kul. At this point it turns northwards and enters a rugged mountain-country. The entire western portion of the basin drains by means of the Kemchik towards this point. The Kemchik—or The Little River—drains a considerable, but a drier region, and its smaller rainfall lessens the amount of its water-volume. Its sources lie in the semicircle of ranges formed by the Western Syansk, the Sailugem, and the Western Tannu-ola. In the case of the first two, the sources rise on the slopes of mountains which do not get the maximum amount of rainfall; and in the case of the Tannu-ola, even its northern slopes, whence rise the other tributaries of the Kemchik, are considerably drier than the southern slopes of the Western Syansk. There are a few lakes in the Kemchik basin, but they are not a feature of it, as is the case with the sources of the Bei-Kem. In fact, generally speaking, it appears that the lakes are already partially desiccated, and in some cases have no outlet. The Kemchik unites with the Ulu-Kem in a rugged hill-country, and, in conjunction, they flow northwards through a narrow defile—called the Kemchik Bom—in the Syansk border-range. This is the only outlet to the drainage of the basin. For a hundred miles the river, which now becomes the Yenisei in name, winds through a labyrinth of mountain ranges, drops from 1,600 ft. to 900 ft. in its passage through the Syansk barrier, and flows out on to the Abakan steppe, the threshold of Siberia.

Great water-ways, especially if running through the heart of a continent, and in a country where travel by land is peculiarly difficult and communication easily cut off, tend to largely attract life and trade, and to give vitality to a region which might otherwise remain undeveloped. If it were not for the waters of the Upper Yenisei, the whole Uriankhai basin would have remained unbroken ground and untouched by the outside world.

POLING DUG-OUT CANOES UP THE AMIL RIVER.

The river forms the one means of easy transport, and the three main sources, the Bei-Kem, the Khua-Kem, and the Kemchik, open up lines of communication to the farthest corners of the basin. Men can pole their canoes up-stream at the rate of from twenty to thirty miles a day, and by the use of rafts they can convey great cargoes of fish or merchandise down-stream at a speed of even fifty miles a day. The outlying colonies which we afterwards came in contact with in the upper basin, and which seemed to us so cut off from the others after our traverse of the forest-route, are in reality within a ten-days' journey by raft of the Siberian town of Minnusinsk.

The navigation of the rivers within the basin is not accomplished without serious drawbacks. The Ulu-Kem is not free from ice until mid-April, and after that date the navigation is often obstructed by sudden floods. Then, on account of the incredible amount of timber brought down by the floods, all boat-work is stopped. A recent Russian traveller estimated the velocity of the Ulu-Kem, in normal water, at from three and a half to four miles per hour, whilst in flood the velocity exceeded seven miles per hour.

The other obstacles inside the basin are the rapids of the Bei-Kem, which the Siberians are in the habit of negotiating by means of strongly built rafts on the downward journey, and by the portage of their canoes when coming up from the lower reaches. The Kemchik Bom obstructs the passage of all up-stream navigation from the Minnusinsk plain to the Ulu-Kem, and it is only by the use of good rafts that the boatmen drift down-stream through the gorges and over the rapids. The canoes and boats on the rivers of the basin remain there permanently, whilst rafts are specially constructed for the passage of the Kemchik Bom. The sale of the timber of which these rafts are constructed, adds quite a nice bit to the pockets of the adventurous watermen who manage them, and who easily sell it for firewood in the treeless Minnusinsk steppe.

The distance between Cha-Kul on the lower Ulu-Kem and Krasnoyarsk is 920 miles, and the difference in altitude is 1,115 ft. The greatest proportion of the drop, however, is concentrated into about 100 miles, which constitutes the passage of the river through the Syansk Range, the difference in altitude here being over 700 ft. in the hundred miles. We did not actually make the passage of the Kemchik Bom ("Bom" means gorge, or defile), but, from all accounts, it affords excitement on account of the series of rapids which make navigation dangerous. The Kemchik unites with the Ulu-Kem in a gorge not more than 30 yards wide, where the current is estimated at 40 miles an hour.

North of the tributary called Uss the most dangerous rapids exist, and from here onwards for another fifty miles the river drops by successive falls to the level of the plain of Minnusinsk. Experienced pilots are in the habit of running cargoes from the Bei-Kem and Ulu-Kem down to the Siberian Yenisei, and, with such men to depend on, the journey can be accomplished without much risk. The journey from Cha-Kul to Minnusinsk is reckoned to take from three to five days.

There are, unfortunately, no statistics of the meteorology of the basin; such statistics would be of the utmost interest as showing more clearly the cause for the contrasts of scenery. The winters are severe, but not of the severity of the open Siberian Plain. Much snow falls in certain localities, whilst others are remarkably free. At Skobieff, for instance, I was told that the cattle manage to feed themselves throughout the whole winter, which shows that the meadow-land cannot be covered with snow to any great depth. The open areas, such as the Dora-Kem in the Upper Basin and the Cha-Kul region in the centre, do not experience much snow, and in consequence it is in these open localities that the natives congregate during the winter months. Snow lies deeper and remains later into the summer on the northern forested ranges, but the Tannu-ola, with a considerable snowfall on its northern flanks, has but little on the south, and the snow soon melts away in the spring.

The rainfall of the basin has the same local variations, the fall being the heaviest in the north and east and lessening in the south and west. July is probably the wettest month. We experienced, in this month, rain-storms of exceptional violence, and long duration, both in the north-east and in the central part of the basin. On the Upper Bei-Kem, on July 10th and 11th, there was a continual downpour lasting twenty-six hours, and—throughout that month violent thunder-storms were to be seen at all points of the compass. At Cha-Kul, at the end of July, the Ulu-Kem rose to a flood-height on account of heavy rain in the upper part of the basin, and at the same season in the same locality we noticed the daily phenomenon of awe-inspiring thunder-storms generating on the western Syansk and following along that range towards the east, without affecting the inner basin.

The driest portion of the basin is undoubtedly the south-western region, which stretches along the south bank of the Ulu-Kem and Kemchik, and which lies between those rivers and the Tannu-ola. The Kemchik region is especially dry, and it possesses a better climate than any other part of the basin; for, being sheltered from the north, south, and west, the Kemchik gets but the residue of the heavy rains coming from the west, which are mostly caught by the Syansk and Sailugem ranges. This region of the Kemchik gets an earlier summer, which is a great asset at so high a latitude. The area best suited for colonization I should place as the zone where the forest and the steppe conditions are waging war on each other. This zone, which is neither too dry nor too wet, runs in a belt across the centre of the basin. The chief Siberian settlements—such as Safianoff's, Toran, and the Uiuk—are all situated in this zone.

Broadly speaking, the climate can be described as mid-continental. There are sharp and sudden changes and great variations between the summer and the winter temperatures. Ostrovsky gives the extreme ranges of the thermometer from 30° Fahr. in winter to 103° in summer. The only reliable readings for summer temperature taken by us were at Cha-Kul, on the lowest part of the floor of the basin, and in the open zone of the steppe. Here during three days, from July 24th to 26th, the thermometer gave an average maximum temperature of 101° Fahr., and a minimum temperature of 51·5° Fahr.

The reader may do well to fix in his mind the exact position of the few routes which cross the basin, and the passes which allow traffic in and out of it. It has already been shown why the surrounding border-land of mountains controls the ways of communication; it now remains to describe the actual routes. Two fea-

SNOW-LINE IN THE SYANSK MOUNTAINS.

tures determine the position of the tracks which enter the basin, namely, the position of the passes and the location of the Mongolian and Siberian centres of trade which the routes connect. Minnusinsk is the only town on the north, and Uliassutai and Kobdo are the only settlements on the south of the basin; we find, therefore, only two main routes running between these towns. Many little passes cut the ranges at unexpected and out-of-the-way places; but these, and the tracks which cross them, are only used by small traders and trappers.

The Syansk is habitually crossed by travellers in four places. In the east there is the Algiak Pass between the Upper Amil and the Sisti-Kem (altitude 4,482 ft.). This is the most direct route between the villages of the Amil and the upper basin, but it is little used on account of the paucity of travellers in these regions. The second pass to the west is the Uss-Uiuk Pass, an easy and well-used track connecting the colonies situated in the two valleys of those names. Between this col and the impassable jumble of hills surrounding the Kemchik Bom lies the third and best-known route —the Kurtushi—which connects Cha-Kul, the chief centre of the basin, with the north. This pass is, according to Kriloff, only 4,320 ft. in altitude; but Chalon, who apparently went by the same route, gives 6,625 ft. as the altitude of the watershed. West of the Kemchik Bom, connecting the Kemchik Valley with the Abakan steppes to its north, is the fourth pass, called the Shabin-daba. The route which crosses this pass may be described as the only feasible trade-route which connects Siberia and Mongolia, by way of the Upper Yenisei basin.

These four routes enter the basin from the north, and pass out on the south by two main passes and several subsidiary tracks. On the west is the Borashay Pass (at 6,854 ft.), leading direct southwards to Kobdo; a more important route, however, is the one which branches off from this track at the point where it crosses the Kemchik River, and leads eastwards along the southern edge of the basin to a pass called the Shamar-daba, which crosses the Tannu-ola and leads to well-populated and important centres of Mongol life on the Tess River, to the trading centre at Uliassutai, and the religious centre of Urga. This line of communication which runs between Uliassutai and the Abakan steppes is the old caravan-route which has always been in use. The track entirely avoids forested or wet country; no difficulties or obstacles are found *en route*, and it represents the line of march of all the ancient invaders of the Minnusinsk plains. A portion of this road has been built up by human agency into a fine high-road, which alone shows the importance which must once have been attached to the route.

Between the Cha-Kul Valley and the Kemchik River we found a well-built high-road, six yards in width, raised above the level of the surrounding steppe and having a ditch on either side. The surface was as smooth and well-metalled as an English high-road. Passing caravans, which generally make a row of deep parallel grooves caused by the horses or camels following each other in single file, here had made no impression on the surface. It ran with Roman directness between the two points here mentioned—a distance of about fifty miles.[1] It

[1] Howorth, in his *History of the Mongols*, recounts, amongst the doings of a certain Lobdyang Taishi—one of the Altai Khans of North-western Mongolia, in 1657—the building of "a winding road which he made over the mountains called Khonin-Tag, for the passage from Mongolia to Siberia"; it was, no doubt, a portion of this route that we discovered.

appeared incredible to us that any volume of trade could necessitate the building up of so formidable a route. Its object remains inexplicable. The area it crosses needs no road-building to make transport possible. The ground is hard, smooth steppe, suitable to every kind of traffic; therefore road-making seems to be a labour-wasting folly. Were the country soft, wet marsh-land or damp forest, there might have been some reason for the arduous labour this work must have entailed. All we can infer from its presence is that once this region must have been of greater importance, many more caravans must have been in the custom of using the route, and a greater amount of communication must have existed between Mongolia and Siberia.

This route, as I have explained, is the only one entitled to the position of a trade-route. The greater portion of it can be used for wheeled traffic. From Uliassutai over the Tannu-ola to the Kemchik, the route is passable for carts; but the passage of the Syansk over to the Abakan steppes is, I believe, impossible for anything but pack-animals. The Kemchik-Borashay route is feasible for camels and just passable for carts, for the pass has a very easy gradient and there are no obstacles in the shape of rocks; in fact, there would be nothing to hinder the building of a route for wheeled traffic between Kobdo in Mongolia and Minnusinsk, neither would it entail great labour or expense. As a matter of fact, it will be seen, in our descriptions of North-western Mongolia, that there is another and easier outlet for Mongolian trade, namely, the track which leads over the Altai Mountains direct to the head-waters of the Ob. Thus the Tannu-ola route can only be considered a route of secondary importance. All other tracks in the basin must be put down as only passable for pack-animals, and only at great expense could they be built up into roads for wheeled traffic.

Between the basin and Mongolia there are several tracks that are less known. The route, for instance, between Cha-Kul and Lake Ubsa can be used in preference to the Borashay Pass, whilst in the far east the head-waters of the Khua-Kem are connected with the region of Lake Kossogol and the upper tributaries of the Selenga. In the far west the traveller can pass across the head-waters of the Kemchik River into North-western Mongolia, and even over into Russian territory to the head-waters of the Ob River. These tracks are, however, scarcely used except by explorers, or wandering hunters. I have stated elsewhere that the far eastern wall of the basin, which divides off the country of Lake Baikal and Lake Kossogol, is also cut by several passes of no great altitude; but these are only reindeer-paths and native tracks, which do not help, in any great measure, to relieve the impenetrability of this part of the basin.

These are the main topographical features of the basin, the short résumé of which will, I hope, enable the reader to realize the conditions under which we travelled, and the natural features which preserve the region untouched by outside influence; and, also, to emphasize the causes of the peculiar position this region holds in relation to its ethnology, flora, and fauna. From this it will be noted, that the basin of the Upper Yenisei holds a very large area of land untapped by ways of communication, and consequently remaining unexplored. Broadly speaking, the regions lying along the main rivers are best known, for these grant ease of transport. The drier steppe-region is also better known than the densely forested ranges. No part of the basin has been systematically mapped, and the compilation of the map accompanying this volume has been of exceptional difficulty.

For the would-be explorer much untouched ground remains. In the far north-eastern corner, to the east of our route, at the head-waters of the Chapsa and Chebash, is a very large area of "new" country. The head-waters of the Bei-Kem and Khua-Kem would be well worth a visit, and the whole region lying between those rivers would repay examination. From our experiences in the Chedan Valley of the Tannu-ola we are at liberty to say that the whole of the north side of that range is unmapped. The Kemchik Valley north of the main river is fairly well known, but the ranges surrounding the valley are not depicted on the maps with that degree of certainty which results from actual surveys, but rather from rough sketches and much guess-work.

CHAPTER V

THE HAUNTS OF THE URIANKHAI

I SHALL now resume our narrative at the point where I broke it off by introducing the account of the physical features of the basin, as suggested by the view from the summit of the Syansk. On June 15th we were heading southwards, towards the heart of the basin, and as we left the spacious, untrammelled views which were granted to us from the highlands, and plunged once more into the obstructing forest, we felt ourselves bitten by a still keener desire for further knowledge. Where did those rivers have their sources? What was that jagged mass of towering peaks which rose out of the jungle far to the east? Where lurked those silent, shy forest-lovers, the reindeer-keeping Uriankhai, whose haunts we were seeking? These were the questions which presented themselves to us and bewildered us by the amount of work their answering entailed, by the physical difficulties in our way, and by the shortness of our allotted time.

Our first concern, after crossing the Syansk Mountains, was to make a depôt of our belongings on the banks of the Sisti-Kem, a small tributary of the Bei-Kem, on whose head-waters we chanced to find ourselves. We soon found that the difficulties of travel and transport in the basin were exceedingly great, and that it would be a hopeless undertaking to move with a heavy caravan

RAFTING DOWN THE SISTI-KEM.

118]

through the forests. Lightly equipped parties must make lateral journeys, whilst the heavy caravan must be kept to the water-ways, and to the main route. Since we were now on the head-waters of the rivers, and our main direction was down-stream, we were enabled to use the river-transport to great advantage.

We therefore halted for a few days at the huts of a Russian pioneer on the Upper Sisti-Kem, and despatched our men into the forest along the river-banks to fell the dry and dead timber suitable for raft-building. The existence of considerable areas of dead forest was a feature of the basin, and in large measure this appeared to be due to human agency. The native Uriankhai owned to the intentional burning of the forest, so as to cause open patches in it, which would make the hunting of certain game less arduous. The fires, as a rule, killed, but did not burn down, the large trees, and only served to clear the forests of the smaller vegetation and young pines. Over these areas there quickly grew up a dense jungle of small scrub and thickets ; the pines never again won the ground which they had lost, but were supplanted by deciduous trees. The dead timber, thus left standing, after a few years of seasoning gave us the most excellent material for raft-building.

The men were occupied for three days in felling the timber, and in building a raft capable of holding all our kit and nine of our men, and this they accomplished in the most workmanlike manner with the aid only of axes. There was neither nail nor bolt in the whole structure, which was fastened together by wooden pegs and ropes of twisted hazel. For ease in steering, and with a view to shooting the rapids of the Bei-Kem, the raft was not constructed on too large a scale ; and two long sweeps, in front and behind, gave us more or less complete control of the steering. She was composed of seventeen pine trunks, and measured 50 ft. in length, 20 ft. in width at the stern, tapering to 12 ft. at the bows. On this we transported all our belongings for a day's journey down the Upper Sisti-Kem.

Then, from a passing trader, we obtained some news of the region to the north-east; he told us of the valley of the Chapsa, left affluent of the Sisti-Kem, and of its head-waters under high snow-peaks; he also told us of the whereabouts of an encampment of Uriankhai, who belonged to the true forest-dwelling, reindeer-keeping section of the tribe. Consequently, at the mouth of the Chapsa we roped up the raft to the bank and arranged for an exploration of the Chapsa and the regions beyond.

The plans for our movements entailed considerable forethought and arrangement. There had to be three distinct parties moving independently. The horses had to go unladen through the forest along the river-bank, the raft and the main party to go down-stream to the mouth of the Sisti-Kem and to await on the banks of the Ulu-Kem the arrival of the third party, who, with light kit and a few good horses, made the journey of discovery into the unknown north-east. All these parties needed supplying with provisions, and with instructions in case of eventualities.

At the mouth of the Chapsa we found an ideal camping-ground, where a lawn of grass under fine larches lay alongside the clear, swiftly flowing stream. Here we stopped and organized our campaign. The raft was despatched down-stream with all the kit we did not actually need; the spare horses went along the river-bank to the place agreed upon, namely, at the point where the Sisti-Kem enters the Bei-Kem, and with a few lightly laden pack-horses, three men, and enough food for twenty or twenty-five days, Miller, Price, and I set out, and headed up the valley towards the north. Our position at this point, as will be seen by the map, was in the north-eastern part of the basin, and, as we were travelling to the north and north-east, we had a great area of unknown country ahead of us. If the reader were to study the maps made at an earlier date to those published in this volume, he would note the boldly marked highlands, and the apparently well-mapped river-courses; but all these are imaginary. We did but little to elucidate the problem; a vast area remains for a future pioneer.

We regarded this lateral journey as an essential one, in order to touch again, and if possible to cross, the Syansk Range at a point hitherto absolutely unknown, and also to find the reindeer-Uriankhai at home in their native forests. We intended to travel north, and to map the Chapsa River up to its source, thence we planned to turn eastwards, and to strike the next lateral valley—the Shive, or the Ugut—which valleys are such a prominent feature of the Russian maps. We were surprised, however, to find that these great waterways only existed on the maps, and that we quickly reached valley number three (the Kamsara) without finding number one and number two in the course of our journey!

Passing up the Chapsa Valley at walking-pace, measuring our distances by time and pedometer, and marching with prismatic compass continually in use, we surveyed the country as far as was possible under the trying circumstances. The region was less densely forested than any we had hitherto seen. We were now within the larch-forest zone, having entered it at a point immediately south of the Ainar River, a left affluent of the Sisti-Kem, some seven miles to the north of the mouth of the Chapsa. With the appearance of the larch, we found a much drier and consequently a much more open type of country.

On the second day after leaving the Sisti-Kem we first came across traces of the Uriankhai; indeed, on the banks of that river our interest had already been aroused by the "skeletons" of their tepees and the rows of neat wooden pegs in the ground, to which the herdsmen were in the habit of tying their young reindeer. We were working our way slowly up the valley, mapping as we went, when the caravan was suddenly brought to a standstill by a rude barricade which had been thrown across a narrow rift of the valley, leaving little room to pass along the bank between the river and the hills on either side. The presence of man's handiwork in the solitary and apparently uninhabited forest increased our enthusiasm, and we eagerly pressed forward expecting, at any minute, to accost some unsuspecting reindeer-herdsmen.

Our actual introduction to the Uriankhai was, however, a very amusing incident in our journey, although disastrous results might easily have followed. For the sake of companionship on a long journey, I had, whilst in Siberia, bought a dog, which, owing to his squirrel-hunting capacities, bore the Russian name of "Belka." Belka was pure white, of a breed highly prized in Siberia by the fur-hunters, and much in use on the post-roads as watch-dogs for the government mail-carts. On this journey he had full scope for his hunting powers, and he proved invaluable to me as a collector of small animals. He caught rats and mice all the way from the Yenisei to Chinese Turkestan, the skins of which now adorn our National Collection in the British Museum, and there was no species of big game after which he did not have a hunt.

On this occasion, as usual, Belka was ranging ahead of the caravan. He had appeared uneasy ever since we had left the raft; but I did not realize that it was a new strange beast that he had scented, and that for days he had been keenly moving up wind on the trail of the reindeer. The scent drew stronger, and suddenly there sprang up right in front of him a pure white reindeer. The result was electrical; off went the reindeer, and off went my dog, and a mounted Uriankhai, who appeared from the forest, followed in hot pursuit. Luckily the reindeer managed to out-pace his pursuer at the start, and, before any harm could be done, the dog was pulled off the trail, and we eventually made friends with the herdsman, who was as much astonished as we were. By signs we urged him to take us to his home, and, leading us up a side-valley called Ala-su, he soon brought us to a pleasant meadow-land between forested hills, where, on a sunlit sward, close under the shadow of the forest, clustered the peaked tepees or wigwams of an encampment of Uriankhai. We rode up the valley, wending our way amongst groups of reindeer, startling by our sudden and strange appearance many a young Uriankhai herdsman, and eventually arrived at the encampment.

It was strange to come suddenly upon these quaint and interesting people, living their retiring, self-centred lives away in the depths of this remote part of the world. It must be noted that the Uriankhai are a peculiar people, restricted in their range to a remote basin, which is so difficult of access, and so cut off from the world, that their very affinity with other races is both vague and uncertain. The Upper Yenisei basin they claim as their own, but beyond its border-walls they cannot pass. In no other country can we come in contact with the true wild Uriankhai—the Soiots of Russian literature, who call themselves "Tubas."

We pitched camp, and were ably assisted by every man, woman, and child who could lay a hand on any of our belongings. We saw no sign of the exclusiveness and shyness which is generally attributed to them; on the contrary, falling in with them as we did, appearing from the forest, suddenly, without intention and without any ostensible cause, they welcomed us as curious and interesting visitors, who were content apparently to give them presents without asking anything in return, and who spent most of their time holding up "magic-boxes" or looking at the sun, which was their way of expressing our zeal in taking photographs and making observations.

Such a sight was well worth coming so long a way to see, and it will remain vividly impressed on my mind. In the evening the slanting rays of the sun caught the rich sepia and white of the birch-bark coverings to the tepees, and showed them up against the dark forest behind, the curling smoke of the "wigwams" rose in blue films, and the reindeer trooped homewards for the night, herded by small boys and old women; then the silent night—broken only by the grunt of the herds—settled down upon the quiet valley in this far-removed and remote corner of the world, and hid from view the quaint encampment. On these occasions one

AN ALPINE LAKE BELOW ULU-TAIGA

THE URIANKHAI ENCAMPMENT OF ALA-SU.

[248]

experiences intense delight and great satisfaction in having again found conditions of life, and a strip of country, which has in no way been spoilt by the hurrying march of civilization, but which possesses intact its old-world character.

We spent several days at this encampment, making the best use of our opportunities, for the true reindeer-keepers are but a very small proportion of the whole tribe of Uriankhai, and the most difficult with whom to get in touch. They are, moreover, of all the Uriankhai, the least influenced by outside elements, and in consequence have kept their peculiarities as regards type, language, religion, and modes of life in a greater and closer degree than any of the others. These people belonged to the Toji clan, one of the five sections of the Uriankhai of the Upper Yenisei basin. The purest and most typical of the original Uriankhai are the clan of reindeer-keepers—to which division these people of Ala-su belonged. From the fact that only a small portion of the Toji clan, and of one other tribe—the Mardi—are reindeer-keepers it will be seen that those dependent upon reindeer, and in consequence the more interesting of the tribes, are in actual number a very small portion of the whole, and are in distribution the most limited and the most isolated.

The encampment was composed of twenty-seven tepees, pitched in groups in a very luxuriant meadow-land, at an altitude of about 3,500 ft. above sea-level. Here we had the Uriankhai in their summer haunts, carrying on an easy existence and depending solely for their subsistence on the produce of their herds of reindeer and on their success in the chase. The vegetation was so rich that the people, although accounted nomadic, were very little so, the necessity for migration being thus reduced to a minimum. The reindeer-keepers did not move their encampment out of this valley all the summer, their nomadism consisting of two great moves during the year—in spring and autumn—when they made their shifts to and from their winter quarters.

Perhaps the most important impression left on us was the peculiar isolation the encampment enjoyed. We traversed miles of country in this part of the basin, yet these were the only people we came across. Their nearest neighbours were those who lived in small groups of tents at the mouth of the Kamsara, nearly fifty miles away. I call it important because this fact of a rich land, of wide extent, being inhabited so sparsely as is the Upper Yenisei basin, does call for investigation, and does point to a probable deterioration and degeneracy of the inhabitants.

Of the ethnographical characteristics of the Urian-khai, we chiefly noted the quite phenomenal variety of type which members of the same encampment exhibited. No description will prove this variation so well as the photograph reproduced on page 204. Here, in a family group belonging to the Ala-su encampment, the facial features of each individual present the most marked differences, and seem to point to the mongrel condition into which this remnant of the Ugro-Samoyede family have sunk. The Mongol type is very pronounced in some cases, and in others it is remarkable by its absence. When we consider that these people are the descendants of an intermixture of the aboriginal inhabitants of the Yenisei and the old Turki or Uigur nation, influenced by and infused with a strong Mongol element, this variation is not to be wondered at. We could, however, distinguish the reindeer-keepers from other sections of the Uriankhai by their less Mongolized appearance.

Nothing interested us so much as the peculiar conditions under which these people lived. Never have we seen a tribe whose life-history was so completely fashioned by their environment. From time immemorial a race of hunters, possessing the inherent traits of a wandering people dependent solely upon nature, they exist as a type most fitted to survive under the peculiar physical conditions in which they live. In such a region the only domesticated animal which could be of service to man is the reindeer, and it is in this isolated locality, at the extreme southern limit of its range, that we found the reindeer living both in a wild and in a domesticated state, but under conditions which seem to us to point to its slow but certain extinction in the course of time.

The Uriankhai, of the reindeer section (we may well call them thus, for the Siberian races specify amongst themselves the different tribes, according to whether they use dogs, reindeer, or horses), were dependent upon their reindeer herds for their very existence, only two other interests entering into their lives, namely, those of birch-bark and wild game. With these three means of subsistence their lives were complete, and when we dived into their smoke-blackened tepees and noticed their clothes and household belongings, we realized how complete was their dependence upon nature. All the tepees were covered with sheets of birch-bark, sewn together into a patchwork, and supported by poles of spruce. The interiors were remarkably empty except for household utensils of birch-bark and reindeer skin, hunting and trapping apparatus, and heavy winter-clothing in the shape of reindeer-skin coats and reindeer-skin rugs. We occasionally saw a Russian kettle or a cooking-pot, but nowhere in Central Asia have we seen so little outside influence as we did here.

On the reindeer centred the chief interest of their lives. In and out of this encampment wandered as many as six hundred of these strange animals. Of their history and peculiarities we shall have more to say in another chapter; here I only wish to point out the complete dependence of the Uriankhai on the reindeer. The reindeer supply him with food, clothes, and transport. The animals easily endure the winter months without risk of injury, and the heat of summer is compensated for by the higher altitude to which they are driven during the hot months. Yet we noticed that, in the valley of the Ala-su, in June, the reindeer herds were suffering from the heat. The herds spent the entire day under the shade of the forest, and at evening only did they troop out into the open meadows. The altitude at which the nomads camp in summer is not, of course, as high as the region where the reindeer would naturally be found, as shown by the haunts of the wild reindeer at the sources of the Chapsa River, which was situated at a height of from 5,000 to 6,000 ft. The open country above the forest-area, which is in its character the true reindeer-ground, runs up to a height of 7,000 ft. above sea-level, and strange it is that in those localities we never saw the domesticated herds.

We used to watch the reindeer on hot days panting under the shade of the pines; during cloudy and cool weather, however, they range over the meadows, feeding at will. They are, for the most part, unherded by the nomads, and at dusk the beasts return of their own accord, not only to the encampment, but to the actual

URIANKHAI "TEPEES" AND REINDEER-HERDS.

128]

tents of their rightful owners. At evening, too, the women deal out a small share of salt, which, at this season, they greatly desire. The natural history of the reindeer, the variety of their colouration—ranging from pure white to dark brown, and the details of their management, were studied by Miller, and every reference made in a future chapter on this subject is due to him.

One of the chief objects of this lateral journey was to decide the question of the existence of the wild reindeer, for, although several travellers, from Marco Polo onwards, have recorded the existence of the tribes of these regions who are in the habit of utilizing "stags" for riding purposes and thereby showing us their knowledge of the domesticated reindeer, yet there has been no proof of the species ranging in a wild condition in this southern locality. Through exhaustive inquiries we got to know of the existence of wild reindeer in the ranges to the north of the Chapsa Valley. But we could not gain very detailed information. We asked whether the domesticated beasts ever wandered off and joined the wild ones, but to this the natives replied that their reindeer were afraid of the wild ones if they happened to come in contact, and that, when lost, they never mixed gotether.

The Uriankhai also owned to the hunting of the wild variety, but never to catching them alive and domesticating them. We subsequently proved these assertions to be correct. The reindeer exist, in very small numbers, in a wild state, on portions of the Syansk Range; these are probably the remnant of the greater herds which once, long ago, formed the original stock from which were acquired the now domesticated race belonging to the Uriankhai.

By gentle persuasion and by offers of presents, such as Russian gunpowder, tobacco, and knives, two hunters were engaged to accompany us up the Chapsa Valley to the haunts of the wild reindeer, it being our intention to carry out the exploration of that region, and to be, at the same time, in a position to determine other questions of natural history.

Accordingly, we left the encampment and continued our survey up the main Chapsa Valley. Interesting geographical features now occupied our attention, and the regions which opened out ahead of us were full of natural beauty and topographic phenomena. To the east rose a rock-range of most remarkable indentation, culminating in a high cone at its southern end, close to the valley of the Ala-su. We eventually mapped this range and climbed its highest point. The actual valley of the Chapsa now presented a dry, open aspect, covered with juniper-trees, mountain-birch, and small scrub. Higher up, at a point one mile above its junction with the Ala-su, the valley-bottom was filled with old moraines. For a considerable distance we travelled up and down over its hills and hollows, wherein lay many a little lake of turquoise blue which added charm to the scenery. This was the lowest altitude at which we found traces of ancient glaciers, the lowest end of these moraines being only 3,600 ft. above sea-level.

A short lateral expedition was now decided upon. From our camp in the main valley at the junction of the streams which we named the Great and Little Chapsa, Miller made an excursion after reindeer, whilst Price and I climbed an isolated mountain-group called Tash-Kil. These peculiar rocky uplifts were so remarkable a feature of the scenery, varying so much one from another, that we ascended as many as we were able to approach in different portions of the basin.

The ascent of the Tash-Kil group of the Chapsa Valley was one of the most tiresome climbs we had yet attempted. The slopes were composed of huge granite boulders, overgrown with moss and lichen, and the crevasses between the boulders were choked with dwarf rhododendron and alder; we scrambled from boulder to boulder towards a summit consisting of small granite blocks. Four hours' climbing brought us to the top, which we found to be very different in character to the point we attained on the Syansk Range near the Algiak Pass. Here was a sharply serrated ridge, instead of a flat-topped table-mountain, and the jagged edge was cut into the most fantastic shapes by wind and weather. A dense haze hindered us in our survey-work, and hid all distant view, the exceptional value of which, in aiding us in our endeavour to unravel the problems of the topography of the land, can be scarcely exaggerated. Miller had hunted a large extent of country, but had found nothing of interest beyond the shed antlers of a reindeer.

At this point we discovered the independence and unreliability of our Uriankhai guides, who refused to accompany us any farther, in spite of offers of reward which ought to have tempted the avarice of any ordinary reindeer herdsman. We were forced, therefore, to plunge ahead without guides up to the sources of the Chapsa, where we spent many days amongst the upland-flats, bogs, and jungles, and in climbing the ranges, which formed the most intricate water-parting we had yet experienced.

Interesting days we spent in strenuous endeavour to

map as much of the region as possible. At daybreak we would start off in different directions, with gun or compass, and, partly on foot and partly on horseback, we would range over wide areas, finding lakes, valleys, rivers, and ranges, entirely new to the pre-existing sketch-maps of the region. At dusk we would return to our tents in some flower-strewn meadow, where the evenings, often extending late into the night, were spent in writing and plotting our route-surveys, as well as skinning specimens of birds or animals. This work was accompanied by the persistent attention of a million mosquitoes, against which we built up the usual circle of smoking fires without much result. We did, I think, in those days, the maximum amount of work with the minimum amount of comfort.

Although at this season the country was entirely uninhabited, yet the existence of narrow paths, obviously used by reindeer, showed that the Uriankhai were in the habit of coming up here at some season of the year, and the presence of tepee-poles showed us where they encamped. Here, we eventually learnt, were the autumn camps of the Uriankhai, the men coming up to hunt and trap, after sending their households down to the lower portion of the basin. By way of food we found a few duck, capercailzie, and hazel-grouse; but for the most part we became Russian in our choice of diet and lived almost entirely on tea and bread.

The mapping of this region was an excessively difficult task; for, though the work was fascinating by its originality, it was tedious and overpowering by its magnitude. Here were thousands of square miles of absolutely unknown country laid out before us. We rode up new valleys and found new lakes; ranges never before seen by appreciative human beings showed up through the mists, only to be hidden again from our hungry eyes, for bad weather or haze made the gaining of distant views very uncertain, and peaks once sighted were often never seen again. We had to search diligently amongst a maze of bogs and lakelets for the water-partings. Looking down into a valley, it was often impossible to tell whether it flowed towards China or Siberia, and a group of lakes in a marshy flat might quite possibly drain into entirely different river-systems. We climbed tediously through dense forests up on to a ridge, only to find all view obstructed by trees and our time and labour lost. Moreover, when horses were "going down" on bad ground, and packs coming off, and there was neither track nor view, and we were days from our base, it was easy to forget to "take time" or put down our calculations. Thus it was with the greatest difficulty that we plotted the traverses and put together a map.

But those days alone in the forest and on the hill-tops, with note-book, compass, sketch-book and camera, were at the same time full of delight and interest; we could scarcely sleep at night with the longing to look into the next deep valley, to discover the way the lakes drained, and to gauge the altitudes of the high peaks. Our survey-work here was accomplished by prismatic compass, and the altitudes were fixed by hypsometer. The chief features of the country were not as difficult to put on paper as was the actual feat of moving over the country to see what it contained.

The region in which we found ourselves on reaching the head-waters of the Chapsa was typical of the nature of the Syansk Range. Imperceptibly almost, we passed out of the Chapsa River system and encamped in a locality which (as it took us some time to discover) actually drained direct into Siberia by way of the Kandat or Kazir Valleys. We had passed over the Syansk divide without realizing that we had done so, and besides having done this we found that we also were within a short distance of the head-waters of the Chebash, one of the main affluents of the Kamsara River. The altitude of the actual divide between these different river-systems was a little below 5,000 ft. above sea-level; and this point constituted the actual watershed of the Syansk Range between the Kandat, the Chebash, and the Chapsa Rivers. Nevertheless, we were still surrounded by the typical uplifts rising to 8,000 ft., which, standing up as landmarks, alone showed us the main direction of the Syansk.

From various peaks in the neighbourhood we looked with ambitious eyes towards the north-east, where great problems await the pioneer explorer; but the magnitude of our task forbade further expeditions in this direction, and we could only note the leading features of the region. The character of the land which lay spread out before us was a vast expanse of level country covered with dense forest; we saw no breaks in its sombre canopy, no stretches of open land or steppe. Occasional gleams of light told us of rivers running to swell the waters of the Kamsara, and of lakes which lay in the heart of the jungle, unvisited and unfished except by some more ambitious, wandering Uriankhai in the course of a hunting expedition.

For a long distance no ranges rose out of the taiga, and the impression of the region was one of appalling monotony. So far away, indeed, was the nearest moun-

LAKE CHAPSA.

tain in the east and north-east, that we came to the conclusion that this distant range which we saw must have been the main ridge of the Syansk. We noticed a fine rock-crested ridge running in a semicircle, and forming the north-eastern wall of the basin, but between this bend and where we were standing there appeared to be a big gap in the Syansk. We noticed no sign of a watershed, and were in doubt as to where the actual divide between the Chebash and the Kazir Rivers was situated. To the south of us lay the isolated Chapsa Range, and on the west rose the Kandat group which extended some way beyond the Siberian side of the watershed.

With regard to the numerous lakes which we discovered in this locality, their existence seems to point to this north-eastern corner of the basin possessing the same lake-land characteristics as the far eastern region, at the sources of the Bei-Kem and Khua-Kem. If we could have continued our surveys farther towards the east we should probably have been able to prove that the whole area is dotted with lakes. The most notable sheet of water we chanced to find was a long, narrow lake situated at the northern end of the Chapsa Range, which, in consequence, we named Lake Chapsa. Its character as a crag-locked mere, with rocky, forested shores, and clear water full of fish, rendered Lake Chapsa one of the most pleasing additions to our knowledge of this wild land.

During our exploration of this region we had our only encounter with the wild reindeer. In spite of long, hard days over the Kandat Range, where they were supposed to exist, Miller had no luck beyond that of tracing their haunts by old horns. As is so often the case with the hunting of a scarce beast in a difficult country, the chances come to the person least looking out for them. Whilst returning from a long day's expedition on foot, I chanced one evening to sight a reindeer in a country where I least expected to find them. He was on a brilliant patch of green pasture amongst the pines, and at quite a low altitude, and not on the open top above the forest. As he slowly grazed and moved through the rich long grass in the slanting light, he looked almost pure white against the green. I was unarmed and let him go undisturbed, but returned the next morning at daybreak with Miller, who, in spite of finding the reindeer in exactly the same locality, and in spite of a whole day's stalk, found the country so excessively difficult that he never got up to him. This was the only occasion on which we actually saw wild reindeer.

Apparently, at this season, they live very low down, in the shade of the forest, where they feed on the rich herbage. The density of the forest protects them, and at the same time hinders the hunters; consequently they still survive, though in small numbers. In winter the deep snow in the jungle drives them on to the bare hill-tops, where the wind-blown summits are clear enough of snow to allow them to feed. The range of the wild reindeer is inexactly known; we should be inclined to put it down as very restricted and confined entirely to those portions of the Syansk Range which extend from the Upper Sisti-Kem eastwards, and thence southwards to the neighbourhood of Lake Kossogol. So far as we could ascertain, there was no record of their existence on the ranges in the interior of the basin, such as the mountains between the Bei-Kem and Khua-Kem, nor is there ground suitable for them in the Western

Syansk; and certainly reindeer would not find favourable haunts anywhere on the Tannu-ola ranges.

By July 2nd we had finished our programme in the Upper Chapsa Valley, and had returned to the Uriankhai encampment by the Ala-su River. Before starting eastwards, however, we made an ascent of the highest point of the Chapsa Range—a rocky, cone-like summit, which stood up conspicuously to the north of us. Leaving the main camp pitched close to the Uriankhai encampment, in the Ala-su Valley, Price and I undertook the ascent of this peak, named Ulu-taiga—The Great Unknown—by the fearsome dwellers in the forests below. Miller remained at the base-camp, partly owing to sickness, and partly so as to be able to study the reindeer more carefully, and, if possible, to procure a specimen.

As was our wont on these side-trips, we started off very lightly laden, taking all the baggage we needed on our riding-horses. Our outfit consisted on these occasions of nothing but a great-coat for covering at night, bread, meat, tea, and sugar for food; as well as a prismatic compass, note-book, cameras, botanical tin and geological hammer, boiling-point apparatus, and, as often as not, a shot-gun.

Most austere and rigorous religious principles forbade any conscientious Uriankhai from accompanying us on these visits to the mountain-tops. We even found it difficult to get answers to our questions as to the existence or absence of mountain-ranges and snow-summits. Such weird localities were beyond the scope of their imagination. The genii of the storms and the elements lurked in those uncanny places where man had no need to go. Every summit of barren rock, which stood sentinel above the dark, sullen forest, was holy ground, the haunt of spirits, the abode of the gods. These spirits they alike venerate and avoid. Every hill-top throughout this part of Asia rejoices in the title of either "bogdo," *i.e.* holy; or "taiga," *i.e.* the wild, the unknown, the incomprehensible; or "Khan," *i.e.* King or chief. Every prominent feature is associated with some myth, every mountain is a monarch, every lake and river a deity. Thus it was that we were always self-dependent on these mountain journeys, and on our own initiative we had to steer as straight a course as possible towards the summits we wished to climb.

On this occasion we assaulted the lower slopes of Ulu-taiga early in the morning, and, by undergoing the fatigue of a thirteen-hour day, succeeded in reaching its summit. For the first four miles a thick cedar-forest, of the usual impenetrable nature, hindered our progress, and necessitated leading our horses. Rocks, soft grounds, and fallen timber did their best to obstruct us, and the usual difficulty of obtaining a view caused us to follow a very circuitous route. At a higher altitude the dead timber formed one of the most troublesome obstacles that nature could successfully place, in order to impede the progress of man. The trees generally fall in a given direction, and in the fall they tear up their roots, which stand erect, thus forming a tangled net-work resembling the most impassable fence. It invariably happened that our line of march was in a diagonal direction to these barricades, so their interfering qualities can well be imagined.

Emerging from the tree-zone at 5,400 ft., we found an alpine lake of exceptional beauty, situated in a rocky cirque; here we left our Russian horseman in charge of our belongings, whilst Price and I, alone, continued

"TAIGAS," OR WILD-PLACES.
Rocky uplifts above the forest-line.

the ascent on foot. With ruck-sacks on our backs, we climbed over rock-skrees to where the giant forest dwindled to mere dwarfed scrub-like bushes,—miniature pines bent and deformed by continual winds and inclement weather. Beyond the limit of tree-growth we had three hours' stiff climbing over granite boulders, devoid of growth, and did not actually reach the summit till past five in the evening. In consequence we had but little time for taking panoramic views, compass-bearings, and altitudes; however, the lights at this late hour compensated us for all other shortcomings, the views we obtained from the summit of Ulu-taiga being beyond our hopes.

The highest pinnacle of Ulu-taiga was a rocky cone, steep-sided on the south and west, and dropping off sheer on the east and north. As was the case in our previous experiences of the taigas, we were conscious again of the strange, uncanny atmosphere which pervades these lonely, rocky uplifts, these granite sentinels of the basin. We overlooked the entire basin of the Chebash, a featureless sea of forest. The immensity of the region enforced itself upon our minds; the utter loneliness of its waiting lands appalled us—within that whole wide region there was probably not one single human being. For true wildness and savage grandeur the panorama could scarcely be surpassed. It is difficult to give an impression of the gloom of these huge woods, of the colossal masses of granite, with their fantastic contours, of the solitary heights that towered upward to where the winds blow chill, of the labyrinths below in which reigned a perpetual twilight, of the foaming torrents and sluggish rivers, all held in the grasp of the dark, deep forest.

The onlooker over this vast scene experienced no

relief from the oppressive silence which pervaded the surrounding atmosphere. There was no ibex or hill-game inhabiting the crags; even the bird-life was scarce—the number of different species could be counted on the fingers—whilst marmots, whose cheery whistle generally enlivens the silence of the snow-line on all Asiatic mountain-ranges, were here conspicuous by their absence. I cannot remember finding more than one species each of animal and bird-life on the summits above tree-line. On nearly every mountain-top we came across a pair of ptarmigan, and the granite skrees formed most suitable homes for innumerable little "picas," or "tailless hares," whose quaint habits and piping note were as great a joy to the others as they were to me, who was intent on collecting them. The shooting and retrieving of these miniature conies was an exasperating task. When shot they almost invariably managed to fall down the crevasses amongst the boulders, or to struggle into their holes before death seized them. Many a dead pica escaped the chance of immortalization by being added to the National Collection in London, owing to the stony rocks which formed his refuge, and under which his little body was irretrievably lost!

We slept beside a huge camp-fire that night, by the edge of the alpine-lake where we had left our belongings, and next morning returned by an easier route to the valley of Ala-su and our main encampment. We soon learnt by experience that, by following the crests of the forested ridges, we should find the pines less closely grown, and consequently the marching less tiresome.

During our absence Miller had succeeded, after much bargaining, in purchasing a specimen of domestic reindeer. Although the reindeer herds were ample for the needs of the tribe, and although, having no outside demand, no marketable value was attached to them, yet the Uriankhai were exceedingly loth to part with even a single beast. The offer of a price which was far in excess of the value of the beast had no effect. When fifteen roubles (30s.) was offered, there was no competition amongst the different tent-holders to realize a little money; apparently it had no charm for them. All our trade-goods, too, were spread out in a tempting array, with the object of ensnaring the fancies of some passing Uriankhai herdsman; but although knives, needles, soap, musical instruments, coloured beads, and automatic pipe-lighters amused them, yet they did not seem to think them worth a reindeer. Some vain old ladies were greatly taken with strips of red and yellow velvet, but they had nothing except reindeer milk to offer us in exchange, and this we accepted at our fixed price of three needles or three safety-pins per bowl.

However, a fine specimen of the domesticated reindeer was eventually procured, done to death, and skinned by Miller. Its horns (in velvet, of course), adorned our packs on horses, oxen, and camels all the way to Eastern Turkestan, and were a proof to the tribes we encountered, *en route*, of the far-distant land from which we had come. The difficulty of procuring good types of reindeer-horns, was increased by the fact that the animals shed them whilst at the lower camping-grounds, and the largest specimens were always spoilt, for it is customary with the Uriankhai to saw off the tops of the longer horns, in order to facilitate the passage of the reindeer through the dense forest.

On July 4th we started our caravan in an easterly direction with the object of passing into the basin of the

Chebash and eventually into that of the Kamsara. Travelling, as usual, without guides, and with no indication of the right direction except a broken reindeer-trail, which as often as not ended in swamp or was lost in the forest, we steered due east until we struck a large river whose course turned us towards the south-east and eventually due south. The region was without any remarkable physical features; low hills or broad flat valleys made travelling monotonous, and surveying difficult.

Some of these valleys, however, attracted our attention as being veritable paradises for colonization. They were of a far more extensive and open nature than the average, and our caravan wandered through rich grass-lands, dotted with pine and larch groves, and through mile after mile of rich pasture-land, unoccupied and ungrazed, yet presenting the most inviting aspect. We noticed the unique opportunities such a land afforded for agricultural and pastoral effort, and wondered at the lack of inhabitants. The whole country appeared to be awaiting the coming of a greater population of a more virile and more progressive people, who would utilize and develop its great wealth. Mention will be made in a subsequent chapter of the progress of Russian emigration into this region, of the reasons for its stagnation up to the present, and for its probable revival in the near future. The fact of the Uriankhai being a "small people" in a land of great possibilities and without serious drawbacks, shows that they are without recuperative powers, and are, without doubt, well on the downward path.

Although the greater portion of the country we traversed between the Ala-su and the mouth of the Kamsara was of this excellent type, yet we passed through a considerable area of fen-country. On the watershed

FALLEN TIMBER.

between these two river-systems, for instance, we fell foul of bogs, which hindered us and lost us one of our horses; indeed, it is a wonder that any baggage-horse escaped, for the soft ground, intermixed with rocks and straggling roots of the forest-trees, gave many occasions for breaking limbs.

The advanced season of the year had produced a torment of mosquitoes and horse-flies, and, as we floundered through these marshes, we traversed the worst locality at the worst season of the year from the point of view of flies. During the whole day life was made hideous. As the horses brushed their way through the undergrowth the mosquitoes and flies rose up in swarms and settled on them and on us. The higher scrub would then brush the horses free from mosquitoes, and leave red smears where the repleted insects had been killed. The disturbing of the undergrowth caused the air to be filled with a real horror of many insects, which drove the horses mad. Giant green horse-flies and small black flies tormented the animals during the whole trek, and did their best to annihilate us. The line of the caravan could easily be distinguished by the cloud of insects which hung in the air above it, and it was with difficulty that we succeeded in keeping our eyes open. Never, even during an eighteen months' journey across tropical Africa, did I find it necessary to wear gloves and a veil in the day-time as I did here. But even these precautions were of little avail against the insects. At night we managed, by use of nets and a circle of smoky fire, to get some sleep; but work, such as writing or plotting maps, was quite out of the question.

On the fourth day after leaving the Ala-su, we struck a big river, which we guessed to be the Chebash, and, following it down for some six or seven miles, we found that it joined with another fine stream which entered from the north, and which we knew to be the Kamsara. A great river, a wide valley bordered by old river-terraces of great height, and a mixture of pasture-land and rolling hills covered with open forest, composed surroundings of a stirring and invigorating character, most pleasing to us after the turmoil of the taiga and the rough mountain-tops. We emerged on to the banks of a great water-way, which is to this region as the main thoroughfare is to a crowded city; all life and interest concentrates on it, being, as it is, the principal line of communication.

On a flat beside the Kamsara, a few miles from its point of juncture with the Bei-Kem, we found a group of log-cabins—the homes of some adventurous Siberian colonists,—and, pitching our tents beside their crude but homely dwellings, we answered their many eager questions as to who we were, and did our best to satisfy their curiosity.

ON THE UPPER BEI-KEM

CHAPTER VI

THE HEART OF THE UPPER YENISEI BASIN

On our subsequent journeys in the land of the Uriankhai and through the heart of the basin, where the ease of river-transport relieved us of the labour of forest-travel, and a more open country gave us greater freedom of movement, we gained many vivid impressions of which descriptions and word-pictures can only give inadequate expression. The Bei-Kem region, above Kamsara, brought us to a land of sunny meadows and shadowy forest, a land of "rolling grass and open timber" dotted with tranquil lakes, coursed by dancing streamlets, and intersected by great swirling rivers. Here we had the bewitching variety of meadow and forest, of hill and plain. We could ride on horseback across downy grass-lands, and appreciate the utter freedom of the down-lands, without being impeded by the obstruction offered by forests or wearied by the monotony of a region which is all steppe. Here came not only a sense of movement, but the sense of space; there were distant views which were keenly devoured after the curtailed views of the forests through which we had struggled, in order to reach this El Dorado.

For contrast, we could wander through patches of fairy-like forest, which were not dense enough to hamper one or to exclude all view, but where the larches half obstructed the sunlight, and the ground was chequered with trembling shade, and where, through breaks in the larch-groves, we gained vistas of a beautiful world of sun-lit prairies, and bright, colour-splashed lowlands carpeted with wild-flowers. Here, too, was a lakeland of a thousand lakelets, whose waters formed the sources of the Great Yenisei, and where great fish rose and the Great Northern Diver laughed ; the whole forming a very paradise of beauty through which we passed on horseback or in canoe.

With the help of skilled Siberian boatmen, we were poled up-stream in our canoes at a greater speed than we could have accomplished the distance by land, and with far greater enjoyment to us. Jolly days we spent lying back in the dug-out canoes or on the raft, whilst drifting down the quiet reaches of the Bei-Kem, and strenuous days we experienced when rapids lay in our course and jeopardized our safety. Romantic camps, too, we made at night on some bar of shingle, twixt the dark, silent forest and the racing river. This was a freer country than we had hitherto experienced, and more easy to move in, but even here in the background we always had the view of distant ranges, whose forested flanks rose to barren and rugged summits which formed a rock-girdle around the basin, and gave us the impression of being hemmed in, and cut off from the outside world.

The "down-lands" and open pastures, where the main section of the Toji tribe of Uriankhai live, are situated on the banks of the Bei-Kem, to the south of Kamsara, and are broadly known as the Dora-Kem steppes. They are, in fact, the chief centre of Uriankhai life in the upper basin, and we were desirous of visiting them, for the existing physical conditions of this region are very different to those which surround the reindeer-keeping tribe whom we had accosted in the depths of the taiga. In order, therefore, to make the best use of the short time at our disposal, and to increase the range of our maps and the scope of our work, we divided forces. Miller and Price undertook to visit the Uriankhai of the Dora-Kem steppes farther up the Bei-Kem, whilst I determined to join the main caravan which was awaiting our arrival at the mouth of the Sisti-Kem, arrange its future course, and then visit the region between the Bei-Kem and the Khua-Kem, which was merely represented on the maps by blank spaces, or by half-guessed rivers and mountains.

The junction of the Kamsara with the Bei-Kem is a point of junction of two routes which lead out of the basin into the Baikal province of Siberia. We were never able, unfortunately, to get very exact information regarding these tracks. They have undoubtedly been used by Russian traders. M. Safianoff, one of the oldest and most go-ahead colonists of this region, actually attempted to drive cattle from his ranches on the lower Bei-Kem over this route to the Siberian towns of Novi-Udinsk and Irkutsk, and he is said to have spent five months wandering in the mountains, instead of accomplishing the journey in two, as he expected. One of these routes leads to the head-waters of the Kuzu-Kem, right affluent of the Kamsara, and over the divide by a pass of 7,400 ft. The other route follows up the main Bei-Kem and over a pass of 6,500 ft.

I mention these routes to draw attention to the lack of knowledge that exists of the far eastern end of the basin. For a hundred and twenty miles between these two passes the divide is quite unknown, and, so far as we could ascertain, there are no routes leading to it. In this region rise the many sources of the Bei-Kem, and a lake-dotted country makes the locality one of exceptional beauty, interest, and indeed of economic value, for these lakes represent untold wealth in the way of fisheries. They are, in all cases, drained by the tributaries of the Bei-Kem, rivers, such as the Azaz and Ee, flowing through and connecting a line of perhaps a dozen lakes. The majority of these are quite small, but there are some, such as Toji Kul and Noyon Kul, which cover as much as thirty square miles.

Miller and Price set out on July 8th in two light canoes, and journeyed up the main Bei-Kem for three days, as far as a "Kuria," or temple, situated a few miles from the left bank of the river in a highly favoured district well populated by Uriankhai. The Bei-Kem River here flows either between high sandstone cliffs, as in the neighbourhood of the junction of the Kamsara, or across the alluvial plain through which it has carved itself a bed between high, terraced banks. The valley on the right bank is wide and open, a rolling country of small hills and grassy flats, backed in some places by higher ground; but the country on the left bank is shut in by a range of hills which runs parallel with and close to the river. Farther south this range gives way, and a fine open steppe-land grants opportunity for a large Uriankhai settlement. Here are the headquarters of the religious community of the upper basin, and the presence of a Kuria, or Buddhist temple, adds additional interest and importance to the locality. Away on the east bank of the river, on the Dora-Kem prairies, is the residence of the "Noyon," or chief of the Toji clansmen, while all over this region, and especially around

THE KURIA OF THE UPPER BEI-KEM.

DRIFTING DOWN THE BEI-KEM.

the Kuria and the dwelling of this chief, congregates the main section of the Toji tribe.

The pastures and prairies of the Upper Bei-Kem support the largest community of Uriankhai that we encountered, for here alone did we find them living in considerable numbers and in close proximity to each other. On the flats beside the river were the tents of the Toji herdsmen, living in communities of from ten to thirty families. The Toji used, for the most part, the familiar birch-bark tepees, but the richer men possessed a winter abode in the form of a felt-covered yurt, of the kind in use throughout Central Asia. In summer the tepees were occupied in preference to the felt-tents, but in winter the latter were used, and, on account of their greater warmth, must have been a boon to their owners; there were not very many of them, however, for only a small percentage of the tribe were wealthy enough to possess two abodes.

On the neighbouring hills grazed flocks of sheep, goats, and horses, and in the more luxuriant pastures beside the streams, cattle of a remarkably small breed grew fat during the short but pleasant summer. These natives of the upper Bei-Kem steppes have no cause to move their encampments very often during the year, and when they do migrate it is not very far, for the majority remain in the same valley during the whole twelve months. The Kuria, and the permanency of the chief's abode, go far to prove the more or less sedentary habits of these people, for a numerous population is always found in the neighbourhood of each of these buildings. In winter the resident population is augmented by the arrival of Uriankhai from the surrounding ranges, men who come either to trade or to settle their quarrels, as well as those who desire to make a yearly pilgrimage to the Kuria. Many tribesmen, too, come down with their families and winter in the lower valleys, so with the gathering together of the various clans, the upper Bei-Kem must at that season present a lively appearance. Little snow lies on the open land, and the herds can be fed without difficulty.

The Toji tribe is in easy communication with the south, tracks lead over to the wide valley of the Khua-Kem, and onwards across the Tannu-ola to the much-frequented Tess Valley, and to the pasturages and settlements which exist in fair numbers on the route to Uliassutai. Other, but less-known routes, lead direct across hill and dale to Urga.

After disembarking from their canoes, Miller and Price visited the Kuria on the day of an interesting summer festival, being lucky enough to witness one of the most curious of religious ceremonies. The description of this festival we will leave for the present, in order to introduce it into the chapter containing all our observations on the religious beliefs and customs of the Uriankhai. The Kuria was found to be a remarkable building, showing an unusual combination of the Chinese and Russian style of workmanship. It is said that the Kuria was built about ten years ago with the aid of Russian workmen; this appeared to be proved by the presence of many log-built houses, for who else but the Russians could have acquired the art of trimming and joining pine-logs? The temple itself boasted of Chinese characteristics in the architectural form of its roof, possessing, as it did, upturned eaves admirably carved to represent evil-looking monsters.

Around were many log-huts, inhabited by the guardians of the temple, and also by the young Urian-khai novices who had consecrated their lives to the service of the temple. Each hut was isolated by a palisade of pine-logs; thus their seclusion was complete. The presence of praying-wheels was inevitable, though the tower from which the lamas called the brethren to prayer brought to mind that well-known custom of followers of the faith of Islam.

The interior of the Kuria contained the usual miscellaneous collection of banners, painted silk-scrolls, and sacred musical instruments, as well as a library of a hundred and fifty religious books, and many idols. Three of the latter were of special interest, for they possessed features unlike any other Buddhist idol that we have seen in Asia, the aquiline noses and long hair giving them a cast of countenance not usually represented in Buddhist pictures or sacred figures. It was with deep religious zeal that the small community of lamas practised the most exact ritual. An evening service, witnessed by my companions during their visit to the Kuria, commenced by two lamas ascending the tower and calling their brethren by blowing mournful notes through large white shells. The lamas and the novices turned up in full force, each with a red shawl thrown across the shoulder, and, vigorously turning the prayer-wheels on entering the temple, they took up their positions, sitting cross-legged on the divans. The head priest then rattled off the prayers at express speed, giving additional emphasis to certain passages by the ringing of a little brass bell. Simultaneously other enthusiasts incessantly turned prayer-wheels, and away in another building the noise of drums and cymbals greatly added to the din, and increased the impression of religious fervour.

This experience of observing the outward expression of the Buddhist faith amongst a people who were originally Shammanists, showed that Buddhism has the appearance of attracting the Uriankhai; but it was obvious that they did not follow the religion with the zeal shown by the Mongols, and this rather brought the conviction that, at heart, the Uriankhai remain, as formerly, nature-worshippers.

Leaving the Kuria, Miller and Price crossed the Bei-Kem to the east, and visited two small settlements belonging to Russian emigrants. This remote part of the basin has attracted a few of the more daring traders and ranchers by reason of its containing a large population demanding trade-goods, as well as on account of the capacity the land possesses for the feeding of flocks and herds, and for the making of butter and cheese. These pioneers were eager to show hospitality to my companions, and, with their help, the journey was continued eastwards to the Lake of Toji Kul. All the country they traversed was steppe covered with short grass, and presenting possibilities of becoming a fine stock-raising district in the future. Patches of larch-forest, and, by the rivers, narrow margins of willow and birch, relieved the barren appearance of the landscape, while the presence of many old burial-mounds showed that the region had, in olden days, been a favourite one, and thickly inhabited. Toji Kul is situated in a rolling country, where the courses of ancient glaciers are easily seen by the existence of moraines; indeed, from our observation on all the lakes that we chanced to see in the upper basin, we are inclined to believe that they

LAKE-LAND AT THE SOURCES OF THE YENISEI.
Toji Kul.

152]

owe their existence to the changing condition which must, of necessity, follow a previous greater glaciation.

Toji Kul, with its wide expanse of clear, still water, its grassy banks and forested islands, its broken coast-line of quiet bays and bold promontories, backed by wooded hills, was an attractive scene of great and exceptional beauty. Park-like country surrounded it, and although scattered tents of Uriankhai showed here and there along the lake-shore, this splendid land seemed, for the most part, to be lying fallow, and unutilized by man.

Toji Kul is considered to be a sacred lake; sacred "obos" are erected in prominent positions as guardians of the lake, and the natives have, up till now and on this account, been able to restrict Russian advances and retain the wealth of its fisheries for their own use. The natives frequent the neighbourhood of Toji Kul in the spring and autumn months, the latter season being the most favourable for fishing. By means of hooks and nets, the latter being beautifully made of horse-hair, they catch with ease all the fish they require for their own use and for the purpose of trade with the Russians. The natives make but poor use of the fisheries considering the incredible numbers of fish. Their methods are too crude and they themselves lack zeal and energy; although living in a land of lakes and rivers, they have not even learnt to build boats or canoes, and are still dependent upon small rafts for water-transport. They have shown their wisdom, however, in proclaiming the holiness of Toji Kul, and in forbidding the Russians the use of its fisheries, lest its sacred waters should thereby be profaned.

Away in the forested ranges to the east of the lake

dwell small encampments of reindeer-keepers, about whom nothing seems to be known beyond the fact of their existence. In winter they are said to come down and encamp on the shores of the lake, and a few visit the Russian settlement near the Bei-Kem for trading purposes. This section of the Toji tribe who inhabit the lake region are called "Kul [or Nor] Soumin," which means "Lake People," "Kul" and "Nor" being respectively the Turki and Mongol for lake, and "soumin" being a tribal division. The whole Toji tribe consists of four soumins.

After visiting the Noyon of the Toji Kul, who dwelt in the centre of a large encampment of his followers, close to the Russian settlement of Safianoff, Miller and Price embarked in canoes and drifted down the river, reaching the main encampment at the mouth of the Sisti-Kem in the course of two days.

Meanwhile, I carried out my plans with fair success. After leaving Kamsara I rode down the right bank of the Bei-Kem, through pleasant scenery, and in one short day's journey reached the mouth of the Sisti-Kem, where I was pleased by the sight of our main party snugly encamped on a grassy meadow beside the river. Tents were pitched, ready for my arrival, the raft lay tied up to the bank, and the horses looked well as a result of two weeks' grazing in the luxuriant grass; in fact, our plans and arrangements had worked excellently, and all parties had carried out their special duties with care and precision.

I rested at this camp a few days, and made arrangements for the despatching of men with the horses to Cha-Kul, where we should again need their services. We ourselves proposed to continue our journey by raft down the Bei-Kem and the Ulu-Kem as far as Cha-Kul, which is a small settlement of Chinese and Russians situated on the lower Ulu-Kem, some 180 miles distant. On July 11th the twenty-four horses were sent off under the charge of three men, for whereas we, in the raft, expected to traverse the 180 miles in three or four days, the men and horses had to be allowed a full ten days to cover the rough track which runs along the bank of the river, parallel to the Syansk Range. The raft was re-constructed and strengthened in anticipation of rough usage on the Bei-Kem rapids, and all details of supplies received careful attention.

Near our camp was another of those isolated ranches belonging to a Siberian settler, named Skobieff. It will be noticed that the settlements we so frequently came across in our wanderings form quite an economic feature of the basin. They exist, at intervals, all over this region, wherever there are suitable localities. In certain places considerable numbers of emigrants have settled together and formed regular colonies, but in others, such as here—at the mouth of the Sisti-Kem—and at Kamsara—the available land is not sufficient for more than a ranch or two. A river-frontage is essential to the existence of these outposts of civilization. The rivers are the life of the basin; all colonists settle, if possible, alongside them, and use them as their high-roads and fishing-grounds. Indeed, there is nothing to tempt the new-comers to settle away from the rivers, the difficulties of transport alone forbidding colonization elsewhere. This is the reason for our finding the settlements only along the main rivers, and in most instances at the point of the juncture of the tributaries with the main streams. The position of these colonies, both politically and commercially, brings forward some interesting facts which will be discussed at length elsewhere.

The Uriankhai population in this district was very small. A few families only frequented the neighbourhood of the Siberian settlement, and some scattered encampments were said to exist on the south bank of the Bei-Kem. To ascertain the conditions under which the Uriankhai lived, in order to compare them with the reindeer-keepers of the Toji tribe, I paid a visit to a chief whose tepee was pitched on the farther bank of the river. The Bei-Kem was here flowing very swiftly in several channels. To cross these we had to use canoes, whilst the horses were swum across by the Uriankhai accompanying me. Their method of doing this was at once original and successful, proving to me that these Uriankhai were naturally watermen of ability. My guide rode one horse into the current, driving the others before him, until his horse was out of its depth, then, slipping off its back into the water, but keeping hold of the long mane, he allowed himself to be thus towed across the flood, chanting a peculiar song as he went.

After a two hours' ride from the south bank of the Bei-Kem, I arrived at a small encampment of four tepees. One of these tents belonged to a chief, and was especially large; it measured thirty paces in circumference, and was composed of over a hundred poles. The more settled habits of these people, who, unlike the others, herded only horses and cattle, was shown by the fact that this chief had built a small log-hut near his encampment, which he used as a store-house for his belongings. A group of horses, carefully protected by a circle of smoky fires from the voracious attacks of flies,

OVERLOOKING THE UPPER YENISEI BASIN.

AN URIANKHAI ENCAMPMENT.

stood in a bunch under the shade of some neighbouring larch; and cattle of a peculiar build—small, stumpy, and short-horned—grazed in the meadows.

These people told me of tracks which led south-eastwards to the upper parts of the Bei-Kem, where, they said, large encampments of Uriankhai existed; but they knew of no routes to the southwards towards the head-waters of the Tapsa, a valley of some importance on account of its placer gold-mines. On the ranges to the south they declared there were reindeer, both wild and domesticated; but my interpreters were so unreliable, and the Uriankhai had so little conception of truth, that I feel obliged to doubt this assertion. From information given to us later, I should prefer, rather than believe this statement, to risk contradiction by saying that reindeer do not exist in the ranges between the Bei-Kem and Khua-Kem westwards of latitude 96° E. That game abounds in this district is evident from the profusion of skins adorning every Uriankhai's home. Roe-deer, musk-deer, and moose were the most numerous, and stood as a good proof of the skill of the hunters, who were dependent upon muzzle-loading rifles of an antique pattern, traps and pitfalls, not only for their supply of meat, but for skins as wearing-apparel, and for furs as a trading medium.

Of the extensive area which lies between the Bei-Kem and Khua-Kem we have very little direct knowledge. A rarely used route passes through its central portion from east to west, from the Upper Bei-Kem to the Tapsa Valley; for the rest, the topography of this region remains unmapped. From rising ground near the mouth of the Sisti-Kem I caught a glimpse of the highlands, which rose in a jagged ridge some distance away from the south bank of the Bei-Kem; so I at once set off in a canoe with three men and as little baggage as possible, driven by the keen desire to fill in as much of the map as I was able.

During the next few days I experienced the joy of canoeing on the quiet reaches of the Bei-Kem amid most enchanting scenery. It was delightful, on a hot day, to drift down in mid-stream, and I was unable to resist drawing a contrast between this water-trip and the hot, tiring struggle that a land-journey would have entailed. We merely lay back in the canoe and enjoyed at a distance the sight of dark, forbidding palisades of pine-trees which lined the banks. Our canoes at one time lazily glided over some silent, sequestered side-channel, protected by islands from the main river; at another we raced through the threatening torrent where the waters roared over a rocky bottom; we steered clear of giant log-jams piled high on submerged islands, and paddled past long, shining bars of sunny shingle, which invited us to rest. This idyllic travelling was varied by strenuous plunges into the tangle of forest and swamp, which extends between the river-bank and the foot-hills of the nameless ranges to the south. I managed to reach the ridge in two places, to survey a considerable stretch of mountain, and to add half a dozen rivers to the map.

The point from which I made the first excursion to the southwards was some eighteen miles to the west of the Sisti-Kem. Here a pleasant valley of a comparatively open nature led up to the north, where the Karagatch River has its source in the Syansk, somewhere to the west of the "White Mountain," which we climbed on first entering the basin. A group of four or five houses stood at the mouth of the river, on the banks of the Bei-Kem, and I noticed that the colonists had commenced to cultivate the soil.

After crossing the Bei-Kem, I found the country to the south very flat and for the most part marshy. The larch and the birch were replaced by the cedar, and the ground was exceptionally wet and consequently covered with a growth of moss. I rode for six hours without touching hard, dry ground, and until the foot-hills were reached I found the travelling very tedious. There were no traces of habitation and no tracks to show that it was even visited by man; yet the Uriankhai, I was told, do visit this region in winter, in order to hunt and trap, using reindeer for transport, horses finding no food in such a land. Game was evidently very abundant here. I repeatedly put up roe-deer, and saw traces of moose and wapiti.

On reaching a ridge of 7,000 ft. altitude I found that I was on the outskirts of a rough mountainous region which extended east and west, and connected across the Bei-Kem River with the Sin-Taiga and Tashkil offshoots of the main Syansk Range. The whole ridge was very steep and rocky, and although it attained an altitude of about 8,000 ft., I found very little snow lying upon it. Southwards there was a veritable labyrinth of rugged ranges, and so broken were they, that I could not even make out where the course of the Bei-Kem cuts through the barrier which this uplift forms across its valley.

My next ascent of this same range was made from a base some fifteen miles to the west, namely, from Sabie—another settlement of Siberians on the north bank of the Bei-Kem; but my time was shortened by the sudden appearance of the rest of our party drifting down the river on the raft, and I had no opportunity of making more than a hasty inspection of the range to the south, from a summit of 7,000 ft. This short trip enabled me to locate the main valleys of several important rivers, whose mouths we had noticed, adding their contribution of water to the Bei-Kem, as we slid past them in our canoe. Large areas of dead forest, and a certain suggestion of dryness on the mountain-tops, coupled with the appearance of a little grass, suggested the beginning of a change in the flora. From this point of vantage I gained a wide view of the middle Bei-Kem, as well as of many of its right and left affluents.

This bird's-eye view, which enabled me to look down over the forest, taught me an interesting fact about the distribution of forest and steppe. The south bank of the Bei-Kem was densely forested, and, so far as I could see, with no break in the afforestation. The north bank also was forested as a whole, but it was distinctly noticeable that at each point where a tributary entered the Bei-Kem there was to be seen a break in the forest-zone, and open meadow-land appeared in place of jungle. Long, narrow, wedge-shaped areas of open-land marked the position of the right affluents of the Bei-Kem and formed encouraging openings for colonization, of which, as already mentioned, the Siberians have not been slow to take advantage. These isolated patches of steppe are the first attempts of steppe-flora to overrun the forests. Steppe-conditions are gaining ground, and they first make their appearance beside the rivers, in valley-bottoms with the most southerly aspect.

The village of Sabie is a typical example of a Siberian

ON THE LOWER BEI-KEM.

Showing the mountain barrier dividing the lower Bei-Kem from the upper.

settlement in the Yenisei basin. It must be remarked, however, that Sabie is the only real village which exists in the upper basin; that is to say, in the region above the Bei-Kem rapids, for no other settlement in the upper parts can boast of more than a few houses. It will be noticed, later on, that the mountain-barrier, where the Bei-Kem rapids are situated, forms a well-marked line of demarcation stretching across the basin. This line divides the little Siberian settlements of the Upper Bei-Kem from the larger colonies which have taken up land in the favourable zone lying in the transition-stage between dense forest and open steppe. The Sabie Valley is wide and open, its deforested area is correspondingly extensive, and the village at its mouth with frontage on the Bei-Kem is large in proportion to the land available for colonization. Karagatch, the last small settlement at which I halted, was the first locality where I had noticed attempts at cultivation, but at Sabie there was to be seen a considerable area of land broken for tillage. The attempts of the settlers in this direction are, however, not altogether successful. Rye succeeds fairly well, but wheat often fails, being more liable to damage by early frosts.

Trade in fur, fish, and wapiti-horns furnish a better means of livelihood than agriculture, commerce in wapiti-horns being a remarkably remunerative business on account of the great value which the Chinese attach to them. Sabie is situated on the edge of a fine game-country; in fact, wapiti come so close to the village that it is an easy and profitable undertaking to capture the younger animals alive. These the colonists keep in enclosures (as is the custom in all localities along the Russo-Chinese frontier where wapiti exist), and take a yearly tribute from the stags in the shape of their soft horns when in velvet. The nearness of the Chinese markets, to which these horns find their way, as well as the existence of many wild wapiti, has caused Sabie to be a flourishing settlement. The inhabitants told us that, during the winter, they employed the Urian-khai, owing to their exceptional skill in forest-lore, to catch the wapiti. The method they employed was to dig pitfalls and to attract the stags to the locality by distributing salt in the neighbourhood; but the pit-falls they only found to be successful so long as the snow covered the ground. The mountains to the south and south-west were the best ground for wapiti, and we noticed their traces quite close to the village on the opposite bank of the Bei-Kem. The horns, when sawn off, are boiled in weak tea, as a preservative, and then sent to Cha-Kul on the Ulu-Kem, where they pass into the hands of Chinese merchants.

The value of the soft antlers to the Chinese is well demonstrated by the price paid for them. At Cha-Kul they were sold in bulk at the rate of ten shillings for a pound's weight of horn, while at other places on the frontier we heard of hunters who got twenty or twenty-five pounds for a heavy pair of horns. As is generally known, the Chinese place great faith in the medicinal properties of the stags' horns, and, considering the extra-ordinary collections which fill the average chemist's shops in a Chinese town, there is no reason why stags' horns should not be included. If the Celestial puts his trust in bears' paws, vultures' feet, and the bones of pre-historic beasts, it is not surprising he finds comfort, or a tonic, in the fresh horn, which naturally contains the best blood of the period of rapid growth. But it is doubtful whether the drug, as sold at the Pekin pharmacies, contains a tonic approaching in value the exorbitant price asked for it.

Having now been brought into close contact with the Siberian element in this region, it will be advisable to record all we saw of the colonists who have taken up land in a region which is virtually under foreign rule, and whose existing status is, in consequence, somewhat unusual in its conditions. The actual position of the Russians in the basin will be best understood by a glance at their story from the time when, as colonists and traders, they first began to interest themselves in this region.

The Upper Yenisei basin has always attracted the avarice of the Siberian. As long ago as 1860 the first Russian pioneer of commerce (Vacelkoff, of Minnusinsk), was building depots in the Uriankhai country and opening up negotiations with the native chiefs. The native Uriankhai preferred to relinquish their patronage of the Chinese merchants, and to deal with the Russian newcomers, for they fully recognized the easy and just dealings of the latter and the advantage offered by the close markets of Siberia. These Russian traders were wise enough to generally employ Abakan Tartars as their "go-betweens," with whom the Uriankhai preferred to deal rather than with the Mongols or Chinese. Thus the gradual passing of the trade out of the hands of the Chinese into the hands of Russians was assured when the first merchant from Siberia penetrated into the basin.

The traders did good business during the first years. In those days the most valuable furs were cheap, most things could be bought for tea, and tobacco purchased what tea failed to buy. Adrianoff, in his *Travels in the Altai and Trans-Syansk,* notes that, in 1860, a packet of tobacco bought a sheep, and a cow only cost two packets! Jealousy and race-hatred, however, caused hostility between the Chinese and the traders, and there were instances of Russian stores being burnt, and of general friction between the two parties. In 1869 a commission was formed by the Russian and Chinese authorities to investigate the affairs and to decide the rights of the new-comers, with the result that an indemnity was paid by the Chinese to the Russian traders who had suffered loss, and an understanding was arrived at which would effectually forbid Siberian colonists to establish themselves permanently in the basin. In those days the annual turn-over of trade was put at 10,000 roubles.

Later on, as more traders and colonists began to appear on the scene, fresh outbreaks against the Russians occurred. The Chinese apparently permitted the Russians to carry on trade in the basin, but tried to forbid the building of permanent settlements. The prohibition ruled that not more than two hundred men should congregate together in any one place, that the Russians should not settle except in those places where permanent Russian Consuls were established—such as Uliassutai and Kobdo in Northern Mongolia,—and that traders should not be permitted to make use of any form of dwelling other than tents or boats. This was a determined attempt to stop effectually the actual colonization of the land by Russian settlers. But, from all accounts, the Russians continued to build ranches, factories, and trading-posts. The native Uriankhai neither permitted nor forbade, whilst the Chinese were in no position to

FORESTS AND FLOWER-STREWN MEADOWS.
At 5,000 ft. in the Syansk Mountains.

A SHAMMANISTIC RELIGIOUS CEREMONY IN PROGRESS.

See p. 248.

expostulate. So the colonists increased in numbers, attracted, in spite of a certain fear as to the attitude of the Chinese, by the offer of new homes in a pregnant land, where fishing and grazing-rights were free to all comers, and there was an unlimited supply of grass and fuel.

Observing the situation at the present time, we note that the Russians have won the day, and that the colonists have the advantage of the lands of the Uriankhai, without the disadvantage of a foreign Government. It is altogether a unique position, for the settlers in the basin actually possess the privileges of their own Russian rule. At Turan, where there is a small settlement of houses, we saw a fine log-built building which added dignity to the village. Here it was that the Natchalnik from Usinsk, the Siberian frontier town, came annually, in order to settle the differences between the colonists and to carry on his official duties, just as if he were within the limits of his own jurisdiction. The Government officials at Usinsk consist of this local governor, a secretary, a clerk, and a police-officer with a dozen men under him. The staff is provided with interpreters for the Uriankhai and Mongol languages. These officials hold under their control the entire population of Russian subjects, including Tartars, Siberians, and Buriats, who inhabit the basin or visit it for trade purposes.

We were never able to get at the truth of the actual status of Russian officialdom in the Upper Yenisei basin, or to find out to what extent they hold the native Uriankhai in their power, or to what bounds their influence extends. M. Paul Chalon, who visited these regions in 1904, gives us some information which I have not come across elsewhere, and I take the liberty of quoting him.

"The Russian absorption," he says, "has already commenced. By reason of the Uriankhai preferring to dwell in larger numbers every year on the Siberian slopes of the Syansk, the Russian administration has, little by little, wormed its way into their affairs, and spread its protection step by step to the southern slopes of the Syansk, to the banks of the Ulu-Kem, to the base of the Kemchik, and finally to the territory bounded on the south by the line of military posts, or the Mongol Karauls (which extend along the southern foot-hills of the Tannu-ola). Every year the Natchalnik of Usinsk comes to the village of Cha-Kul, the future Uriankhai capital, where he administers justice, checks the work of the 'noyons' (local chiefs), and listens to the complaints of the residents and the nomads. He is treated with much respect by all the chiefs who come to meet him at the villages where he stops. The present Natchalnik is a most competent man, and it may be said that he has already asserted the Russian protectorship over the whole country, to the great satisfaction of the natives."

How far this is correct I am not in a position to say, but it is certain that Russian protection would be welcomed by the natives, and in view of recent advances made by Mongol princes to Russia, and in consideration of the preference for Russian rule over Chinese rule, it would be strange indeed if these regions do not, some day, fall under the protectorship of the Russian Empire. The Tannu-ola range forms a far more natural boundary between the two Empires than the Syansk Mountains, and is one which is far more easily delineated.

During our conversation with the settlers, moreover, we were constantly questioned as to the existing state of affairs between Russia and China. These ranchers had a fear at the back of their minds of the possibility of trouble with the Chinese, and an undisguised knowledge of the insecurity of their position, should hostilities break out. We were repeatedly asked when the war was going to begin? Whether there were many Chinese in Mongolia? Their questions pointed to the fact that the colonists recognized their isolation and their exile in a foreign land. If a Yellow Peril should arise and march this way, escape across the frontier would be easy and quick owing to the water-ways, for the Russian territory lies down-stream. We are inclined to believe that the entire population could evacuate the basin by water at a few days' notice, if necessity drove them to leave their homes.

Gold is the chief attraction held out by the basin to the Siberian pioneer. The existence of it, practically all over the basin, has caused the springing up of certain out-of-the-way mining-camps; but the extreme difficulties of transport and the isolation of the camps have been responsible for their failure. We came across several placer-mines on the Upper Amil and Upper Sisti-Kem near the Algiak Pass over the Syansk, but the majority of these were shut down. Mines also exist on the Upper Kamsara, on the Tapsa, and on Upper Sisti-Kem, but the only successful one of which we had information is that in the Upper Tapsa belonging to M. Safianoff, the success being due to his possessing sufficient capital. The other mines mentioned may be well worth working, but the owners have not money to work them on an adequate scale. The cheapness of labour, which allows the mines in the vicinity of Minnusinsk to work at a paying rate, does not here affect the situation, for labour and food have to be imported; moreover, these mines are closed all the winter, and the workers shifted long distances to localities where living is considerably cheaper.

The mineral wealth of this part of Asia is a well-established fact ; it is possible that, at some later day, parts of the Syansk may become scenes of activity, leading ultimately to the establishment of thriving mining-camps. Iron and copper are being successfully worked on the Siberian side of the Syansk, these mines, in many cases, being merely the reopened old workings of the ancient Yeniseians. The remoteness of the mines of the upper basin from the Siberian centres alone hinders their successful working, but these are hindrances which may some day be overcome. Russian protectorship, augmented by sufficient capital, would work wonders in connexion with the commercial possibilities of the Upper Yenisei basin.

In regard to the natural wealth of the basin, we must especially mention, as the most important, hides and wool besides furs, fish, and the feathers of water-birds. In the forests which clothe the Syansk Range live the most valuable sables in existence, and an incredible number of squirrels possessing excellent fur, as well as fox, lynx, otter, marten, ermine, glutton, wolf, bear, snow-leopard, and a few beavers. These, together with reindeer, wapiti, and roe-deer skins, besides musk from the musk-deer, supply a fine opening for the keen hunters and trappers, and yield a good return at the markets of Minnusinsk. Fur-hunting supplies the staple means of livelihood for many Siberian colonists, as well as for the native Uriankhai. All the traders in the basin deal largely in furs, and barter all their goods with the Uriankhai during the summer months for the promise of fur payable during the winter. The returns are still large, but the profits have greatly diminished during the last few years. The diminution of the actual number of skins which pass into the traders' hands, as well as the great rise in prices, shows to what an extent this once lucrative business has fallen. The Siberians themselves hunt and trap during the winter months, but their main source of supply is from the natives, who pay in furs for the debts they have incurred with the local traders for tobacco and clothing.

Where the Russians especially succeed is in the development of the fisheries, for here they deal with untouched grounds, and their activity in this direction does not in any way interfere with the natives. The Uriankhai are no fishermen, and although there are certain lakes which they deem sacred, and which they strenuously guard against Russian desecration, yet the fishing of other rivers and lakes they leave as something not worth troubling about. There being no reservation of the fisheries, the majority of Russian residents in the basin occupy themselves with this special pursuit at certain periods of the year. The number of the fishermen is considerably increased in the autumn by the arrival of Siberians from the villages of the Amil, who come over to fish in the upper reaches of the Bei-Kem. The industry must give good returns, for the expenses of the fishermen amount to almost nothing. The dug-out canoes they use cost about a pound or thirty shillings, the rafts on which they descend the river are constructed at no cost, and are eventually sold for fire-wood; even the salt used in packing the fish is easily bought from the Uriankhai for a few packets of tobacco, or a little tea.

It appears that the Uriankhai try to preserve the best fishing-grounds from Russian poachers, and these are generally so crowded with fish that even the natives can catch all they need without much trouble. I strongly suspect that Toji Kul is only considered *sacred* as an excuse for retaining its fisheries intact for Uriankhai use. The mention, by Adrianoff, of a Russian trader leasing a lake for fishing from a Uriankhai chief, shows that there is some restriction against the ravages of the newly arrived fishermen. In this instance, it is said, the Russian fished the lake when frozen over, and made a haul of a thousand pounds' weight of fish from the lake, and of another thousand pounds from the river flowing into it.

There are nine or ten varieties of fish inhabiting the rivers and lakes of the upper basin; of these, trout, salmon, sturgeon, perch, and tench are the most important from the commercial point of view. It is said that the fish move up into the higher reaches of the rivers [1]; that is, they move from the Yenisei of the plains up into the Yenisei of the Uriankhai country, in September and October. This particular season is, of course, also made most use of by the Siberians. With simplest tackle, consisting of a few nets, and by use of flimsy dug-out canoes, they make prodigious hauls. Living in the open in the forest, or constructing small log-huts to

[1] The fish run up the rivers as far as they can in the autumn, in order to spawn in the upper waters. They remain in the upper waters under the ice all winter, and come down (in bad condition) in the spring. The autumn is, therefore, the season for the Siberian fishermen. The wonderful series of lakes at the highest sources of the Bei-Kem tributaries form a unique spawning-ground for the salmon, and, as these lakes are drained and are not standing water, the other fish probably use them as a spawning-ground instead of the rivers, which may be frozen solid in the winter.

SPRUCE-FOREST IN THE UPPER YENISEI BASIN.

shelter themselves, they spend a few weeks of hard work and strenuous living, then, salting their catches in barrels, and building their rafts, they float them down the quiet reaches of those pleasant water-ways, shoot the rapids of the Bei-Kem and Kemchik Bom, and eventually dispose of their fish at the Siberian market-towns.

Having accomplished their task, these hardy frontiers-men return to their log-built villages for the cold weather, or outfit again for a winter's fur-hunt in the forests. In the latter case, they travel with a few light sleighs which they haul up the frozen rivers, and drag through the forests, into the inaccessible depths of a region where the sable still holds his own in spite of the persistent endeavour of man to exterminate him. The Upper Yenisei offers much attraction to the keen fisherman, longing for a new and interesting region in which to travel and strange conditions under which to fish. We heard stories of a great fish which swims in the Toji Kul and other lakes; the Russians call him "Taime," and claim that he runs to eighty pounds in weight and measures 6 ft. in length!

On the Russians depends the development of the commercial advantages of these regions, especially with regard to minerals. Of the latter we can mention iron, copper, and gold, asbestos, lime, rock-salt, and salt from the lake-beds. All awaits development, and all will act as a further incentive to the Siberians, who are ever ready, under the fatherly protection of their own Government, to take up new land and to try new ground, but are forced to hold back when the political state of the country is as uncertain and unsettled as it is at present. The trade is almost entirely in the hands of the Russians. The chief difficulty experienced by these traders is the supplying of articles of which the natives have the greatest need. Tobacco, tea, clothes, cooking-utensils, copper, red-leather, and gunpowder take the place of money, for which they find no use. The native, being lazy and without ambition, sits idle so long as he has sufficient for his needs, and does not bestir himself until necessity forces him again to work, hunt, or sell his stock. Besides this there is ample land awaiting the rancher; there are unlimited grazing-grounds suitable for cattle, horses, and sheep, as well as a certain zone of country quite capable of producing crops.

In the course of our journey down the Bei-Kem we spent a day at the ranch of the most notable pioneer of the basin, the one who has done more to open up these regions than any other man. Dotted all over the Russian map of the basin we see the name of Safianoff. The word is written across blanks, as if to fill in the empty spaces; in reality, the name represents some tiny ranch or trading-station, called after its founder. Forty years ago this pioneer visited Uliassutai, reconnoitred the regions he traversed, and finally settled as a trader on the Ulu-Kem at Cha-Kul. Now he has built himself a house and laid out a fine ranch at the mouth of the Tapsa River on the Lower Bei-Kem, where he occupies himself with experimenting with different breeds of cattle, and with the qualities of various grain, plants, and trees best suited to the region.

M. Safianoff was able to show us the first camels we met in the basin, for his ranch is situated in the zone where the forests give way to steppe, and the climate becomes drier; he also had a surprise for us in the way of horse-flesh. With great pride his Tartar groom brought out a pure Arab and two Russian-bred stallions for our inspection. One of the latter had the great Galtee More for a sire, that Irish-bred "triple-crowned" winner who was sold to the Russian Government for twenty-one thousand guineas. With the help of these he was trying to improve the breed of the Mongol horse, a task well worth the trying, and one which might eventually have far-reaching results. We presume M. Safianoff had the aid of the Russian Government in this matter, and that they considered an unlimited supply of Mongol horses as being well worth such an improvement, taking into consideration the demands for such horses for military transport and for remounts.

M. Safianoff entertained us in his comfortable house, and showed us round his newly laid out experimental gardens, where we saw growing in profusion potatoes, onions, cucumbers, and vegetable marrows. He succeeded with wheat, oats, barley, and millet, was keen to try what could be done in the way of fruit-growing, and had started trials that year with different varieties of apples and melons. It should be noted, however, that all his efforts are dependent upon irrigation, the rainfall being too scanty during the summer months to be relied upon. It was indeed a pleasure to find so ambitious and energetic a pioneer in this very remote region. We believe that M. Safianoff is looked up to by all the colonists as the authority in the basin, and his name is honoured by all Uriankhai for fair and just dealing.

This digression on the Russian inhabitants of the basin, on the scope of their work, and on the success of their endeavours to found permanent colonies, was suggested by our arrival at Sabie—the first settlement of any note which we came across in our journey down the Bei-Kem. We quitted Sabie on our raft on July 18th, having received ample warnings from the inhabitants that below us lay rapids which might prove disastrous to our frail craft. We were told endless tales of broken rafts and drowned fishermen, which, however, in no way prevented our Kushabar boatmen from attempting to shoot the rapids ahead of us.

Almost immediately after leaving the village the open country on either bank began to give place to steep hills, which hemmed in the river, and soon we were drifting down the narrowed channel between high perpendicular precipices which dropped sheer into the water. The river here swept in great curves under the red-coloured cliffs, standing like walls on either hand, above which rose forested slopes leading up to crags towering 5,000 ft. above us. Six men working at the "sweeps" managed to keep the raft off the rocks, until in the far distance the sullen roar told us of the close vicinity of the rapids. On rounding a corner we saw the river ahead of us broken by a white line of foam; the raft was then roped up to the bank some few hundred yards above the first cascade, whilst we carefully examined the rapids and counted the risks.

We found the Bei-Kem rapids to consist of two falls about a quarter of a mile apart, the uppermost of which was the more dangerous. The river was here about eighty yards across, and shut in by steep hills. The danger presented by the rapids was that of the possibility of the raft breaking up on the rocks which reared themselves up out of the foam in the most threatening manner. The right bank of the river allowed no opportunity for portage, the river cutting in under a rock-wall and the hill-side dropping sheer into the water. But

THE BEI-KEM RAPIDS.

174]

the south bank had a narrow, boulder-strewn margin over which we eventually found ourselves struggling with the baggage, for we decided to unload the raft, transport the baggage to a point below the first rapid, and then send the raft down over the rapids with only a few men on board. The remainder of the day was spent in carrying the bales and boxes over the boulders, which were piled high along the bank of the river. We then hauled the raft by ropes up-stream so as to get a good "take-off," and our head-man and two others shot the rapids without mishap, including a twelve-foot drop between the rocks. For a few seconds during this drop the raft was under water, and the men almost lost their hold, but the next moment the quiet reach between the two rapids brought them into safe water.

After a restless night spent amongst the rocks, in too close proximity to the thunder of the waters, we strengthened the raft by the addition of two tree trunks and embarked once more with all our belongings. The lower rapid was passed with the entire party and all the baggage on board, and it was not until we were below it that we realized the risk we had run, and the foolhardiness of our venture. The current was so strong that, even with four men at the sweeps, it was impossible to steer the raft into the main channel, and we had to let her go, trusting to the current to keep her off the rocks, on which we narrowly escaped being wrecked.

The long, smooth reaches below the rapids took us on at a great pace, for the current was strong and deep, on account of the water here being hemmed into a narrow defile. Inspiring scenery lay around us: rugged cliffs bordered the river, and pine-trees clung romantically to the crags wherever they could find root-hold. Winding in great bends, the river passed through the labyrinth of ranges, and later in the day, after a twelve hours' journey, the hills were left behind, and we glided out on to the now sluggish current into a wide and open country, the central portion of the Upper Yenisei basin.

CHAPTER VII

THE CENTRAL BASIN AND THE KEMCHIK

THE mountainous region through which the Bei-Kem River flows for thirty miles, between the points where the Sabie and Uiuk tributaries join the main river, is a country of complex formation and extreme ruggedness. This mountain-wall forms in itself a very important natural boundary-line, and divides the upper portion of the Yenisei basin from the lower, and thereby accounts for the complete isolation of the Upper Bei-Kem region. Above the barrier are beautiful reaches of rapid-flowing rivers, clear, deep back-waters and racing mid-streams, with their typical high-piled log-jams, spits of shingle, and palisaded banks of pine-trees. Above the Bei-Kem rapids are the homes of the Siberian fishermen, with their log-built villages, their canoes, and nets, as well as the isolated ranches of the adventurous pioneers. Below the barrier there extends a more barren land of slow-flowing rivers which sweep in majestic curves across the wide steppe-valleys, a land of deforested hills and dusty plains, a land of altered conditions now suffering, it seems, from the great and far-reaching blight of desiccation—a condition brought about by the slow-moving but certain increase of aridity in the interior of Asia.

That part of the Upper Yenisei basin, which was truly Siberian in character, ended at the Bei-Kem rapids;

below the rapids the land approached Mongolia in climate and in general aspect; a region which, as we came later on to learn, formed in reality a transition-stage between Siberia and Mongolia. For this reason a description of the central basin and the Kemchik is especially important, as showing the life-zones of the region, and the lines of demarcation that separate them.

It was only after passing the Bei-Kem rapids, where the river begins to free itself from the constraint of the mountains, that we first came to observe the novel conditions of the central basin. As we passed through the gorges the appearance of the mountains became gradually drier and less covered with heavy vegetation. The pines became scarcer, until larch-forests alone remained on the hills; later in the day, as we drifted slowly on the bosom of the now tranquil Bei-Kem, the hill-country dropped away, and we came in sight of the central part of the basin. Here we were astonished at seeing that the steppe-country, which had extended its influence over the valleys, was already laying siege to the hills.

At a point just north of the junction of the Uiuk River with the Bei-Kem, we noticed that the hills were destitute of tree-growth on their southern flanks; but on their northern faces the larch forest still held its own against the war of desiccation waged by the arid conditions creeping in from the south, and slowly but surely overcoming it. Along the river-margin the poplar, birch, and willow grew in scanty array, owing their very existence to the proximity of the water-way. The southern foot-hills of the mountain-barrier presented that marked termination of forest and grass-lands which is so typical of Inner Asia. We saw phalanes of larches standing in lines along the crests of the hills, and extending down

SHOOTING THE BEI-KEM RAPIDS.

ON THE WATERSHED OF THE TANNU-OLA,
Borashay Pass.

the northern slopes, but on no portion of the hill-sides facing south were trees able to exist. On the lower hills forest was entirely absent.

With the change in flora came new types of fauna and new conditions of human life. We left behind us the reindeer, the beaver, the moose, the wapiti, the capercailzie, and the hazel-grouse; these all were a part of the northern forests, and did not extend south of the Bei-Kem barrier. As we drifted into the neighbourhood of the Ulu-Kem we saw the yurts, or felt-tents of the nomadic Uriankhai, and noticed that the owners themselves differed essentially from their kinsmen of the upper basin. These Uriankhai kept herds of sheep and goats, in place of the reindeer, cattle, and horses owned by the tribes of the upper basin, and the first sight of the camel greatly astonished some of our Russians.

We looked southwards with unbroken view across rolling steppes to the faint, distant outline of the southern border-range—that of the Tannu-ola—beyond which lay the great expanse of immense Mongolia; and we enjoyed the keener and dryer atmosphere of the open lands after the enervating humidity of the jungles.

The change became complete when we had drifted on to the broad waters of the Ulu-Kem. Nothing here remained of the scenery to which we had become accustomed during our stay in the upper basin, but we were now by slow degrees learning the true character of the central basin. Once on the Ulu-Kem, we made fair pace down its single channel. and, covering eighty miles in twenty-five hours, we arrived at the settlement of Cha-Kul, where, finding a grassy flat beside the river, to the west of the village, we tied up the raft to the bank and pitched our tents.

The existence of Cha-Kul is due to its exact position on the Ulu-Kem, this being the starting-point of all up-stream navigation, and also to its precise situation at the junction of the two main trade-routes which cross the basin and connect Siberia with Mongolia. Cha-Kul has little to recommend it beyond the fact of its important natural position, and its existence as the chief trade-centre of the basin ; no pleasant prospects or fertile lands making it attractive in other ways. Yet the neighbourhood is gradually assuming the look of a permanently settled locality, tracts of land are being opened up, irrigated, and cultivated, and the nomadic Uriankhai are becoming partly sedentary. Cha-Kul has, in fact, all the appearance of becoming, in the future, a centre of some importance, the capital perhaps of the Uriankhai " reserve."

A road is in construction which will join up Minnusinsk with Usinsk ; and if this route is prolonged as far as Cha-Kul it will have an immense effect upon the importance of this place, as it would mean a direct line of communication between the Yenisei province of Siberia and North-west Mongolia. This route would, there is every reason to believe, become a powerful rival to that of the Altai, which, at the present moment, absorbs all trade from Mongolia, and carries it to the towns on the Ob, such as Biisk and Barnaul. With the growing importance of Mongolia to Russia, this line of communication must, of necessity, be opened up sooner or later, for at present there is no real and adequate connexion between the two countries from the Altai to the religious centre of Urga, a distance of about nine hundred miles.

The Cha-Kul settlement is situated on the south bank

of the Ulu-Kem in a treeless steppe. The rather dirty and squalid houses of the mixed inhabitants gave an unsightly air to the town. The "compounds" of the Russian traders alone stood out as containing well-built and permanent dwellings of some pretension. Of these, there were only ten, the remainder being the log-built huts of small traders, such as half-bred Tartars, or Russianized Uriankhai, and the clean houses of a few Chinese shopkeepers. Cha-Kul showed a remarkable mixture of types. Men from odd corners at the back of Asia congregated here—Mongol, Buriat, Tartar, Muscovite, Celestial, and half-wild Uriankhai. The Russians held the greater part of the trade, which consisted largely of cloth-stuffs, knives, tobacco, guns, household utensils, and cheap trinkets utilized as a means of exchange with the natives in return for wool, hides, and furs.

The Chinese element was, however, not to be discounted, for it was noticeably on the increase, the Chinese being by far the most pushing tradesmen. At the Chinese shops only were we able to obtain small change for hundred-rouble notes, and the cleanliness of these shops in comparison with other stores was most marked. There were about forty Chinese in Cha-Kul, all of whom had come from Uliassutai, either as private traders or as agents of large firms from the big towns of China, who are in the habit of sending their agents to the most remote corners of the Empire. It was said that these Chinese had only started their business during the last five years; if this was true it showed with what avidity and keenness the Celestials were pushing forward even in these far-off regions, and how greatly their influence was tending to increase.

We found that Cha-Kul supplied us with food-stuffs,

such as tea—which was imported at remarkably low prices by the Chinese—flour, sugar, salt, and meat; eggs were scarce, and rice unprocurable. It was obviously necessary for us to live, in native fashion, on the products of the country. We had not seen a shop for two months until we arrived at Cha-Kul, and we had no reasonable hope of seeing another for the next two months. Luckily, we had now to employ native labour instead of that of our meat and bread eating Russians, for I do not know to what huge size our caravan would have grown, if we had been obliged to supply a staff of Russian followers with food. The natives, being accustomed to arranging their own food-supply and at the same time requiring very little of it, the food question gave us no anxiety.

At Cha-Kul we occupied ourselves with arrangements for the onward march, plotting surveys, and writing notes. We sold the raft to an enterprising Chinaman, who bought it either with a view to a journey to Minnusinsk, or to use as firewood. We paid off our Russian servants, who either rode, walked, or returned on rafts to their homes in Siberia; two of them, however, we thought it wise to retain, so as to obviate the difficulty of being entirely dependent upon the natives. This necessitated a halt of five days, which we spent in carefully exploring the neighbourhood of Cha-Kul.

Southwards, the plain bordering the Ulu-Kem runs in level reaches to the foot-hills of the Tannu-ola, some twelve miles away. These foot-hills climb in very gradual grades to the featureless, snow-patched ridge of the main Tannu-ola, the southern wall of the basin, and the watershed between the Arctic and the inland Mongolian drainage. No sign of forests appears on these

YURTS UNDER LARCH-FOREST.
In the Chedan Valley.

mountain-flanks, the hills looking barren and dry, yet, as we came to discover later, green valleys and forested slopes were to be seen when once we reached the heart of the range.

The environs of Cha-Kul presented some interesting studies as regards the economic conditions of the Urian-khai. Here we found instances of the wandering nomads becoming domesticated and even sedentary in their habits. Often we came across the strange and unusual sight of their felt tents being pitched in the ordinary way, with an annex consisting of log-built cattle-pens and various enclosures for the flocks. The most unmistakable sign, however, of a settled life was the existence of a large extent of cultivated land lying to the south of the town, and stretching for some way up the valley of the Cha-Kul River. Millet seemed to be the most favoured crop, but wheat and rye were also grown. Kriloff, the botanist, who was here in 1892, mentions that barley is also sown. He also remarks that "if the water is sufficient, the land is well cultivated with millet, and if the water-supply fails owing to the drying up of the several branches of the Cha-Kul River, then the fields have a most desolate appearance."

This shows that the water-supply is uncertain in this locality, and this fact proves the remarkable difference between the rainfall of the northern border-range of the basin—the Syansk—and that of the southern wall—the Tannu-ola, where the Cha-Kul River has its source. The locality is most suitable for irrigation works. The Cha-Kul River, after leaving the hill-country, divides into four streams, and for ten miles meanders across a level plain before reaching the Ulu-Kem. Two of the streams never reach the main river, as the irrigation works rob them of their water-supply. This flat country, capable of irrigation, measures about five miles in length by ten miles broad, and it is evident that, if the natives had sufficient initiative, the whole of it could be cultivated. We noted large areas of land lying fallow, but whether this was of necessity, or merely on account of lack of effort, or of failure of the water-supply, we have not exact information enough to say. Beyond the limits of the irrigation canals, barren steppe—devoid of vegetation—held sway, and the outlying spurs of the ranges were entirely destitute of grass, or growth, with the exception of small thorny scrub and varieties of steppe-plants.

We were here compelled to forgo water-transport, and to take to horses once more, our intention being to visit the Kemchik region in the western part of the basin before crossing the Tannu-ola Range into Mongolia. From a local chief we engaged men and animals to take us to the valley of the Chedan River, a southern affluent of the Kemchik, which, we were informed, was the residence of the chief of the Kemchik tribes and the quarters of a considerable population of the Uriankhai.

Leaving the Cha-Kul, we journeyed during an entire day over a barren and waterless steppe, a part of this trek leading along the great roadway described in a preceding chapter. During the later days (23rd to 29th) of July we experienced very hot weather; the thermometer went up to 101° in the shade and the temperature was intensified by the glare of the open country and the complete lack of shade. The great heat told both on us and on our caravan, none of us being accustomed to the open steppe, where the heat rising from the ground was almost as great as the direct rays of the sun;

during the first day's trek our Siberian horses became so exhausted that many of them completely gave out. By evening we had climbed up to over 3,000 ft., and, with thunderstorms to clear the air, we managed to get cool again.

The waterless character of this region well illustrated to us the dry climate this portion of the basin enjoys,—as compared with the rest, a small stream we camped at being the only water-supply on the great road between Cha-Kul and Biakoff on the Kemchik, a distance of fifty miles. The next day we passed over an outlying spur of the Tannu-ola, where larch-groves gave us welcome shade; but, beyond this, our route lay over barren country again, until, at dusk, we arrived at a broad, fertile valley where a number of yurts and a large Buddhist temple spoke of an important centre of Uriankhai life.

For six days we made our main camp near the temple, whilst lateral expeditions were undertaken to the north and south. Price visited the main Kemchik, and the little lake called Sut Kul, which lies in the hills to the north of the river, whilst I made a rapid survey of the Chedan up to its sources in the Tannu-ola.

The whole of the Chedan Valley in its central portion was a fine camping-ground for the nomads. The three-mile-wide valley-bottom was so level that the river-course had been diverted with ease, and the water caused to meander all over the flat in many different channels, thus irrigating the soil and enriching the pasture. The pasture zone was bordered on either side by a stream of water, and there were four other channels besides the main river-bed itself, which, by the way, contained scarcely more water than the subsidiary channels. The subsidiary channels appeared to be artificial, for we noticed that from them innumerable little canals were led off in order to allow the water to be continually overflowing and saturating the meadows. The Uriankhai herdsmen had thus cleverly utilized ordinary methods of irrigation to freshen and renew their pastures; in consequence they had no fear of a summer drought, and were not forced to shift their camping-grounds. Only the northern half of the Chedan Valley contained good land for the herdsmen; the southern half was forested and useless for pasture. The northern half, however, furnished sufficient ground for a large population, great flocks of sheep, and a certain number of cattle or horses.

Close to our camp was a particularly luxuriant piece of meadow-land, and here was situated the Kuria, with its group of buildings composing the lamaseries; and in the near vicinity stood the great white-felt tent of the Noyon, or chief of the Kemchik. All tended to produce an imposing and animated scene, a scene often come across in Central Asia, where life is concentrated into narrow zones and where outside these zones "all is desert." The white walls of the square-built temple stood as a landmark for many a mile, and gave a distinctive air of settled life to this nomad's-land. Curling smoke drew attention to where the yurts were picturesquely pitched, half hidden under the shade of giant larches; while herds of horses and flocks of sheep grazed on meadows so luxuriant and so exquisitely green that these meadows might well have been part of an English landscape, were it not for the presence of Uriankhai horsemen and red-robed Buddhist priests.

The day after our arrival we exchanged visits with

CHIEFS OF THE KEMCHIK URIANKHAI.

186]

the deputy of the Noyon, for the chief himself had gone on official business to Uliassutai. Here, for the first time, we met a man of real rank and importance; certainly the dignity and race-quality of the Kemchik chief was beyond question, and struck us forcibly after our dealings with the degraded tribes of the upper basin. We can well imagine that a stronger element of Mongol blood might be possibly mingled with the blood of the Kemchik people, for this region is more in touch with Mongolia than are the other portions of the basin. Here pass the caravans which are responsible for bringing in new ideas, and for arranging opportunities for closer communication with the outside world; and the importance of the district is shown by the fact that the Kemchik Noyon is acclaimed as the paramount chief of the basin.

After exchanging cards in Chinese fashion, we visited the white-felt yurt which served both as a court of justice and as an official residence. Hung up by the door were instruments of torture, as a sign of office, and as a warning to evil-doers. Amongst these, we noticed, were such instruments as the heavy leather ear-boxers, the finger-crushers, and various kinds of whips. The interior of the yurt was beautifully clean, and decorated with blue cloth and red felt, whilst around the sides stood divans and cabinets of Chinese make.

The Noyon's deputy and retainers were fine-looking men; they were wearing their official uniforms and Chinese hats as an emblem of office. They seemed surprised to hear that we had come from Siberia and yet disclaimed the honour of being Russians; neither could they understand why we had no papers to show them, other than our imposing-looking Chinese passports from

Pekin. Our conversations were carried on by interpretation from English into Russian, into Chinese, and back again into Uriankhai, the local Chinese trader acting as interpreter to us and also as translator of the passports.

A promise of transport was accorded us, but it was very apparent the favour was not willingly given, nor were we treated with the respect which any Russian, with his well-known and highly valued local passport, would have received. We found ourselves hampered by the fact that we were still within the bounds of the Uriankhai country, which is shut off apart, and kept as a reserve for the Uriankhai tribes; the reservation being so strict that no natives are allowed to pass out of it beyond the line of guard-houses, which decide the southern limit of the native territory on the south of the Tannu-ola. We were promised transport, however, as far only as one of these posts lying three days' journey away.

The Chedan Valley is of distinct importance as being on the direct route which cuts across the basin from the plains of Minnusinsk and Abakan to Mongolia; its northern end is also crossed by the route which diverges to Uliassutai. We acquired a certain amount of information respecting the Upper Kemchik Valley, and, from all accounts, its character is the same throughout as that of the Chedan Valley. The entire valley seems to be well populated, its climate is the most favourable of the whole basin, and its pastures are capable of supporting large numbers of sheep and horses. In its characteristics the Kemchik Valley is an improvement on the more arid Mongolian plateau on the south, or the Abakan steppe on the north, representing as it does a somewhat broken country of hill and dale, of even temperature and of moderate rainfall.

In spite of the proximity of the Kemchik Valley to Siberia and the comparative ease with which it is approached, either from the north or south, it still contains considerable areas of unknown and unmapped country. Russian travellers have passed across its northern portion, down the central valley, and up to its head-waters; but the southern tributaries and the whole of the northern flanks of the Tannu-ola which drain into the Kemchik Valley are still unsurveyed. Our energies were therefore concentrated, during our stay in the Chedan Valley, on mapping the whole river-valley from its sources down to its juncture with the Kemchik River.

The Chedan River had a length of about forty-five miles, and was composed of two main branches, which flowed parallel for about two-thirds of this distance before joining and passing together into the Kemchik. The road to Mongolia led up the western valley called Kandagai, and this valley we eventually mapped on our way over the Tannu-ola. The eastern branch led nowhere, and was unknown except to a few herdsmen, who, during the summer months, drove their horses up on to the high ground above the forest. This was the main Chedan Valley. For about fifteen to twenty miles this valley continued its flat, meadow-like character, then it narrowed down and its bottom became choked with larch and spruce forest. The bordering hills retained their barren nature on the southern flanks, but became heavily forested on the north. In pleasant side-valleys where there was no jungle I found large encampments of natives, while in the main valley, wherever there were open spaces, I saw yurts, and, occasionally, small fields of millet. In places where the forest overran the valley, and left no available pasture-land, the natives ceased to utilize it, and only a narrow and very bad track remained leading through the forest. The forests on the Tannu-ola were, however, of a very different type from those of the Syansk. The lowest portions were composed of larch and a few spruce; farther up spruce gave way, and cedar took its place, until, upon reaching the highest limits of tree-growth, we found cedar predominating over the larch. The forest was much more open than any we had experienced; there were no bogs, and very little fallen timber to hinder us.

By making a long day's journey from our camp by the Kuria, I succeeded in reaching an altitude of 5,000 ft., and spent the night in the open, just below the limit of tree-growth. The following morning I climbed up on to a bare summit, a spur of the main Tannu-ola. By my position on this outlying spur I got a good impression of the Tannu-ola range, for about fifty miles towards the east and west, and also of the Kemchik Valley. The Tannu-ola range proved to be a ridge of remarkably simple construction. From this point, at any rate, it spread itself out east and west in a narrow, flat-topped ridge with terraced flanks. Its character was so uniform as to destroy its impression of height, and although summits reach to 7,500 ft., and, in its far western end, even to 9,000 ft., it did in no way do justice to its altitude.

It seemed to me that the traveller could pass anywhere on horseback over the Tannu-ola or even along its flanks, such was the evenness of its structure. The only obstacles which might hinder would be those tiresome areas of loose rocks which compose the flat-topped summits, and which it was difficult enough to walk over, but to ride over would be impossible. The whole panorama of the range appeared to be the same in character both towards the east and west. Very far away, beyond the western end of the range, at the sources of the Kemchik, I could discern a great snow-mass, the first view of real snow-mountains that we had seen. The highest pinnacle of this group, which we first observed from the Chedan Valley, remained in sight and stood as a landmark for the succeeding month's journey across North-west Mongolia. It was a great round snow-peak of remarkable beauty, and from its position on our maps must be located on the Sailugem Range to the north of the alpine lake called Kendikti Kul.

Looking from the same point of vantage, towards the Kemchik Valley, I noticed the rough hill-country which bordered the river on its north, and the more open area to its south, while far away to the west the lie of the land gave one the impression of the valley being quite shut in and enclosed by rugged hills. However, a cart-track, which extended for some seventy miles up the main valley, the existence of Kurias and centres of Uriankhai life, showed that the region was well-favoured, and that in between the hills there must have been luxuriant valleys and good pastures. The notable difference between the highlands of the Tannu-ola and the other ranges in the basin was that they produced a certain amount of pasture suitable for horses to graze on during the summer. We repeatedly saw large herds of horses on the highest ridges, where the natives drive them, to avoid the troublesome flies of the lowlands, and to graze them on the short but succulent mountain-grass.

From the high point to which I climbed I saw no sign of snow on any part of the Tannu-ola that came under my observation, and its name, which literally means "Snowy," seems to be somewhat unsuitable. It is probable, that, owing to the bare, smooth summits of the range, any heavy snowfall they may receive in winter melts quickly in summer. The depression of Lake Ubsa, which lies just over the range on the south, may cause an extra heavy precipitation, as it undoubtedly causes a very heavy snowfall on the Turgun Mountains to the south of the lake, thus making the Tannu-ola, at certain seasons, worthy of its name. But the traveller expecting a fine mountain panorama of snow-topped ranges in the Tannu-ola will be disappointed.

On my return to the main camp we planned our onward journey, repacked our kit, and awaited the promised transport. Meanwhile, a visit to the Kuria amused us, and was most instructive, as throwing light on the influence Buddhism has on the simple nature-worshippers and as showing to what remarkable dimness the "Light of Asia" has dwindled. The Kuria was an imposing building of white stucco, surmounted by a frieze of brown, with blue marginal lines, dotted with white. It was square in shape, with three sides unbroken by windows or doors, and the fourth largely taken up by a portico supported by wooden pillars, which led in to four large folding-doors. Buddhistic emblems surmounted the building at its four corners, and were also carved on the doors.

As we approached, a mob of evil-looking, ill-kempt young lamas and students surrounded us and made insolent gestures, but, by interviewing the head lama, we were permitted to enter the temple; the crowd of dirty,

A KURIA, OR BUDDHIST TEMPLE,
Chedan Valley.

DEGRADED TYPES OF URIANKHAI.
Buddhist Lamas.

brute-like men, boys, and priests so greatly annoyed us, however, that we were forced to leave. This is a remarkable instance of the sudden and complete change which may be effected under the so-called influence of religion. We could hardly recognize our shy, retiring, harmless Uriankhai in this noisy, pushing, interfering mob. The brutal, sensual expression of the lamas stood in marked contrast to the placid, almost fearsome, demeanour of their lay-brothers—the wild woodmen and shepherds. There were said to be about three hundred lamas and neophytes attached to the Kuria.

The interior of the temple was draped with gaudily coloured flags, and hangings of every conceivable hue. Scrolls of silk with coloured pictures of Buddha hung on the walls, and gigantic gilt images stood in glass-fronted cases at the head of the building. The contents of the Kuria mostly consisted of cheap, trashy material from Uliassutai and Urga. A few pieces of old silk and brass-ware attracted our attention, but they were not to be purchased, in spite of our generous offers.

One evening at sunset a curious religious ceremony took place just outside the Kuria. A procession was formed of all the lamas attached to the temple, and these, dressed up in all the finery of old silk robes, carrying banners, blowing trumpets, beating drums, and firing guns, marched out to where there had already been erected an "obo," or small shrine made of branches and brushwood. The accoutrements of the head lamas were covered with red and yellow silks, the trumpets they carried were 12 ft. long, and, being made of brass, were so heavy that it needed a small boy to support the end whilst the priest blew at the mouthpiece. The drums were equally unique, the hide of which the drum was made being dyed green, with red-and-yellow devices painted upon it. On reaching the obo the procession formed up into line, the gun-bearers fired two volleys, and then with great ceremony the high-priest set the obo on fire, and when properly alight the whole assembly circled round the fire until it had burnt itself out.

The Kurias of the Upper Yenisei basin are generally located near the residences of the Noyons, or head-men, and therefore in the most largely populated localities. There are six in all: three in different parts of the Kemchik Valley, one in the Elegess Valley, on the south side cf the Ulu-Kem, one in the Upper Khua-Kem region, near Lake Teri Nor, and one in the Upper Bei-Kem district. All are under the direct control of the Dalai-Lama at Urga, and the lesser lamas are in constant communication with that important centre of Mongolian religious life. These temples are the only permanent buildings which are associated with the everyday life of the native, and they doubtless do a great deal to attach him to certain localities, both by reason of his religious fears and as forming a centre for barter and trade.

When at last, by considerable effort and the aid of bribes, we acquired the use of eight oxen and half a dozen men, we were in a position to think of moving the expedition forward. The expanse of the Kemchik Valley, and the shortness of time, determined us to leave the basin and cross into Mongolia. We therefore loaded up the eight oxen with the entire kit, each ox carrying two horse-loads, and moved on very slowly towards the Borashay Pass, which leads by way of the Kandagai branch of the Chedan over the Tannu-ola.

The Kandagai Valley resembled the Chedan in scenery, but a well-used route led up it, and by an easy gradient we crept up to the summit of the pass. The passage of the Tannu-ola was full of interest and surprises. In the course of a two days' journey we passed from 3,190 ft. in the Chedan Valley up to 6,854 ft. at the watershed and eventually down to 5,000 ft. on the Mongolian plateau beyond. We appreciated to the full the unusual topography of this region,—the terraced flanks of the Tannu-ola, the long, gradual incline which led up to the watershed, and the sharp but slight drop-off to the Mongolian plateau on the south. As we accomplished this last trek in the Yenisei basin we noted with growing interest that the scenery, the flora, and indeed the whole atmosphere of the region was changing. Although we had no high altitude to attain, and no difficult pass to climb, we realized that we were on the eve of coming across a great transformation, that this southern wall of the basin formed an important dividing-line, and that, after accomplishing its passage, we should arrive at an entirely different land, offering us still greater opportunities for the study of new races of people and unique physical conditions.

The actual watershed was a rounded ridge almost flat at its summit; here the forest grew as dwarfed scrub, and the miniature trees appeared to be wind-worn and storm-battered. Higher ground lay on either hand, in the shape of flat-topped, terraced ridges, which rose some few hundred feet above the tree-line. This, then, was the threshold of Mongolia. As our mixed caravan of oxen and horses crept to the top of the pass, and wended their way slowly down the southern side, we made a detour to the west in order to climb to a point of vantage from which to gain a view of the new country that lay ahead of us. From a flat-topped ridge we gazed back once more into dark, stormy Siberia, whilst before us, as a contrast, lay the pale-coloured steppes and plateaux of Mongolia, giving a strong impression of intense light, of aridity, and of a profound unrest.

CHAPTER VIII

THE URIANKHAI AND THEIR REINDEER

"THEY have no horses, but in the stead of them they tame certain wild beasts which they call Reem, being of the just bigness of a Mule, with rough hair like an Ass, cloven feet and branched horns like a Harte but lower and with few antlettes. I suppose that this thing was somewhat known to the old writers, although received in manner by an obscure and doubtful fame. For they also write that certain Sythians do ride on Hartes."

Thus Richard Eden, as long ago as 1555, recorded for the first time in the English language the information he had gathered of the "North east Frosty Seas and Kingdoms lying that way," and thus he gave us the first intimation of the reindeer-keeping tribes of Northern Asia.

Marco Polo, too, passed on to us the information he had gained during his journeys in Cathay, and mentioned certain people, inhabiting a region along the Northern Frontier of the Chinese Empire, who were a "wild race and lived by their cattle, which were stags, and these stags they used to ride upon."[1] In the few

[1] These references apply broadly to the forest-dwelling tribes of Southern Siberia near Lake Baikal, and cannot be taken as specially referring to the Uriankhai of the Upper Yenisei region.

references we have of these people we find emphasis is always laid upon the fact of this (to them) unique custom of keeping and rearing "stags" as a means of livelihood, as well as for transport. The existence of the reindeer-keeping races in Southern Siberia appealed strongly to the imagination of the writers on China, who had perhaps never come in contact with the Lapps, Finns, and Samoyedes, representing the reindeer-tribes of the far north.

In spite of the knowledge handed down to us by these old writers, it did not seem to be known until we visited the land of the Uriankhai in 1910 that a race existed within the confines of the Chinese Empire, a certain section of which was entirely dependent upon the herds of reindeer for their subsistence, and that the reindeer even lives in a wild state on the ranges bordering Siberia and Mongolia. Russian travellers were aware of it, and it is a proof of our complete ignorance of Russian literature that this special information never came through to the rest of Europe. But it is not only this peculiarity in their customs which is of such interest, it is the strange fact of the very existence of these people, every detail of whose life-history, every record of whose habits, haunts, and religious ideas is of peculiar historical value; the Uriankhai representing, as they do, the remnant of an ancient race dwelling in seclusion in the very heart of a great continent.

In a previous chapter, when describing the ancient inhabitants of the Abakan and Minnusinsk steppes, the origin and early history of the present-day Uriankhai was also mentioned. I showed that the original inhabitants of the plains of the Siberian Yenisei were gradually ousted by stronger incoming races, such as Uigur and

URIANKHAI WOMAN AND HER CHARGES—THE YOUNG REINDEER.

19 8]

Tartar, and on this account eventually pushed back into remote regions, such as the tundras of far Northern Siberia and the forests of the Upper Yenisei basin. During those periods of racial upheaval the ancient Yeniseians, or Tubas—as they were called—fell under the influence of many other races, but those who retreated to the backwoods of the Upper Yenisei preserved their original type better than might have been expected, on account of their complete seclusion. After the varied course of the history of the Uriankhai, and their final retreat from Siberian Yenisei to the Upper Yenisei basin, we hear of them again in the sixteenth century as belonging to one of the six divisions into which the Mongol people were divided, which means that they were by that time incorporated in the Chinese Empire. It was in this century, no doubt, that the boundaries of the territory given over to them were delimited, and the Upper Yenisei basin became their recognized home.

The name Uriankhai, or Uriangut, is Chinese. It was first broadly applied by the Chinese to the tribes along the Siberian-Mongol frontier, who live in the forested areas; and the term would thus include the Tubas of the Upper Yenisei basin, the Uigurs of Lake Kossogol, and the Tunguses of Trans-Baikalia. The word simply means "Forest-dweller." At the present day the term is solely applied to the inhabitants of the Upper Yenisei basin, and to a small tribe who live on the eastern flanks of the Altai. A better title for the tribes of the Upper Yenisei would be their own name for themselves—"Tuba," for this specifies these people alone, and cannot be extended to any other forest-dwelling race. Tuba is not a tribal name, but the title of the once intact, but now scattered, nation of Samoyedes. The word "Soiot," which is the name usually applied by the Russians to these people, is, I imagine, a case of mistaken identity. The first Russian visitor found the Uriankhai living under like conditions, and with like customs, to the true Soiots of Central Siberia, and, imagining them alike, hastily called them Soiots, whereas in reality the two tribes have nothing in common.

The Russian traveller Klementz says that the Tubas were originally a race of Samoyedes inhabiting Southern Siberia, who gave the name to the right affluent of the Yenisei, the Tuba. The descendants of these Tubas inhabit the vicinity of Minnusinsk and speak a Turkish tongue (Abakan Tartars ?). The name of Tuba was mentioned for the first time in the Chinese Annals of the Ta dynasty. These records speak of a certain tribe—"Doubo"—living in the mountains, and devoted to the chase and to robbery. The Persian historian Raschid-ed-din mentions these same tribes as inhabiting "the forests of Mongolia" at the time of Jenghis Khan. Amongst other things he recorded names which correspond to the Uriankhai clan of the present day—such as Oïnar and Ondar. The next reference to the Tubas, or Uriankhai, was made by William of Rubruck in 1255, who included the name Orengai amongst his list of tribes, who dwelt in the region to the north of Mongolia.

The near neighbours of the Tubas who dwell on the shores of Lake Kossogol divide themselves into two clans, the Darkat and Uriankhai, the latter calling themselves "Uigur." The Darkat are, however, of the same race as the Uriankhai, but speak the Mongol language. The Abakan Tartars, who dwell in the region occupied in the old days by the Yeniseians, and their descendants, have also affinities with the Tubas, especially as regards language. Great familiarity and sympathy exist between the two people, who hold each other in as great esteem as if they were of the same blood. In physical features, too, they have much in common, and there is little doubt that at one time they were socially and politically identical one with the other. Adrianoff called the language of the Uriankhai "Tartar," and noted how easily his Tartars from the Abakan spoke with the natives of the Upper Yenisei basin. Kastren, speaking on the knowledge we get from the study of languages, recognizes the Tubas as a tribe of Samoyedes, having been subject to Turkish (Uigur) influence, and having adopted their language; but it is difficult to place them in regard to their close neighbours the Soiots, Tunguses, and Buriats, for all traditions are forgotten.

The Uriankhai, or Uriangut, the remnant of the Tuba nation, at the present day are confined to the region enclosed on the north by the Russo-Chinese frontier, which runs between the Eastern Altai and Lake Kossogol, and on the south by the line of Mongol guard-houses, or Karauls, which are placed at intervals along the southern foot-hills of the Tannu-ola. This area is chiefly occupied by the basin of the Upper Yenisei, as described in Chapter III., but it includes also the strip of country beyond the watershed of the Tannu-ola, namely, the southern slopes of that range as far as the above-mentioned Karauls."[1] The area prescribed to the Uriankhai is roughly about 52,555 sq. miles. Beyond this boundary they do not roam. On the south they are

[1] The inhabitants of the Kossogol basin are ethnographically the same as the Uriankhai, but are much more Mongolized. Their territory is geographically cut off from the Upper Yenisei basin, and belongs to a different administrative division.

hemmed in by the Mongol guards and forbidden egress; but on the north a freer country allows those who desire to do so to visit the towns and villages of Siberia. Restrictions are scarcely necessary, for the Uriankhai are of a most retiring disposition, and do not often trouble the outside world. Not so long ago, however, the Uriankhai ranged over the northern slopes of the Syansk Range into the region at the sources of the Kandat, Kazir, and Tuba Rivers, but now they only visit the northern side of the watershed in order to hunt in winter. Over the whole of this area the Uriankhai are sparsely distributed in isolated encampments. Certain regions are quite uninhabited, whilst others, on account of more favourable conditions, are comparatively densely populated.

It would be difficult to give an exact estimate of the number of Uriankhai. Many of the tribes have never been seen by any traveller, and in summer, when the Uriankhai are alone approachable, the encampments are distributed in small, isolated groups over large areas of dense forest, and in valleys whose very existence is quite unknown. M. Paul Chalon places the maximum population of the basin at 100,000 souls, and the Chinese reckon the Uriankhai country as forming one "Aimak," or territorial division.

The Uriankhai are divided into five principal tribes, whose names and whose distribution are as follows:

(1) The Toji tribe, holding the whole of the Upper Bei-Kem region at the eastern end of the basin, their territory being bounded on the south by the Khua-Kem and on the west by the Utt River, and their chief centre being on the Dora-Kem steppe, where the residence of their Noyon, or chief, and their Kuria are situated.

(2) The Saljak tribe, inhabiting the region of the

south of the Khua-Kem and ranging as far west as the valley of the Elegness.

(3) The Mardi, a small clan living in the confined area between the Rivers Utt and Uiuk.

(4) The Oina, who hold both banks of the Ulu-Kem on the north and south, between the territory of the Saljak, the Mardi, and the Kemchik. Cha-Kul may well be taken as their western limit.

(5) The Kemchik[1] tribe may be classed in one or two sections. The entire population of this western portion of the basin—the Kemchik Valley—comprises nearly a third of the entire population of the basin. These are classed together or separately. In old days two hereditary chiefs kept their own sections apart, but latterly the Chinese have endeavoured to place them all together under one Noyon.

These main tribes are subdivided into numerous clans, who collect together in encampments, and claim certain geographical areas as their own. It is difficult to say to what extent the main tribes are separated one from the other; but we are inclined to believe that the divisions are dependent on the exclusive rights to certain pasturages and hunting-grounds. Within the basin the Uriankhai move about as they wish, each section or tribe keeping to its own allotted area for grazing or hunting, but beyond the boundary of the Mongol guards they dare not pass. The area allotted to them serves as a reservation, which is a favour granted by their Chinese rulers, in the same way that the territory of each Mongol chief in Mongolia, and of each Kalmuk tribe in

[1] The Kemchik was, in the time of Jenghis, inhabited by Kirghiz and Kem-Kemjuks, closely allied Turkish tribes, who lately, in the seventeenth century, migrated to Dzungaria and farther westwards. They are the origin of the true Kirghiz, the Buruts—Black, or Rock Kirghiz.

Far Western China, is reserved intact for that chief or tribe, thus preserving their independence.

The Uriankhai are at the present day all under the suzerainty of China. They were probably an independent people until the coming of Jenghis Khan in the thirteenth century. Then they became subjects of that great conqueror. Later on, the allegiance which they at first owed to the Mongols passed eventually to the rulers at Pekin. Jenghis is still worshipped amongst the Uriankhai as a deity. All good things are attributed to the great Mongol chieftain; he taught them, they say, to sow wheat and to make irrigation-canals. On the death of Jenghis the Uriankhai came under the rule of his third son, Gesser Khan. With the establishment of the Manchu dynasty, and the fall of the Mongols, the Uriankhai passed under the suzerainty of the Emperor at Pekin, and ever since they have been under the administration of a Chinese official of military rank, resident at Uliassutai. They differ, however, from other vassal tribes in that their chiefs are not considered of much account, and do not pay homage in person to the Emperor at Pekin.

For each separate tribe there is a Noyon, or local chief, who is responsible for the taxes of his section and for the local government of the people under his charge. The Noyons of the minor tribes—the Toji, Saljak, Oina, and Mardi—are responsible to the chief Noyon of the Kemchik tribe, whose precedence is recognized throughout the basin, and who, in his turn, is directly responsible to the official of Uliassutai for the taxation and affairs of the whole Uriankhai people. Some writers say that there is another intermediary between the chief of the Kemchik and the Uliassutai official, in the person

URIANKHAI TYPES,
Ala-su encampment.

"THEY HAVE NO HORSES, BUT IN THE STEAD OF THEM THEY TAME CERTAIN WILD-BEASTS WHICH THEY CALL REEM."

of the Amban of the Tess,—a well-populated region on the south of the Tannu-ola, in the Ubsa basin; but, as this region is not inhabited by Uriankhai, and its Amban does not represent Pekin officialdom, it is difficult to understand what business the two can have in common, unless it is an instance of one more grasping hand through which the taxes must pass, and one more greedy official claiming his share of the spoil.

It is noteworthy, however, that in the old days the "Khan of the Ubsa district" was considered to be paramount chief of these regions, his power extending far into Siberia, and he held all the Uriankhai in subjection. Howorth mentions that, in the early part of the seventeenth century, numerous embassies passed between Russia and the Altan Khan, who then had his residence beside Lake Ubsa. "Altan Khan" was a title held by all the Khans of the Ubsa confederacy. He was evidently a frontier chief of great importance, he exchanged many presents with the Czar of Russia, and eventually took an oath of allegiance to him. But later on his power failed, the Abakan and Yenisei tribes broke away from him—and have remained Russian subjects to this day, whilst he himself became free from any dealings with the Czar. Whether the Altan Khan owned the Tess region or the Turgun highlands, or both, and whether we can trace the remains of his kingdom in the Dalai Khan of the Durbets, who to-day hold the whole Ubsa basin outside the Tess Valley, we cannot say.

It will be seen from this that the Uriankhai are well looked after, and in spite of the fact that they are at the farthest corner of the Empire they still have to pay in full their yearly tribute. The suzerainty of Pekin gives a standing to the local chiefs, who are only too willing to raise the tribute in return for a recognition of their authority. The rich grind the poor, and the strong bully the weak, with the result that there is a growing tendency to look towards Siberia as a land of freedom. With the gradual influx of Russians into the Upper Yenisei region, and the growth of their trade and influence, this tendency will be increased, and the absorption of the Uriankhai by the Siberians will be but a matter of time.

Besides the Noyons there are a considerable number of smaller chiefs—heads of encampments or heads of the richer families—and still lower in order are the herdsmen, who form the bulk of the population. Besides these we have to reckon with the religious community, which, as in other Buddhist countries, includes a large proportion of the population. The lamas hold a strong position, having much influence over the affairs of the tribes, and by using this influence they drain the already overtaxed herdsman of his patrimony.

The Uriankhai pay tribute to the Chinese officials, but are not called upon for military service. Chalon estimates the yearly taxation of the Uriankhai to amount to about 60,000 roubles, all of which passes into the hands of the official at Uliassutai. The tax paid by the ordinary Uriankhai is supposed to represent a tenth part of his herds, or he may pay the tax in furs of equal value; we imagine this, however, to be a very nominal amount, as the wild forest-dwellers, especially the reindeer-keepers, would be difficult subjects to bring to justice if they wished to evade the law. The local chiefs all get their share, and the bulk of the population exists in serfdom owing to the continuous extortion of tribute. The taxes are payable in any form: mares, cattle, sheep, and goats are supplied by the steppe-dwellers; furs by the reindeer-keepers; feathers, eagles' tails, the down of aquatic birds—such as swans, ducks, geese, and grebes —are brought in by the lake-people of the upper basin.

Adrianoff, the Russian traveller, says that the division of taxation is thus,—the entire Uriankhai people compose one "Aimak"—a Chinese term, denoting a large territorial division—and are liable to pay, as tribute, one thousand "oureghe" in a year. An oureghe is used as a tax unit per thousand head of cattle, and must equal the value of three sable-skins. Thus the Uriankhai people owe, as tribute to China, the value of three thousand sable-skins in the year.

So far as I can find out, the system of taxation is thus,—the tax is levied on each yurt-holder, according to the total number of cattle owned by the inmates of the yurt, whether it be a whole family or a single individual. The poor herdsmen, who own neither yurt nor cattle, are free from taxes. The others pay in proportion of an oureghe—three sable-skins, or one hundred and twenty squirrel-skins, per thousand head of cattle. Thus the tax may vary from a few squirrel-skins upwards, according to the wealth of the owners.

If the tax remains the same now as it was then, and the number of sable-skins demanded has not been reduced owing to the increased value of the sable, we are sorry for our friends the Uriankhai. We presume, however, that all such values are very uncertain. The comparative values of the furs are interesting; a man may bring a sable, or forty squirrels, or six wolves, or six martens. A snow-leopard is accounted equal in value to twenty squirrels, a wolf, and a marten, whilst a fox-skin is the same value as twenty squirrels. These were the proportionate values of long ago; but we hope, for the sake of the overtaxed natives, that a revision of the laws has been made, owing to the gradual extermination of the fur-bearing animals.

It is difficult to deal with the social and economic conditions of the Uriankhai as a whole, for the tribes vary much amongst themselves, owing to the different conditions under which they live. The habits of the Toji tribe are as unlike those of the Kemchik as they are those of the Mongols. We might group all the tribes of the upper basin together, and describe them as being the most typical, and at the same time the most independent of outside influence. The tribes of the central and lower basin again differ, in that they have come more in touch with the Mongols, their country approaching Mongolia in physical features. The Toji, the Saljak, and the Mardi live in more or less similar surroundings. They all have the forests as their habitat, and the wet taiga as their playground; they live in the tangled jungle or on the luxuriant meadows, and their habits are entirely moulded by their surroundings.

To these three tribes of Uriankhai, then, we must look as having the most marked characteristics. The Uriankhai must undoubtedly be placed amongst the category of nomad races, although, as a matter of fact, their nomadic tendency is somewhat undeveloped. It remains an advantage to them to be able to shift their abodes; for this reason their dwellings, in all cases, are portable and easily moved. There are occasions when settled abodes would be an advantage, and the building of them quite feasible, yet so far they have not found it necessary to erect permanent homes. The Abakan Tartars of the Minnusinsk region have for long built their quaint huts of logs—permanent dwellings—in exact re-

REINDEER-HERDS GOING OUT TO FEED.

production of the felt-tents they formerly used; but not so the Uriankhai, for, even when they dig canals and sow fields of millet, they still camp beside their lands, and still use their movable tents.

The habit of nomadism varies also according to the possessions of the tribes in the way of flocks and herds, and the different treatment the stock requires. The reindeer-keepers, for instance, must perforce visit the higher regions during the heat of summer, for the preservation of the reindeer, which cannot stand the high temperature of the low country. Reindeer delight in and require, intense cold, and it is strange to find that this animal, which ranges to within ten degrees of the Pole, is able to exist at this low latitude. Only the geographical position of the region—in the heart of a continent—and its plateau-like nature compensate for the latitude, and make their existence possible. But even then the reindeer require special handling, and we can put down the migrating habits of the clans who keep reindeer to the necessity of finding cool summer resorts for their welfare. But the owners of cattle, horses, sheep, and goats need not necessarily migrate farther than the ordinary changes of pasture demand. Consequently the reindeer-Uriankhai are the most migratory in their habits.

Let us look at the annual programme of this branch of the Toji tribe. In spring, as soon as the hot weather melts the snow, the herdsmen shift from their winter quarters on the shores of the Toji Kul, or along the banks of the Bei-Kem. Rolling up their strips of birch-bark, and packing their few belongings on the backs of the reindeer, they travel through the narrow forest-paths to the luxuriant meadows, which are situated at about

3,500 ft. in altitude. The poles of their tents they do not need to carry, as they keep a stock of these in their winter quarters and another stock at their summer resort. This insignificant fact shows with what regularity their migrations are carried out. These migrations are not wanderings in search of pasture, as is the case with many nomad tribes, but well-established yearly moves from one camping-ground to another.

For four months during the summer the reindeer-herds are kept in these high regions. In autumn the tribes begin to move again; the men go off in small parties to hunt for furs in the more distant ranges, or into the forests, which are never penetrated on any other occasion, whilst the women and the herds are sent down to the winter quarters. Winter is the season for trade with the Russian settlers, for winter means spare time, the herds requiring small attention. The scattered encampments then meet at the popular winter resorts, and much traffic and trade is carried on between the various tribes. Summer is essentially the season for attending to the breeding of flocks and herds, amongst nomadic tribes throughout all Asia.

The remainder of the tribes, those who own flocks and herds and possess no reindeer, move their homes according to the supply of pasture, which in most localities is so rich and plentiful that the migrations scarcely deserve the name. All summer and winter these Uriankhai may be found in the main Bei-Kem Valley, their tents being pitched on the open downlands or in the forests. The shepherds, who use the open lands, are less able to reside in one particular locality than are the cattle and horse herdsmen, owing to a scarcity of pasture which necessitates the changing of their grazing-grounds; but even *they* move about in a lesser degree than the reindeer-keepers.

The great wealth of grass in the upper part of the basin and amongst the forests tends to scatter the population. Small encampments are to be found dotted at intervals over large areas, the natives being free to wander where they will and take their choice of innumerable luxuriant pasturages. But in the lower part of the basin, in the more arid areas, the population is restricted to narrower zones. The pastures are poorer, and consequently the movement in search of grass becomes greater. Certain areas are capable of supporting the flocks and herds throughout the summer's heat, and on these areas concentrate the bulk of the Uriankhai population; it is in these same localities that signs of sedentary habits are forthcoming.

Yet another force, that of religion, is responsible for influencing the distribution and movement of the tribes. The building of temples and lamaseries—the only signs of absolutely settled life in the Uriankhai world—is necessitated by the presence of the religious element, and this may have affected the nomads, by causing a kind of desire towards centralization, which will gradually tend to make them less migratory. The temples, or Kurias, form a centre for administration and trade, as well as for the purposes of religion. The chiefs reside in the neighbourhood, Siberian traders pitch their tents near by, and the bulk of the population congregate here during the winter months. The position of the Kuria indicates more or less the headquarters of each tribe, and probably also denotes the whereabouts of the best-favoured localities.

The domestic economy of the Urankhai is simple in

the extreme. There are few nomads whose existence depends on such simple requirements as those of the reindeer-keeping Uriankhai. Imagine a people who live on the produce of a single species of animal life, who depend on it for their food, clothing, and transport, and for their other needs rely entirely on the gifts of the forest and of nature. Nothing else affects their lives but the wild game and the roots of the taiga; nothing disturbs their tranquillity beyond the possibility of evil spirits destroying their herds. They want very little, and are contented.

The reindeer-keepers belong chiefly to the Toji clan, and are to be found mostly in the far eastern and north-eastern corner of the basin; there may be in existence a small section of the Saljak tribe who keep reindeer on the head-waters of the Khua-Kem, but we are still doubtful whether reindeer-encampments exist or not on the ranges between this river and the Bei-Kem. Apart from this probability only small numbers of reindeer-keepers are to be found amongst the Oina tribe on the south side of the Syansk. Thus the range and distribution of the domesticated reindeer inside the basin is remarkably small. To the east they extend over the Syansk into the region of Lake Kossogol, but beyond that lake no reindeer-tribes are to be met with, until one comes across the Tunguses, in the forests to the north-east of Lake Baikal. The existence of wild reindeer in these regions seems to prove that undoubtedly the reindeer-keeping clans must have been resident here for a very long time. No matter what may have been the movements of the other tribes,—even if they formerly belonged to the Minnusinsk region, the reindeer-keepers must, at any rate, have always lived in the highlands of the Syansk. Probably in the old days they ranged farther north than now, for there is no geographical boundary, no physical obstacle, to obstruct them; they probably lived then in the ranges overlooking the lowlands of the present-day Minnusinsk, where dwelt their kinsmen who owned cattle, horses, and sheep. The wild reindeer of the Syansk must have been the original type of the domesticated stock, for there is no reason to suppose that the Uriankhai migrated into the regions of the Upper Yenisei, bringing their reindeer with them.

For this and many other reasons we devoted the most careful study and observation to the reindeer-keepers and their encampment in the Ala-su Valley; so crude a race were they, and so completely dependent were they upon nature, it was difficult to imagine a people existing in such a primitive state in the present century and at the same time in such close proximity to other civilized races. The effect of their environment has protected them from outside influence, and the Uriankhai live on, unaffected and uninfluenced by their near neighbours. It is on account of the natural difficulties of the country, of the mountain-crossings and of the dense forests, that the Upper Yenisei basin has remained thus isolated and untouched by outside influence. Strangers have not been tempted to penetrate its wilds, and the indigenous tribes, revelling in their seclusion, have no desire to leave its solitudes. Shyness, independence, fear of intrusion, and superstition are for this reason characteristics of the reindeer-keeping Uriankhai, who in consequence hide themselves in the forests, and live as best they can on the beasts they herd. They are a tribe which must soon disappear through the introduction of a stronger and more go-ahead people, or by the mere importation of intoxicating drinks, for it is evident that we are dealing with a race who are on the decrease, their numbers being already small and the introduction of fresh blood being very rare. The fact of these small encampments being found in a region brimming over with wealth of pastures and showing thousands of square miles of untenanted lands full of possibilities, proves that the reindeer-keepers are no longer capable of increasing their species.

Living isolated existences, dependent upon their skill in hunting and their knowledge of reindeer-breeding, the Uriankhai have become, in consequence, both self-reliant and independent. Their lives do not show any particular hardship, for pasture is ample, food easily procured, and they have no enemies; we have here an example of a nomad race who are not forced to make any great effort, who are more or less settled in ideas, if not in their actual manner of life, and who are never driven to fight, raid, or make expeditions out of their own territory.

The Uriankhai are consequently self-reliant when dealing with their own affairs, but they are altogether at a loss and full of fear when they encounter things they themselves do not clearly understand. A look of both sadness and melancholy is stamped upon their faces, as might be expected in a people who are in constant fear of the gods of the mountains, rivers, and forests, dreading the evil spirits that haunt the land, and whose whole time is taken up with propitiating these spirits lest harm befall them. Such a people are easily dominated by any one with a strong hand, or possessing a show of superior knowledge, and we found the chiefs grinding down the poor, the Shamnan witch-doctors

A MELANCHOLY URIANKHAI.

having absolutely their own way, and the Buddhist lamas living on their lay brethren.

The Uriankhai is lazy and independent; he works only when he has a desire to work, and would far sooner run wild in the forest hunting the roe-deer and the maral and live in comparative poverty, than work for the Russian colonists and earn a good wage. He is a child of the forest, and has no desire to better himself. This has hindered his advance and doomed him to perpetual serfdom. Hidden away behind the ranges, in the depths of his forest-home, the Uriankhai has eked out his existence, wholly independent of outside influence. The Mongols and Chinese have successfully demanded tribute from him, the Russians have tried to employ him, and have indeed succeeded in doing a certain amount of trade with him; but all the Uriankhai really wants is to be left alone. His shy, wild nature prevents him from frequenting the villages or towns. He may pay a hasty visit to the trade-centres in order to exchange a few furs for tobacco and gunpowder; but his forests attract him most, and he hurries back again, not to be seen perhaps for another twelve months. The Russian trader advances him the few luxuries he indulges in—such as tea, snuff, and tobacco; for the Uriankhai has no ready money, and eventually, after a successful hunting-expedition, the goods are paid for in furs. An Uriankhai may even be lucky enough to pay off his debt for the whole year at the Russian trader's store in the course of one month's fur-hunting. Such easily gained success is no incentive to advance.

In appearance the Uriankhai are of a mixed ethnological type. Taking them as a whole, we can divide them into two sections—those of the upper basin and those of the Kemchik, two natural divisions which are impressed on us, also, by reason of certain physical and climatic differences between the regions inhabited by the two races. The inhabitants of the upper basin, and especially the reindeer-keeping clans, are the least touched by Mongol influence, whilst those of the Kemchik are the most influenced by the outside world. The variations between the two types are from almost pure Mongolic features to almost typical European, this divergence in type being noticed throughout the community irrespective of the two different divisions, although the Kemchik race approach more nearly to the Mongolic type than any other.

The encampments of reindeer-keepers on the Ala-su showed us what remarkable variations of features this one clan of Uriankhai possessed. There was no one type, and scarcely two individuals had like characteristics. On the whole, they were of rather small build, lean and wiry, which gave them the appearance of being quick and agile; but some were sturdily built and well-proportioned. According to Price's estimates, the average height of a man was from 5 ft. 4 in. to 5 ft. 6 in., and that of a woman from 4 ft. 6 in. to 4 ft. 7 in. Their facial features showed either the typical Mongol characteristics, namely, the "drawn" upper eyelid which forms an almond-shaped eye, and broad, prominent cheek-bones, or European features, with eyes large and round, noses often thin and aquiline, and with scarcely any prominence of the cheek-bone. The latter type is the most common in the upper basin, whilst the former is more conspicuous in the Kemchik. Amongst the reindeer-tribes the hair was mostly black, straight, and rather fine; but light, and even auburn, hair was common. This was especially noticeable amongst the children, the percentage of adults with auburn hair being considerably smaller. The Kemchik tribes were, on the other hand, dark, of taller build, with very high cheek-bones; and, according to Klementz, they can be always easily distinguished from their kinsmen of the upper basin.

The existence of auburn and fair hair amongst these people is a fact of exceptional interest, in point of view of proving or disproving the much-discussed question as to what part environment can play in modifying racial characteristics. Our observations only amount to placing on record another instance of the presumable modification of type by environment, a theory of which Professor Ridgeway of Cambridge is so keen an exponent. I am here stating the case—for and against—as suggested to me by criticisms which Professor Ridgeway has been kind enough to make. To put it shortly—the Finns, who are kinsfolk of the Uriankhai; have become a tall, fair race in their northern home; the recent discovery, also, of "blond"[1] Eskimo on the Arctic Coast of North America is another instance of the supposed effect of environment in producing this characteristic. Of course, the first conclusion one jumps to is that these characteristics are due to outside influence, such as the Siberian trader in the case of the Uriankhai and a lost Norse colony in the instance of the Eskimo, as Stefansson—their discoverer—thinks them to be. Amongst the Uriankhai, at any rate, it is a remarkable fact that the largest proportion of the blond type exist amongst the reindeer-keeping section, who are the *least* touched by outside

[1] I use the term "blond" on the strength of Stefansson's statement that out of six to eight hundred individuals, about 50 per cent. have "blond" or light brown eyebrows, and many have fair beards and blue eyes.

influences, and are of the most primitive stock; whilst the other Uriankhai who are in easier communication and contact with foreigners do not show this tendency to blondness.

It is also of significance that this section (the reindeer Uriankhai) live at a *higher* altitude than the rest. Taking into consideration, therefore, the fact that altitude acts like latitude in determining physical characteristics, we have an additional reason for reindeer-keepers possessing a greater percentage of the blond type than the Uriankhai who live at lower altitudes, and an additional proof in support of the theory. As has been pointed out elsewhere, the Upper Yenisei basin, although situated in Latitude 52°, has, owing to its high altitude, the conditions of, say, Latitude 64°—altitude compensating for latitude—and thus the reindeer-keeping Uriankhai live under almost the same conditions as the Finns.

On the other hand, we know that a foreign element does come in contact with the Uriankhai, and the suspicion of foreign visitors, to whom the existing blondness may be due, is added to by the fact of the presence of certain diseases. Yet, in spite of all other propositions, might not these characteristics be due to the influence of the ancient Uigurs, with their "light hair and blue eyes," as described by the Chinese annalists of that period?

Both men and women grow their hair fairly long, the women wearing it in two or three plaits and the men dressing it in the form of a pig-tail behind, but shaving the fore-part of the head. Apart from this the Uriankhai is remarkably hairless. He does occasionally grow a small moustache, and still more rarely cultivates a straggling

AN URIANKHAI FAMILY.

beard. In these ways he resembles the Mongol type rather than any other.

The Uriankhai dresses almost entirely in skins, except during the heat of summer, when he puts on a loose garment such as all Chinamen wear, made of blue material traded from the Chinese merchants. This is a recent innovation, and is the only garment he wears not typical of the Uriankhai. In cold weather this garment would be replaced by a heavy coat of sheep or roe skin, worn with the roughly tanned leather outside, and edged with a black velvet band. Their foot-gear is very peculiar, as it resembles almost exactly that of the Eskimo, namely, a long soft boot made of well-tanned furs. These boots are made of many separate pieces of fur, the leg-skins of roe-deer or of musk-deer being a favourite material. The Uriankhai wears on his head either a little conical fur-hat or a head-gear which, so far as I can ascertain, is quite peculiar to these people. This consists of a cap made of black astrakhan, with fur inside and coloured cloth on the outside, with a couple of tails of blue and red material hanging down at the back. This is the most common head-gear, even in summer, throughout the Uriankhai territory; but we never met with it beyond the borders of the basin. A leather belt round the waist, with a Russian-traded knife, a Mongol flint-and-steel, and a Chinese pipe completed his outfit; these, with a Buddhist charm hung round his neck, leave him ready to make his way through the Uriankhai world. When he wears out a garment he hunts for skins, or exchanges a fur or two for a new one. When his pouch is empty he borrows tobacco off the nearest trader until he has success in the forest, and in the same way he stocks his tent with the few requirements necessary to him. The young girls dress almost exactly like the men, but married women wear garments longer and looser in make.

The extraordinary simplicity of these reindeer-keepers is best shown by the type of food with which they find it possible to support life. In summer reindeer-milk is the staple diet, supplemented by the roots of a herb called Kandic,—a liliaceous plant which they dig up with hoes in the forests. In winter they live on the powdered roots of this herb and on the salted meat of the game they killed in the previous autumn. Reindeer-meat is a rare delicacy, the killing of the beasts being considered an extravagance as long as there is wild game to be found. From the traders they buy tea, and, if able to afford it, sugar and a little wheat-flour. The food of the other tribes consists of mares'-milk,—or "kummis," cows'-milk, cheese, and mutton, according to the produce of their herds. They mildly indulge in smoking and snuff-taking, though the desire for an intoxicant is as strong in the Uriankhai as amongst the Mongols. Spirit is made out of fermented mares'-milk by a crude means of distillation. The cost and trouble of this method of distillation, however, forbids many from indulging in these spirits, and so far the race has been little affected. But, given the wholesale introduction of strong drink by traders, the Uriankhai would undoubtedly succumb. This risk of deterioration is increased by the prevalence of nameless diseases which are obviously deeply rooted in the race.

On account of the poverty and simplicity of the Uriankhai, Russian merchants find small scope for trade and barter. A people who themselves make all that they need, and have no desire to better themselves, are of no use to those searching for good markets. As before mentioned, birch-bark is used for the manufacture of all vessels, and camp-gear; and what is not bark is skin. The women are wonderfully skilful at dressing the hides. With the aid of milk and a wooden-toothed implement they work the skin until it becomes as soft and as fine as if it were tanned under the most scientific methods. The tents are generally full of roe-deer skins prepared ready for making up into coats, or reindeer-hides for saddlery and mats, and of wapiti- or moose-skins used for harness and camp-gear, and various other furs for trading purposes. The only articles of foreign make used by the reindeer-keepers are tea, blue cloth, tobacco, gunpowder, and an occasional iron cooking-pot or kettle.

The land of the Uriankhai is a most wonderful fur-bearing country, and supplies them with a medium for barter and exchange, without which they would be in a bad way. Hides, salt, wool, and butter, besides the sale of live stock, make up the list of produce sent out to Siberia from the country of the Uriankhai. Salt, of which there are large deposits, comes from the southern slopes of the Tannu-olu, north of the Ubsa Lake. Adrianoff estimated the export at 15,000 poods (1 pood = 36 lb.) at the cost of a rouble a pood. Gold, which must be included in the list of the riches of this region, does not materially affect the Uriankhai, though the Russians who work the mines may employ a certain amount of Uriankhai labour. If, in the future, the native Uriankhai are capable and willing, there may be a great demand for their labour at a good wage.

There are many interesting facts in connexion with the ordinary domestic family life of the Uriankhai. They show, for instance, much appreciation of their women, partly for the reason that they are not very numerous, but more especially on account of the great desire they have to possess children. The women do most of the home work, it is true; but the men, in their turn, take over all the responsibility for the misdeeds of their wives! Chalon mentions the incident of a man being bastinadoed in the presence of his wife until she confessed to the felony she had committed! The universal desire for children shows that their upkeep presents no anxiety to these forest-dwellers; more mouths to feed is no burden to them, so long as they can ensure the continuation of their families. This desire is principally for boys; girls are not needed in the same degree, the custom of the country being that, on the death of the father, the property is divided amongst all members of the family equally. A number of girls in a family causes, to that family, not only loss of the name, but also the loss of a certain amount of property. The wish for a number of boys also results from the desire of these Buddhist parents to be able to give one or more of their offspring to the Lamaism.

The daily labour and the struggle for existence is not severe enough to exclude amusement from the life of an Uriankhai. Although of melancholy disposition, he occasionally indulges in music, which represents no doubt an outward expression of himself. He sings, for in-instance, and plays a flute, not by breathing out, but by drawing in, his breath, the results being most mournful and pathetic. His special accomplishment is an imitation of the bag-pipes, and besides this, the witch-doctors' drums and trumpets, and a curious two-stringed violin, complete the list of his musical methods. The

Uriankhai music is probably of special interest to the ethnologist, being peculiar to these people, and filled with the melancholy of the race. Amongst the Mongols we never heard any music resembling it.

The Uriankhai has no artistic sense as far as we could see; though the wood-carvings and the rock-drawings may possess some originality. These carvings were used to adorn the little obos, or shrines, where it was the custom to place offerings to those gods who protected the herds, or who were themselves the special guardian-spirits of the hunters. We recognized camels, reindeer, cows, sheep, deer, sable, and beavers. The figures carved in wood were apparently original in conception, if somewhat crude in design; they were of great interest as an example of true Uriankhai work. Other patterns, such as those on the furniture of the temples, on the banners, on the musical instruments, on the lamas' vestments, and on all uniforms worn by the chief men, were of Mongol or Chinese origin.

With ample spare time at their disposal, it is curious to note that the Uriankhai have learnt no other form of amusement beyond that of horse-racing and wrestling amongst themselves. These pastimes they have acquired from the Mongols, and they are practised in the basin only at places where considerable Mongol or Buddhist influence exists. The reindeer-keepers do not indulge in such sports, unless it be on the occasion of their annual visits to the Kurias with the object of attending a religious ceremony, this serving as the occasion for a kind of fair or festival.

Miller and Price witnessed such a wrestling-match at the termination of a religious ceremony, held by the Toji tribe on the upper Bei-Kem steppe, a description of which will well compare with Mr. Campbell's account of a similar match seen by him in Mongolia. Miller mentions that, at the close of a free meal provided for those attending the ceremony, "a dozen of the younger men stripped to their loin-cloths and began at once to wrestle. The two competitors advanced into the ring with leaps and bounds, whilst their 'seconds' held a hand in the air. . . . It resembled a 'catch as catch can' style of wrestling, it being the game to seize any part of the body. At the close of the bout the victor performed a curious sort of dance round the ring, slapping first his thighs and then the ground with his hands. After prostrating himself before the holy mountain, he received a prize of cheese from the hands of the Noyon and the head lama; this, after tasting, he magnanimously threw to the crowd, much to the enjoyment of the small children who scrambled for it."

Campbell witnessed wrestling-matches on the occasion of the Mongolian "Derby," the wrestlers trying their skill *during* the time the race was in progress. "It was always a layman against a lama," he writes, "a tournament of Church *versus* State, and the sympathies of the onlooker usually sided with his own representative. Kicking was in order, and most of the wrestling was a mere exhibition of force; but now and then a dexterous trick showed long practice or great quickness. . . . In the majority of cases the bout began by an orthodox grip, neck to neck, and shoulder to shoulder, and ended by a trip or a violent throw. The comical feature of the contests was the preliminary challenge. Each, as he emerged from the dressing-tent and came in sight of the 'gegan' (local chieftain) brought himself by a series of standing-jumps to the pavilion, sprang as high

AN URIANKHAI LAMA.

A WRESTLING MATCH.

in the air as he could, bowed low with a smack of the hands to the ground, followed this by a couple of high springs, turned round and leaped into a minatory position in the centre of the plot, where he waited until his adversary had accomplished a similar performance." After the bout "the victor, by a fresh series of leaps, accompanied by whoops, presented himself once more to the 'gegan,' prostrated himself, was invested with his hat, and given a double handful of cheese-scraps, which he partly ate and partly scattered amongst the onlookers."

A remarkable and interesting performance, a survival, no doubt, of many ancient tests of strength and valour which the Mongols must have revelled in, during the palmy days of their greatness. One point is especially noteworthy in these competitions between Church and State, namely, that the results usually end in an easy victory for the *Church,* which seems to prove that the lamas are the strongest and best-developed, and yet, curiously enough, in the influence of lamaism we look for the cause of Mongol decadence.

The life-history of the reindeer-keeper is written in the herding of his beasts and in hunting, these pursuits occupying his whole time when not lazily lounging in his tent; and, as he makes his wife and children carry out, not only most of the camp-work, but also help him with the care of the herds, the owner of a tepee in the Upper Yenisei basin has a very good time of it! In hunting, however, he finds a real scope for his trained skill, and in expert knowledge of forest-lore he is probably unsurpassed. It is no uncommon sight to see a couple of small boys, not exceeding fourteen years of age, start off from camp on a hunt extending over a period of several days. Mounted on their small, wiry horses, they ride off into the forest, having nothing with them but the clothes they wear, their long guns across their backs, and a skin of fermented reindeer or mare's milk attached to their saddles.

The guns they use are the ordinary long-barrelled muzzle-loaders, such as are used everywhere on the outskirts of the Chinese Empire; but they differ from most guns that we have seen elsewhere, in the remarkably long forks attached to the fore-part of the barrel as a support. All the native hunters of Central Asia use supports of this kind, but usually on a smaller scale. We imagine that the length of those used by the Uriankhai is necessitated by the heavy undergrowth over which they have to shoot. Dressed in dirty leather clothes of a neutral tint, with head bound up in an old handkerchief and soft fur moccasins on his feet, the Uriankhai hunter creeps through the forest with as little noise and as little show as does the game which he is hunting. To this kind of life he has been inured from youth; he is as much at home in the taiga as he is in a tepee. His unequalled skill as a hunter is due to his dependence upon wild game, not only for his meat-supply, but also for his clothes, the produce of the reindeer supplementing this requirement and supplying transport.

Before the importation of firearms the Uriankhai made good use of the bow; but bows and arrows have now died out, and we found difficulty in obtaining a specimen of these weapons, which the hunters used in earlier days for the killing of game. They must, indeed, have been well skilled in wood-craft if they succeeded in stalking such large game as moose and wapiti in dense jungle, for to slay such with arrows is a fine achievement. The bows were about four feet in length, and were made of a single broad piece of spruce. The method of freeing the arrows was peculiar, approaching as it did that of a crossbow in method, the string being kept by a support at a greater tension than a man could pull, and the arrow being fired off by the pressing of a kind of trigger.

The hunting of large game is not the chief ambition of the forest-dweller; his great desire is to procure plenty of skins and meat for his own use, and furs for the purposes of trade. Roe-deer form his chief meat-supply, musk-deer give him not only good skins, for we saw bags and gun-covers most beautifully made of the leg-skins of musk-deer, but also supply him with musk to sell at a high profit. Moose and wapiti tempt him on account of the abundance of meat they provide, and the great value attached to the soft horns of the stags, as a marketable product for purposes of trade with China. The wapiti he either shoots during the summer when the horns are in velvet, or he traps them during the winter in pitfalls, attracting them thither with salt. The wapiti are kept alive and passed on to the Russian settlements, where a business is made of keeping stags in enclosures for the sake of the yearly tribute paid by their horns.

Apart from these his quarry consists entirely of fur-bearing animals; these he hunts chiefly in the early winter, using guns and dogs rather than traps. The dogs we saw in the Uriankhai encampments were of a peculiar breed, and were said to be remarkable for their hunting capacities. They were lean, under-sized animals of the lurcher type, with prick-ears and very pointed noses. Nearly every tent had one tied up outside, and we can vouch for them being excellent watch-dogs. With these dogs the hunters track the sable, marten, fox, lynx, and squirrel, until they run them to ground or tree them, when they are easily killed either with guns or by digging them out. Uriankhai fur-hunters generally go in small parties and divide the spoils. Centuries of this kind of life has made them adepts—there is no waste of time or labour.

Furs must be procured for sale, and for tribute; so long as there is a demand the Uriankhai procure them. The Chinese still demand that their taxes should be paid, in part at least, in nine sorts of furs, namely, lynx, otter, sable, fox, squirrel, marten, wolf, glutton, and snow-leopard. This is the survival of an old custom, by thus demanding furs the officials took their share of the spoil without much trouble, for furs, which were held in great value in Pekin, represented comparatively nothing to the rough forest-dwellers. Mares also form an item in the list of the products of the country which are acceptable for the paying of tribute, cream-coloured mares of certain localities being in great demand amongst the Chinese officials.

Besides the above-mentioned animals there is still another species inhabiting the basin worthy of record, namely the beaver, for its presence completes the list of the northern fauna extending thus far southwards. A few beavers still exist in the upper tributaries of the Bei-Kem; but they are very rare, and their skins are seldom brought down to the markets. In old days they were mentioned as being included in a tribute sent by the Khan of the Ubsa region, then paramount chief of the Uriankhai tribes, to the Czar of Russia. We read

A YOUNG URIANKHAI.

URIANKHAI HUNTERS.

of "a hundred sables and two beavers" being on the list.

Although hunters and trappers, the Uriankhai are no fishermen; the wealth of the fisheries which surround their homes remains neglected and almost unused except by the "Lake people," as a small section of the Toji tribe are called. Fishing is never adopted amongst them as a profession, although of late years a few ambitious Uriankhai have taken to fishing in the Toji Kul and trading their hauls to the Siberian settlers. They are usually quite content to catch a few fish for their own use in the backwaters and small tributaries, by the help of nets made of horse-hair.

This indifference to fishing may be the reason why the Uriankhai have no skill as watermen; it is a peculiar fact in the life-history of these people that, although living in a land of lakes and rivers, and having constant need of water-transport, they have never yet gone so far as to devise a boat, and, while adepts in the use of birch-bark, have never attempted to construct a canoe of this material. The Uriankhai undertakes great risk when he ventures on to the water-ways, or when necessity forces him unwillingly to cross a river. For occasional fishing expeditions on the lake, or for the conveyance of merchandise downstream, he is in the habit of constructing small rafts.

We remember encountering an old Uriankhai on a raft on the Bei-Kem as we drifted down the river; this raft was a very small one, which he paddled and guided with a single oar; his cargo consisted of a bale of hides. As we allowed him to tie up his raft alongside of ours and to continue in our company, he sang us melancholy songs in appreciation; drawing in his breath to the full, he made a sound far down in his throat—by slowly letting out his breath—resembling that of bagpipes. This is a custom peculiar to the Uriankhai, the nature of the sound produced being not only impressive but strangely in accordance with their somewhat melancholy character.

For transporting baggage across the rivers, the Uriankhai use their horses to tow the rafts. With no harness but a rope passed through a loop tied in the horse's tail, one end of which rope is fastened to the raft and the other held in the hand, the Uriankhai urges his horse across the river. If the horse be in danger of drowning, the rope can be easily released and the horse set free; if the horse prove unwilling to take the right direction, the Uriankhai cleverly guides him by means of a rein attached to a long pole. The method is crude, but highly successful. A raft can be rapidly constructed on any occasion, and horses are always to hand. For ordinary river-crossings the natives are accustomed to swim beside their horses, guiding them, and at the same time aiding themselves by gently holding on to their mane or by their flanks.

The herding of the reindeer occupies the remainder of the time which the men of this tribe devote to work, for the herds form the chief item in the domestic economy of the encampments. It is really a wonderful sight to see these beasts moving about amongst the tents or over the surrounding meadows. They are free to wander where they like, and are often away for days without returning to their owner's tent, which they eventually always do. They are remarkably tame, even for reindeer. We were frequently disturbed by the ropes of our tents being pulled by a too friendly reindeer, and

SYANSK REINDEER.
Brown variety.

SYANSK REINDEER.
White variety.

the upsetting by chance of some salt belonging to our baggage attracted so large a number that we found them a trouble to get rid of. For salt they have a very keen desire, keener than I have noticed in other animals; here it is a common sight at evening to see the women feeding their pet deer with salt out of little leather bags, as they come home to the tents for the night.

The owners mark their beasts by cutting holes in the ears, and disfigure the older ones possessing large horns by cutting the antlers off short, in order to facilitate their passing through the dense forest. According to Miller's investigation:—

"At the time of our visit the horns were all in velvet, yet they were advanced enough for us to judge that some of the deer would later on carry remarkably fine horns. The horns are not free from velvet until the end of August, and are shed in March. The type of horn was rather thick and short, with a large palmation, and many points." In size the beasts were large and heavy, as compared with the Norwegian reindeer. This is also the case with other Siberian breeds, such as the Tunguse, which have been described as finer than those owned by the Laplanders.[1]

"We noted that the herds were, at the end of June, composed of a strange mixture of beasts of two varieties of colour, white and greyish brown, the latter predominating. As there were both white and greyish brown individuals of every age and sex to be seen, we are inclined

[1] "The measurements of a five-year-old male, of the brown type, were: height at shoulder 3 ft. 6 in., length of horn 27 in., girth above brow-antler 5½ in. Number of points about thirty when free from velvet. Another male of the brown type measured 3 ft. 5 in. at the shoulder, whilst a fine specimen of the white type aged about nine years was 3 ft. 8¼ in. at the shoulder.

to believe the natives, who said that there were two distinct varieties. Whether or not these two varieties breed true remains to be proved, but we never saw any that appeared to be crosses. The white breed is the more highly prized, and is the larger and stronger beast. In other reindeer lands, such as Norway, I can find no record of the existence of a white *breed*; but there are certain individual cases of variation in which a reindeer may be pure white. For instance, Du Chaillu, in *The Land of the Long Night*, roughly describes the appearance of a herd of domesticated Lapland reindeer in winter: 'The hair of the majority of the reindeer was grey, very coarse and thick, and almost white under the belly. Some of the animals in the herd were white.' Certainly they are known in the far north of Siberia, for in the Samoyede folk-lore there is often mentioned the 'milk-white reindeer.'

"The wild reindeer seen on the Syansk Range at the head-waters of the Chapsa appeared to have a very dark brown,—almost black—face; neck and body was almost pure white, turning to brown on the flanks, and with a dark line down the back. Fore-legs dark brown in front, otherwise white; the hind-legs were lighter brown in front. This specimen was undoubtedly changing from winter to summer coat. All the bushes where he had been feeding and resting were covered with white hairs. In full winter-coat he would probably be pure white, as in the white domesticated breed. At the time I saw him he was in an intermediary stage. His face and legs, being the first to change, had already assumed the dark summer colour, whilst the white winter-hair still remained on the body and covered the darker coat underneath it. Judging by this solitary specimen, it would appear that the wild reindeer change into summer-coat at an earlier date than those in domestication. In July his long winter-coat has given place to the following: face almost black, neck white, body grey-brown, legs very dark brown in front, insides of legs and belly white. This summer colouration would also apply to the white domesticated breed. In fact, it is chiefly from the appearance of some individuals of the latter in June, when patches of the short summer-hair were visible where the shaggy winter-coat had fallen off, that I have formed my opinion. The dark type would be in their summer-coat, dark brown on the body, grey-brown on the neck, and almost black on the face and front of the legs.

"If my estimation of the summer colouration of the two types be correct, they differ far less at that season than in the winter, though even then the light type, with its white neck and brown-grey body, would be considerably lighter. It is impossible to guarantee the accuracy of these descriptions of the colour of the reindeer, owing to seeing them at the very worst season of the year. Not till complete specimens in full summer-coat, and with fully developed horns, have been obtained will it be possible to ascertain in what characteristics, if any, the Syansk reindeer differ from those of North Siberia.

"The habitat of the wild Syansk reindeer differs very considerably from that of their northern cousins. The latter roam over the vast mossy tundras practically at sea-level, where nothing grows in the shape of timber except stunted birch, and perhaps occasional patches of wind-blown pines at the southern limit of their range. The former are to be found about the tops of the mountains at an altitude of from 6,000 to 8,000 ft. During the summer months they are exceedingly hard to find, living, as they do, on the upper edge of the timber, amongst cedar and rhododendron scrub. At the approach of winter, when the snow, caught amongst the dense growth, lies to a depth of several feet, they move up on to the open tops, which are blown almost clear of snow. At this season they must subsist entirely on reindeer moss, which grows there in abundance.

"In their habitat, therefore, the Syansk reindeer differ from those of Arctic Siberia (*Rangifer tarandus sibiricus*) in the same way that the mountain caribou (*Rangifer tarandus osborni*) of the upper waters of the Yukon differs from the Barren-ground caribou (*Rangifer tarandus arcticus*) of Northern Canada. Although we saw only one wild reindeer on the upper Chapsa River, there was ample proof, in the shape of droppings and well-worn paths, that there must have been many more concealed along the edge of the forest. They are probably more numerous along the range to the east, there being a larger area of suitable country in that direction."

In July the women of the encampments were busy with the care of the young reindeer, which seemed to need constant attention. All day the little beasts were tied up under the shade of the larch-trees, or under specially constructed booths near the tents. They were fastened by a cord round the neck to a peg in the ground and arranged in rows to enable the parents to find them easily on their return, and to lie down for the night beside their offspring. The older beasts seemed to suffer much from the heat, and never started out to feed until late in the day, which they partly spent lying panting under the shade of the forest. These required very little care, and for this reason reindeer appear to be amongst

HORNS, IN VELVET, OF THE SYANSK REINDEER.

the most easily managed domesticated beasts in the world.

The most important use the Uriankhai make of their reindeer is for transport purposes. All their migrations are carried out with the sole object of finding suitable pasture for their herds, and it is these very herds that supply the transport, for even if they travel slowly they go far. In the high country horses would be at a complete disadvantage, both on account of the soft ground and of the scarcity of grass, but the reindeer is there in his true element. The Uriankhai are thus able to traverse great areas of country, which would otherwise be difficult of access. When the hunters start off to hunt in the autumn they ride their deer, and the same transport is used to convey their families and households down to their winter quarters. The rolls of birch-bark and their other belongings do not constitute heavy or bulky loads, and with small packs the reindeer can move easily along the narrow forest-paths.

The women and children ride as well as the men; it is an everyday sight to see a small boy leap on to any unsaddled reindeer near at hand, and pace off to the other end of the encampment to find a friend or to see some fun that is in progress. No bridle or bit is used to guide the beast; only a rough halter controls him. For travelling purposes a pad of roughly tanned skins, a wooden saddle, and stirrups make riding more comfortable for the natives; but we found these wooden saddles considerably worse to sit on than a bare back.

Besides their use as transport animals and for riding purposes, the reindeer supply their owners with milk and occasionally with meat. The milk is very rich, and during the summer months forms the chief article of diet. When we exhibited a sample of our "trade-goods," such as needles, pins, tobacco, and tea, we were kept supplied during our stay with more milk than we needed; but, as I have described elsewhere, the purchase of a whole beast was a very different matter, the natives showing themselves to be so unwilling to part with a full-grown male that it proved to us the great value which they attached to them as stock.[1] The Uriankhai probably never kill for meat, except under exceptional circumstances. The neighbourhood of their homes abounds in wild game, easily killed at less cost and trouble than that entailed by breeding and rearing the reindeer. On the open lands it is different; on the steppes, where no such game supplies the demand for meat, the nomads are dependent upon the produce of their herds, and either exist meagrely on milk and cheese, or, if rich enough, on such meat as the flocks and herds supply.

Special importance is attached to these differences between the reindeer-keeping Uriankhai—whom I have just described—and the other tribes inhabiting the rest of the Upper Yeneisi basin, who live in very different surroundings and under very different conditions. All other Uriankhai, apart from the reindeer-keepers, can be classed together. Whether we are describing the other section of the Toji tribes in the far east, or the Kemchik people in the west, certain conditions under which they live tend to make them all very alike in customs and character. The most potent influence in causing this resemblance is environment. There is, for instance, no necessity for them to move into the high

[1] It is possible that there is a difficulty about breeding, for a recent traveller (Mr. Bassett Digby) amongst the Tunguses says that the reindeer do not breed well so far south, and that the natives import the best animals from the far north, and pay as much as £6 per head.

country in summer, nor is there much need for them to penetrate into the forests, for they can herd their horses, cattle, sheep, and goats on the open pastures in the lower valleys. On this account we find them distributed in the main valleys, such as the Upper Bei-Kem, where fine prairie-lands and open larch-groves make a shepherds' paradise, and also in all the steppe-country throughout the central and western basin.

An open country, which is easily accessible, has the effect of making these people less shy and more ambitious, with an eye to bettering themselves. They have come in touch with the outside world and have felt the influence of people greater than themselves. Their homes are Mongol in type, their dress half Chinese; they might be possessors of Russian cooking-utensils and they know of Urga—their religious centre—and Siberia, where their furs are sold. Intercourse with the world beyond their remote basin has led to a greater infusion of Mongol blood, which accounts for their divergence in type from their kinsmen of the upper basin. Thus the type of non-reindeer-keeping Uriankhai, especially of those of the far western parts of the basin, is distinctly more Mongol than that of the true forest-dwellers.

These non-reindeer-keeping Uriankhai, who, in point of fact, form the main bulk of the population, live a semi-nomadic life, herding horses, cattle, sheep, goats, and a few camels. The richness of the pasture in the east necessitates little movement, but in the central basin the land is poorer and migration consequently more frequent. All these people use the ordinary felt yurts as dwelling-places, a type of dwelling probably introduced amongst them by the Mongols. The dome-shaped tent made of laths of wood and trellis-work, covered with sheets of heavy felt, is too well known to need description; for these Uriankhai yurts resemble all others in Central Asia, except that they are small, dirty, and badly made,—poor reproductions, indeed, of the magnificent abodes of the wealthy Kirei, or the Kirghiz nomads of the Altai and Tian Shan pastures. Yet some of these Uriankhai are rich in herds, and it can only be the result of their uncleanly habits and utter disregard of comfort which dooms them for ever to live in this somewhat degrading manner. All the Mongols and Kalmuks have the same disregard for cleanliness, their encampments forming a great contrast to those of the spic-and-span Mohammedan nomads. How far these habits may be influenced by their religious beliefs is a question open to discussion elsewhere.

In contrast to the unmarketable possessions of reindeer-herdsmen, the flocks and herds of the other Uriankhai provide a certain surplus for trade. There appears to be an export of butter, and the sale of horses, cattle, and sheep is possible, and probable, owing to the proximity of the Siberian towns. Hides and wool make up the list of marketable products. The native sheep are covered with fine, silky wool, and the "astrakhan" supplied by the lambs commands a good price. The cattle of the upper basin are small, short-horned beasts, but there exists a very good breed peculiar to the Kemchik and Abakan steppes, which is especially adapted to those regions and deteriorates if removed to other pastures. The hides of these cattle fetch a very good price in Russian markets.

The horse indigenous to the Uriankhai country is of Mongol origin. He is a small but well-built animal, rather thick-set, and capable of great endurance. An average pony stands about thirteen hands. The chief peculiarity is the heavy head and shoulders and the round muzzle. For deficiency in appearance the Uriankhai pony atones by living on practically nothing, requiring little care, and by being capable of enduring extremes of weather. With a peculiar amble he carries his rider the entire day without flagging. Great wealth in horses, however, has caused the native never to make use of the same steed for more than one day's journey without a change; thus the native horses have no staying powers after their first stage. White and cream-coloured animals are common; we noticed many piebalds, and a great proportion of the animals had striped legs.

The trouble caused by horse-flies and mosquitoes obliges the owners to seek for open pastures away from or above the forests during the summer's heat, yet, in spite of this, we found encampments with small herds of cattle and horses buried in the forests. Great trouble, however, was taken to ensure their remaining undisturbed, by the building up of a circle of smoky fires around them. It is possible, however, that these particular people were carrying out a migration, and that the forest was not their usual haunt. On account of the mosquitoes and flies, the natives kindly spare the animals the use of their tails, although they are in the habit of hog-maning all their horses, there being a considerable trade in horsehair with the Russian markets.

The harness used by the horsemen is Mongol in character; we noted no peculiarities. The use of the lasso amongst the nomads interested us, however, and made us wonder whether the custom of roping horses originated in Asia. It is unlikely that it was introduced from elsewhere; no other people in Asia, to our knowledge, use the lasso, with the exception of the Mongols. In Mongolia, no doubt, in the earliest ages, primitive man first caught and domesticated the horse for his own use; the knowledge and practice thus gained concerning the capture of wild horses, has been passed on to others by those tribes who spent more of their time on horseback than on foot.

One other salient difference between the habits of these Uriankhai of the western basin and the eastern tribes is the fact that they practise agriculture, which necessarily enforces changed conditions of life. The natives who till the soil become semi-sedentary, although they are not yet actually domiciled in permanent dwellings. The Uriankhai of the central and western basin, who own and cultivate their lands, live in a manner approaching to the more advanced state of the Abakan Tartars. The semi-sedentary habits which they are slowly acquiring indicate an approach to a higher state of culture, and grant the possibility of the Uriankhai becoming in time a more useful and more capable race. This means, of course, that they are coming under the influence of a more intelligent people, and that, if they are not demoralized by contact with civilization,—if they are not ruined by the introduction of drink and disease, the Uriankhai may become a people. Fresh blood would be brought in, and, with the consequent greater traffic and facilities for trade and transport, the risk of deterioration would disappear.

How closely environment is in touch with the moulding of the character and habits of the people is often being proved, but how great an effect environment has had upon the thoughts and ideas, and in shaping the earliest superstitious beliefs of a people, has yet to be shown.

A SHAMMAN WITCH-DOCTOR.

The Uriankhai make an interesting study of a people who live in dependence upon nature, and whose religious ideas appear to be based on a system of propitiation of the gods of nature forced by a craving to avoid harm at the hands of the evil spirits, and to obtain favours from the good ones. Their cult, which is called "Shammanism," or the Black Art, is now only practised by certain tribes in Siberia, and by the Uriankhai; but in old days all the tribes of Northern Asia,—Tunguse, Mongol, and Turki,—were without exception followers of the Shammanistic faith. In all cases, however, at the present day, Shammanism is practised under an outward show of newly introduced religions.

In Siberia the Black Art has been largely destroyed by the introduction of Christianity, and is by law not allowed to be practised; the Turki tribes have embraced Islam to such an extent that it is scarcely possible to find even a trace of Shammanism, whilst in the Uriankhai country Buddhism is the professed religion. Faith in the Shammanistic rites and ceremonies is, however, so strongly ingrained in the people that it may still be considered to be their real belief. As a matter of fact, a study of the beliefs of these people show that they include much higher ideals than the worship of the genii of nature under the guidance of a tyrannizing priesthood of Shammans. And we shall do well to look into their religious ideas, for these are no small influences in determining the history and character of a people. To understand fully the Uriankhai beliefs, we must trace the stages of religious growth from Fetichism to Theism. By doing so we shall see the origin of the higher beliefs, and the early stages of man's attempts to recognize a superior power.

In those earliest stages, primitive man believed that all natural objects had personalities of their own. They treated all natural objects or phenomena of the universe as supernatural, as if they were beings in whose hands the lives of men were but playthings. Every physical feature—every mountain, hill, or hollow, the swift rivers and the water-falls, the rain-shower and the snow-storm, thunder, lightning, and dew, the sun, moon, and stars, all —to the early searchers after knowledge—were living creatures, having minds and bodies of their own. These spirits were, of course, both good and bad, some of them apparently persistently harrying man and troubling him with disaster, others were good in helping and cheering him; but all were to be feared, all were to be appeased by offerings, invoked for aid, propitiated in order to avert evil, or thanked for benefits received. Fear of offending the bad spirits, fear of not pleasing sufficiently the good ones, fear of the fact that, sooner or later, man falls into error, the god is angered, and man in consequence suffers death, it was *fear* that was the basis of the earliest stages of Totemism, or Nature-worship. This cult was universal amongst primitive races from Siberia to Patagonia, and from Lapland to Greece. All peoples seem to have passed through this stage, but there are few now left who remain instilled with the terror of the great god Pan.

In the next stage the natural objects were not considered alive in themselves, but were presided over by special deities, who were only approachable through the medium of Shammans, or priests. Hence the origin of the sacerdotal class. Shammanism, as this stage is generally called, is therefore an advance on ordinary Nature-worship, for deities were recognized. Later still, man gradually came to realize that there were not a great number of different gods, but that there was unity and harmony between the different natural elements, and this great force slowly evolved into the idea of one Supreme Being. But a remnant of the old idea of manr minor deities remained. These were impersonated by idols and images, in attempt to represent in man's image their vague ideas of the protecting spirits.

Now, the Uriankhai present to us the strange case of a people whose religious ideas seem to be a mixture of these several grades of primitive beliefs, from pure Nature-worship to Idolatry and Theism. We have, as a basis, a remnant of true Nature or "Thing" worship, in the prevalence of the deification of natural objects, such as trees, mountains, etc. It is in this respect that the Uriankhai show, by their superstitions, how near they are to nature, and how strangely they have kept to the present day this oldest cult, in spite of an advance of ideas in other directions. As an example of the next stage in the evolution of religious belief, we have the presence of Shammans—a priesthood—in whose hands are all dealings with the supernatural and the next world. Idolatry is exemplified by the use the Uriankhai make of idols and images in representation of the minor deities, such as the guardian-spirits of the flocks; and, strange to relate, by a form of ancestor-worship. The reverence of ancestors is generally to be found at the basis of most Asiatic beliefs. Ancestors are considered to act as intercessors in the next world, and the Shamman priests have the power to call them up, and to apply to them for aid. Amongst the Uriankhai and other Shammanistic tribes the existence of ancestor-worship is found in many forms, as described in Chapter II. (p. 61).

Above all this is a well-established belief in one Supreme Being, who is the God of Heaven and ruler over all things.

I will now show in greater detail the extent to which pure Nature-worship is practised by the Uriankhai, for this is the real basis of his beliefs. Amongst a people living in the twilight of the dark, damp forests, isolated in remote, secluded valleys, shut off from the outside world, surrounded by—and dependent upon—nature, superstition is apt to run riot. The Uriankhai, in his simple and yet subtle belief, sees mystery and feels the supernatural on all sides. His attitude is scarcely to be wondered at. The mystery of the sodden, taiga-clothed hills, the dark, silent valleys, and the mountain-crags which toss their heights above the forest, fill him with awe and crowd his thoughts with dread. The howling wind is obviously a god in anger; the swift-running river-gods hinder his crossing and jeopardize his life, the lonely summits of granite boulders—storm-riven and streaked with snow—are surely the thrones of gods, and not fit places for men. The record of such names as "Bogdo"—holy, "Khan"—Chief, as applied to mountains, show how greatly the Uriankhai and the Mongols venerate the superb, isolated snow-summits, which stand up like thrones of Kings on the wide plateaux.

The rugged crags which rise above the forests in the Upper Yenisei basin are held by the Uriankhai in such awe, that he never on any occasion visits them; he calls them "taiga," *i.e.* the wild—the unknown,—and looks upon them as the abode of spirits. The frequency of sudden storms, of thunder and lightning add to his nervousness. The terror of Pan is everywhere. The Uriankhai sees him in every tree, rock, and stone; he hears him in the silence of the night and feels the closeness of

AN URIANKHAI SHAMMAN DOCTOR.

his presence by day. Who is it who gives him suffering, if not an evil spirit? Who is it who spoils his luck when hunting? What is Chance but the interference of the genii? A people who are absolutely dependent upon nature for all their wants naturally worship the hand that gives so freely, and thus we see that pure Nature-worship still keeps a strong hold on the minds of the people.

A superstitious dread of the genii, both good and bad, makes the Uriankhai's great object in life to propitiate the spirits, lest evil befall him. On every possible occasion the forest-dweller endeavours to keep on good terms with the evil spirits. Any danger encountered in the path, such as a river to ford, or a mountain to cross, in fact, any natural difficulty, is propitiated by votive offerings, with which the nature-worshipper hopes to pacify "Erlik Khan"—the evil one. Votive poles, covered with pieces of coloured rag, are to be seen everywhere, and prove how necessary the Uriankhai finds it to show this respect, in order to ensure his peace of mind. In the reindeer-encampments we found small poles, from which dangled white rags, placed in front of every tent-door to scare away the demons of sickness. The reindeer-herds had other poles specially placed close to their resting-place, to guard them from harm. Never did we climb the summit of a single pass without finding it adorned with a cairn of stones, and innumerable rags of every colour attached to poles, or hung on the trees.

Obos are built at places where special attention is to be drawn to the sacredness of the spot; we have seen these shrines in every part of the Yenisei Basin and in North-west Mongolia. So familiar are they, and so often are they the only signs of human agency in a wild and uninhabited region that the name "Obo" is often printed on our modern maps in regions possessing no other place-names. Many a desert waste is marked off into stages by obos built by zealous adherents to the practice of Nature-worship. It is a primitive attempt to do honour to the deities—an idea which has slowly germinated, with the growth of civilization and religious cult, into broader and more ambitious lines. In wild Mongolia, where men live in tents, the only attempts at building are these small temples, sacred to the worship of the deities; as, in Europe, man's highest achievements in architecture are devoted to the service of his religious belief.

In the forested regions we found the obos made of pine-branches and brushwood—looking from afar like huge, conical-shaped bonfires piled ready for lighting. Sometimes they were in the form of booths, made of branches, into which one had to crawl on all fours, the interior of which could only be seen through the means of striking a succession of matches. Those we entered were found either to contain offerings of food to the gods, or a sacred Buddhist picture, or innumerable wooden representations of the animals herded in the neighbourhood, such as sheep, cattle, or reindeer, of the beasts of the chase, and of fur-bearing animals. The obos serve, in fact, as a depository for the offerings to the spirits who guard the flocks, and to those gods supposed to grant good luck to the hunters. The custom of presenting wooden models of different domesticated animals may be a remnant of the ancient rites of sacrifice, which were so common in all the earlier forms of worship. In old days the tribes were rich enough to afford the sacrifice of a certain number of their flocks

URIANKHAI "OBOS."
In the Upper Yenisei basin.

AN "OBO" AND VOTIVE OFFERINGS.
On the Mongolian plateau.

and herds, but they certainly are not in a position to do so now. The only record we have of live sacrifice at the present day in this region is amongst the Buriats, who have yearly festivals when horses are sacrificed and feasted on. Certain details of these ceremonies as described by Professor Curtin, such as the locality—a hill-top—where they are held, and the wrestling-matches which take place after it, remind us of Uriankhai religious meetings which we witnessed.

There are permanent obos besides the temporary residences of the god, and these are generally built over some venerated object. Chalon makes mention of a large obo at Cha-Kul which was built over a large dead tree-trunk, an especially sacred object, the subject of much veneration; we too saw a pretentious array of votive poles in the same locality rigged up before a cave, which possessed rock-paintings of Buddhist origin.

The obos are generally placed on hill-tops, which are looked upon as the chosen haunts of the gods. Good spirits are apt at times to change their home, and the ceremony carried out by the Uriankhai on the occasion of welcoming a god to his new home is of great interest. Miller and Price were lucky enough to witness such a festival in the Upper Bei-Kem region, and I quote Miller's ready description of the extraordinary scenes enacted by the priests and laymen on that occasion. The scene lay on a grassy hill-top, overlooking a wide panorama of prairie and larch-forest, situated on the left bank of the Upper Bei-Kem to the west of the Kuria which formed the religious centre of the Toji tribe.

"On the hill-top was a square log building with a conical roof, the whole of which was covered over with boughs of trees and larch-poles decorated with strips of white cloth. The entrance was by a double doorway. On the north and south sides were six similar, but smaller, conical-shaped obos, made of branches and brushwood and decorated with votive poles. The interior of the central obo was fitted with a low platform on which were placed four smaller ones—one above the other—and on the top of all was a pyramid of wood inscribed on all its faces with sacred writings. The platform was covered with presents and gifts intended as a welcome to the newly arriving god; there were clay discs stamped with writings and images of Buddha. All the chief animals of the country, too, were depicted in wood, and food-offerings were prepared for the god, and the best 'kummis' was placed at his service in brass bowls.

"The people now began to arrive, and from the lofty position overlooking a wide expanse of country we could see horsemen spurring from all points of the compass towards the sacred hill. The Noyon—or chief of the clan—with his retinue were early on the scene. Dressed in a silk robe, with a gilded hat on his head, he sat under the shade of an awning, especially erected outside the obo, and held a "durbar" as the clansmen arrived. There was much talking, drinking of 'arak' (spirit brewed from fermented milk), and exchanging of snuff-bottles, until a shout from the novices heralded the arrival of the head-lama, whose horse they led up the hill to the entrance of the shrine. He was quite an imposing-looking individual, with his clean-shaven head and terribly wrinkled face.[1] He made no appearance as regards his vestments; for a high-priest he was even

[1] See page 224.

MUSICIANS AT AN URIANKHAI RELIGIOUS CEREMONY.

A RELIGIOUS CEREMONY.

See p. 249.

disreputable, being clothed in a dirty old skin-coat boasting the remnants of fur-cuffs and collar, and he wore a skull-cap of the same material.

"Meanwhile, some hundreds of natives had collected from all quarters, and, as the arak had begun to take effect, the shouting and laughing grew very loud. An amusing incident now occurred. A minor official, who had been despatched by the chief to ride with a message to a priest living at a distance, had promptly ridden off to the nearest encampment and there become intoxicated. He was captured, however, and was led up before the Noyon for punishment. After having his ears severely boxed, he was laid out on the ground and given twenty lashes with birch-sticks, borrowed for the occasion from the sacred obo.

"After this diversion, which all present seemed thoroughly to enjoy, the religious ceremony began. The lamas seated themselves in order of rank, in two rows, facing each other, and the head lama took the top right-hand place. In the centre between the two rows was placed the cooked meat and bags of kummis which was to compose the feast after the ceremony. To the accompaniment of two gigantic brass horns—ten feet in length, cymbals, a drum, shell-horns—which emit the most mournful of music—and a flute-like instrument with a note like a bagpipe, the priests chanted their prayers and kept up a 'fully choral' service for half an hour.

"During that period, I suppose, the god had actually arrived at his new abode, for at the end of the service each member of the congregation in turn prostrated himself and muttered prayers before the entrance of the obo; then the concourse broke up and the whole congregation trooped off down the hill to enjoy themselves. The feast—the main attraction, no doubt, to the nomads who dwelt at a distance—now took place. Lamas and laymen lined up, each in their respective ranks, the Noyon heading the latter and the chief priest the former, whilst food in the shape of meat and kummis was distributed amongst them. A few women, hitherto excluded from the ceremony, now made their appearance and sat behind the Noyon, but took no further part. After the feast there were wrestling-bouts between the young men, whilst the older folk continued to sit over their kummis and snuff-taking."

This ceremony was a peculiar mixture of Shamman and Buddhist rites, and shows how mingled are the two in this strange community of partially converted Nature-worshippers.

So much for the presence of original Nature-worship amongst the Uriankhai. Now let us see how far Shammanism, *i.e.* the actual practice of Black Art by the priest, has got a hold over the people. At the outset it must be noted that this influence is very strong, in spite of tendencies such as the influence of Buddhism and the endeavours of civilization in Siberia to put a stop to the practices of the Shamman witch-doctors. The Shammans hold great influence over the people, their occult powers are still believed in, there being nothing in the introduced religions to take the place of their time-honoured institution.

Great secrecy envelopes the cult, and the Shamman tribes do not care to let others know their ideas. The Shamman doctors themselves are more feared than loved by the people. The priesthood is hereditary, and the skill and magic is supposed to be transmitted from father to son or daughter, without any actual training. The Shammans hold the people in their power, for only through them can intercessions be made with the next world, only *they* can keep on good terms with the evil spirits, and their peculiar art alone is able to keep up the close communication between the living and the dead which is necessary for the veneration of ancestors. The priests make the sacrifices on the occasions of misfortune or death, conduct requests and prayers, are soothsayers, doctors, and weather-prophets, in fact, they run the superstitions of the people for their own benefit.

Where pure original Shammanism is especially noticed, is in the domestic life of the Uriankhai. Buddhism is all very well as a profession; the simple forest-dweller is only too glad to leave all such ritual in the hands of his educated superiors; but when demons of sickness torment his home and the shadow of death comes over a tepee, then the Uriankhai resorts to the black magic, and the practised hand of the witch-doctor is called in to battle with the evil spirits. Miller and Price were on one occasion the witnesses of a struggle of the Shamman doctor with some fell disease.

It was night when they heard the sound of a muffled drum,[1] which warned them that a Shamman doctor was at work in a neighbouring tent, so, walking over to it, they pushed back the flap which formed the door, and

[1] The drum is probably the most original of all instruments used in religious ceremonies. In Shammanism the drum has an exceptional significance. Of all the strange outfit and accoutrements of the witch-doctors, none are considered of any real value but the drum. Without it no ceremony would be of any use. With the drum alone can the Shammans call up the departed spirits. It is the sign of rank of the Shamman priest, and is an heirloom handed down from father to son or daughter, together with the inherited skill or magic.

watched the strangest of spectacles by the flickering light of a smoky fire. "Inside sat two men and a woman on either side of the tent, and at the far end, with his back towards us, stood the witch-doctor. He was dressed in a long buck-skin shirt, decorated with innumerable pieces of many-coloured rags, whilst down his back and from his arms down to his feet dangled strings of red, green, and white tape. Across the shoulders he bore two iron rods to which were attached innumerable pieces of metal. His drum was of wapiti-hide, and he beat it with a stout drumstick, the padded part of this being made of some rare fur. He faced a large piece of yellow cloth—decorated with many-coloured rags—which was hung up to the side of the tent. In his incantations he beat the drum incessantly, first on the right side, then on the left, and even behind his back—varying the strength and tone accordingly. Sometimes he droned a weird, low chant, swaying from side to side and shaking his shoulders so as to make the irons rattle. Then, changing his tactics, he became silent, but increased the violence of his gestures until convulsed with the intense strain; his face became distorted, sweat ran off his brow, and in this frenzy he worked himself up into delirious madness, so much so that the strain became too great, and he dropped exhausted to the ground. One of the onlookers then took the opportunity of tightening the drum over the fire, and after a short rest the Shamman doctor set to work again, but his heavy breathing and occasional groans showed that he was still very exhausted." Evil spirits of sickness and disease are thus exorcised and driven out by the Shamman doctors, who may be either men or women. In the neighbourhood of Cha-Kul we witnessed a like

FLAG INDICATING AN URIANKHAI CEMETERY.

BUDDHISTIC BANNERS.
A religious ceremony at the Chedan Kuria.

URIANKHAI FORM OF "BURIAL."

ceremony in which a woman took the part of the witch-doctor.

When death ensues the Uriankhai dispose of the corpse by exposing it on a hill-top, and leaving it to the wild animals. No form of burial is known to them. Their superstition teaches them that the man who has spent a good life is quickly devoured by birds and beasts of prey, but the others, who have not lived so well, have not this doubtful honour bestowed upon them. The "cemetery" is often marked by a white flag, which warns strangers not to approach too close when a Uriankhai of well-known bad character chances to have recently died, and been there laid to rest.

Turning now to the most interesting part of Shammanism, as practised in these regions, that of idolatry or anthropomorphism. There is obviously a strong sense in these people of attempting to represent to themselves, by idols and images, certain minor deities which they still hold in great reverence. The curious mixture of this idol-worship with a belief in a God of Heaven, which these same people profess, caught the attention of the earliest visitors to the Mongols and Southern Siberian tribes. For instance, Carpini notes that the Mongols "have certain idols of felt, imitating the human face, and having underneath the face something resembling teats; these they place (in their yurts) on either side of the door. These they believe to be the guardians of the flocks, from whom they have the boons of milk and increase. Others they fabricate of bits of silk, and these are highly honoured; . . . and whenever they begin to eat and drink, they first offer these idols a portion of their food and drink."

The most important thing in the life of the nomads

is the well-being of their flocks, and it is quite natural that the guardian-spirit of the herds should receive a special place of honour. Marco Polo relates the same fact, but adds the care of the children and the crops, as well as the guardianship of the herds, to the protecting powers of this idol. "They show him great worship and honour," he says, "and every man hath a figure of him in his house, made of felt and cloth, and they also make in the same manner images of his wife and children. . . . And when they eat, they take the fat of the meat and grease the god's mouth withal, as well as the mouths of his wife and children. Then they take of the broth and sprinkle it before the door of the house; and, that done, they deem that their god and his family have had their share of the dinner."

Besides this they impersonate the "god of the chase," the next most important factor in the lives of these shepherd-hunters. This deity is represented by a roughly stuffed hare-skin, and may be seen hung up in the tent, close beside a modern Chinese picture of the Buddha, and amongst the other bric-à-brac which go to swell the strange collection of relics representing the mixed religious ideas of the present-day Shammanist.

These minor deities are placed in a category by themselves, and called the Gods of the Earth; but above all this primitive superstition and idolatry there is the certain belief in one supreme power over all nature. The Uriankhai, as well, I think, as all Shammanists, recognize a Great Spirit, whom they do not attempt to understand, and whom they call Tengri—the God of Heaven. Carpini says of the Mongol Shammanists that they "believe in one God, the Maker of all things . . . the distributor of good and evil in this world; but worship Him not with prayers or praises or any kind of service." Still more interesting is the fact that they make no attempt to impersonate this Creator.

To the intensely devout Western missionaries, the Mongols in the thirteenth century seem to "differ from all nations of the world, for they do not boast of having any law warranted by God, as many other nations falsely do, but simply by some instinct or movement of nature, say that there is something sovereign above all the things of this world, and that there is a God." This is a most remarkable confession. "Simply by some instinct or movement of nature" means volumes. The Franciscan monk recognized the fact that these pagan barbarians had come to the conclusion, of their own accord, "that there is a God."

In these days the old beliefs are being gradually veneered over with (an almost enforced) Christianity in Siberia, and the most degraded form of Buddhism in Mongolia and the Uriankhai country. It is difficult to say how far these religions are influencing Shammanism, or how much of the original Nature-worship still underlies the outward evidence of the comparatively newly introduced faiths. Shamman-doctors are still always resorted to in cases of sickness, and the sacrifice of horses is still continued amongst the Siberian Buriats. It is doubtful whether Christianity in Siberia has greater power in exterminating the Black Art than has Buddhism in Mongolia; in both cases a good deal of it remains. But the influence of the presence of a foreign race, such as the Russian colonists amongst the indigenous Siberian tribes, ought to have more effect than that of the Buddhist missionaries.

Nature-worship was formerly highly suitable to the

Mongol character, it was a strong, simple faith, in no way weakening to the race, a worship—as Ratzel remarks—"poetic in feeling and artistic in representation." But the growth of a sacerdotal class and the enslavement of the people under the priests produced a state of affairs which, upon the introduction of Buddhism, easily turned the new faith into Lamaism. It is Lamaism which has sapped the strength and destroyed the independence of these people. In consequence, their reputation is not what it was when, as Shammanists, they rose to power and made their gigantic conquests. In Mongolia Buddhist influence has expelled the minor deities of the Shammanists, keeping only "Tengri"—the good spirit—the God of Heaven. But amongst the Uriankhai and the Siberian Shammanists a certain amount of idolatry remains. Indeed, I think, it will be a long time before any faith replaces the cult of the gods of nature amongst the reindeer-keeping Uriankhai.

CHAPTER IX

THE TURGUN HIGHLANDS AND THE INFLUENCE OF MONGOLIA

WITH the passage of the Tannu-ola we started a new stage in our journey. We here left behind us the varied scenery and wealth of life which belong to Siberia, and entered upon the cold, bleak monotony of the heart of the continent. This change brought us to the vast expanses and untrammelled distances of a land, where Nature has built her works on unusually extravagant lines ; it brought us to wider wanderings, to a freer life, and to a journey unimpeded by those obstacles we had experienced up to date. Instead of tangled undergrowth, hidden views and narrow valleys, we were faced by far-flung wastes of the Gobi, and were able to indulge in a lengthened *Wanderlust* the natural result of close contact with its restless inhabitants. We experienced, too, the sense of movement brought about by these vast and barren plains, where the nomads shifted camp far more often than did the tribes of the forest,—who have ample grazing ; and we found real fascination in watching the slumberous movement of the camels, suggestive as it was of long marches over endless steppes and across arid deserts.

Day after day, as we travelled across the boundless wastes of Inner Asia, we were surrounded by views possessing the magic which inspires a man with great thoughts and "makes him long great longings." The stagnant atmosphere of the swampy taiga, was replaced by air as exhilarating and as glorious as ether. The dark, sombre colouring of the Siberian forests, changed to the most vivid contrasts of light and shade, to the varied tones of the pale steppe and of the flower-strewn plateau. Contrasts, in short, such as Nature revels in placing in close proximity, and contrasts which are especially noticeable in the heart of this great Asiatic continent.

It was with both expectation and enthusiasm that we climbed to the top of the Tannu-ola and looked down into Mongolia. This was *the* psychological moment during the course of our journey. A feeling of awe was ours, such as the least enthusiastic man would experience, upon finally reaching the summit of that "Great Divide." At this point the waters parted, the rain which fell on the slopes where we stood, found its way by streamlet, torrent, and gigantic river to the far-off Arctic Ocean; the rain which fell on the other side of the range, was destined to go through a process of slow evaporation in the self-contained saline basins of Mongolia itself.

We stood on the crest of the southern wall of the Upper Yenisei basin and bade farewell to that little-known and secluded region, the investigation of which, had been the initial object of our journey. Behind us lay the Yenisei basin, with its forests, meadows, racing rivers, cloud-capped ranges and lowering storm-clouds. All that impenetrable region, with its peculiar inhabitants, lay *behind* us to the north. Before and below us stretched the limitless expanse of Mongolia, a world of

THE YAMACHU PLATEAU,
Looking east.

plain and plateau, open to view, easy of access, free to all comers, and brilliantly lit up under cloudless skies. Could there be in the world two such contrasts as these, divided by the single breadth of one mountain-range? The magnitude of the landscape was beyond possible description; an impression can only suggest it. The region ahead of us appeared one of unbroken horizons, vast as the sea, and almost as boundless. The eye roamed over a space equal to several weeks' journey, and at a glance covered several mountain-ranges. Plains as large as an English county divided mountain-groups as high as the Alps. Cloud-like, baseless ranges seemed to hang in the air, their snow-fields visible, but their foot-hills invisible, so far away were they below the natural curve of the earth's surface.

The feeling of restlessness which this wonderful expanse brought about, was intensified by the total lack of settled habitation. The inhabitants of this country were as uncertain and restless as the winds which for ever swept across her plateaux. "Here to-day —gone to-morrow" is the motto of the Mongols, and this was so in fact, as their wanderings left no single trace of their existence. One travelled for weeks without the eye alighting on a sign of life, other than the distant glimpse of a hastening horseman, or a string of camels on a far horizon. Then suddenly, by contrast, one arrived at a well-favoured locality where grass and water were abundant, and where, in consequence, one observed the domed tents of the Mongol nomads pitched in close array, and innumerable flocks and herds grazing over the rich pastures.

Into this "new" country we rode down in a storm of rain. We received no warm welcome from Mongolia.

We spent the night near some herdsmen's yurts, and arrived the next morning at one of the Mongol karauls, or guard-houses, which form the southern limit of the territory of the Uriankhai. The local official supplied us with a change of transport animals, and, obtaining horses in place of our sorely tried oxen, we despatched our Kemchik hirelings back to their own land—for even when in the service of distinguished strangers the Uriankhai were not permitted to pass the boundaries of their reserve. Here, for the first time, we accosted representatives of pure Mongol race; truculent-looking rascals they seemed to us, after the reserved and rather timid Uriankhai. The natural influence of the wild life and freedom of the open Mongolian plateau could be traced in their careless and reckless manner; they were loud-speaking, rough soldiery, used to a hard life, apt to bully those below them, but respectful to their superiors.

The karauls stretch like a line of block-houses along the southern foot-hills of the Tannu-ola for about five hundred miles. In themselves they are nothing more permanent nor imposing than felt-yurts,—of larger dimensions than those in general use among the shepherds. Their names, however, are written large on the maps, as if they were permanent abodes; for this reason the traveller is often misled in his calculations, as the karaul he expects to reach, may have been shifted a long distance from its position as shown on the maps. Each link in this chain of guard-houses is about thirty miles long, and every fifth guard-house is of greater importance than those preceding it, the resident official there, having control over the other four.

Once on the south side of the Tannu-ola we had

reached the true Mongolian plateau. Our route led along the southern foot-hills at an altitude of 4,500 ft. above sea-level. To the south, the land stretched out in a long, smooth sweep as far as the depression which contains Lake Ubsa—just distinguishable as a blue streak across the yellow steppe. Far away beyond the lake the country rose again into plateau-land, broken here and there by narrow ranges of rocky hills. The southern slopes of the Tannu-ola were neither well watered nor well timbered. Many of the valleys were waterless—although lines of larch and poplar bordered the dry watercourses. On the main range itself patches of forest seemed to hang on the slopes of the inner valleys having a north aspect, but all outlying spurs were stamped with signs indicative of lack of rainfall. Yet it was fair pasture-land, for we found Mongols in good numbers along the valleys, and we saw immense flocks of sheep grazing over the plains to the south. The abundance of pasture is accounted for by the prevalence of summer rains; these mostly spent themselves on the ranges, but the result of their influence evidently extended some way across the plain to the south. Large masses of cumulus clouds stood over the ranges surrounding the Ubsa basin, showing that even in the month of August this part of Mongolia is anything but dry.

We were now in a land where our passports were handled with respect, for we were dealing directly with the Chinese authorities. Local chiefs sent men to arrange our affairs, transport was procurable at a few hours' notice, and there were always plenty of men about to do odd jobs and any work demanded of them. The karaul of Borgushaitu, where we first accosted the

Mongol guards, was only of the secondary type, yet the transport they provided us with numbered twenty men, thirty horses, and eight oxen; and with this cavalcade we hastened by a forced march to the chief karaul of the district—Bodkhon-Khalat—which we reached the same day. Difficulties of locomotion, such as existed inside the basin, were here entirely absent, as proved by the fact that the first day's trek along and over the southern spurs of the Tannu-ola was thirty-five miles in length, and the heaviest laden horse only took twelve hours in which to accomplish it.

At Bodkhon-Khalat we camped close to the little mud-built block-house, where a Chinese frontier official had his residence. Wang-fu, as he was named, possessed a most agreeable and delightful personality. We dined with him, and he came to tea with us, several times during our stay in the neighbourhood of his post. He kept up quite an establishment; he had Chinese servants and a wife from his own province, and his house was typically Chinese, being built in the shape of a miniature yamen. His present to us consisted of a box of Chinese sweets such as come only from the cities of China Proper; he entertained us throughout with the trained etiquette of the true Celestial. This little outpost of the Empire was augmented by the presence of a Chinese trader who spent the summer here trading with the Mongols, but later on resorted to the Mongol winter settlements of Ulankom near Ubsa Nor.

The presence of a Chinese official at Bodkhon-Khalat much impressed us, proving as it did the growing zeal with which the Chinese were coming to the fore along the Mongol frontier of Siberia. Wang-fu was directly

MONGOL KARAUL ON THE SOUTH SIDE OF THE TANNU-OLA.

under the Governor of Kobdo, the chief (and only) town of North-western Mongolia, his authority extending, solely, to the guarding of the frontier, and his position resembling that of a frontier-agent. He had no dealings with the Mongol tribesmen,—who were directly under their own Khan,—and only interfered with the affairs of the Khanate when he wished for transport, or local aid, in regard to his journeys or those of foreign travellers. He procured oxen and horses for us, and provided us with every help; indeed, we were most agreeably surprised at the welcome and attention we received on first entering this very far-away corner of the Celestial Empire.

During our stay at the karaul we explored the neighbourhood. Price and I moved up the valley of the Saklia (or Saglik) and once again reached the watershed of the Tannu-ola. The Saklia is typical of the valleys which drain the Southern Tannu-ola; its floor is wide and of a very gentle gradient.[1] We travelled up it for twenty miles, from Bodkhon-Khalat to the summit of the pass, without realizing that we were rising from 5,000 ft. to 8,000 ft. The pass at the head of the

[1] The actual valley of the Saklia gave evidence of the peculiar conditions under which the drainage from the mountain reaches the plain. The upper portion of the Saklia has many tributaries entering it from the Tannu-ola, yet none of these affluents reach the main river above ground; all disappear below the surface on leaving the hills. The valley is composed of wide skrees on the north side, and the river runs close under the hills which border it on the south. In its lower portion the reverse is the case. No streams enter from the north, but many do from the Saklia range on its south. The *south* side of the valley is therefore composed of giant skrees which show where the drainage is, but no water flows visibly above ground. Where the valley widens out and loses itself in open steppe the water of the main river gradually disappears below the surface, to appear again on reaching the "water-table" of the Ubsa basin. A line of trees showed the main course of the drainage, but the line was not continuous as it would have been had the flow of water been unbroken.

valley which led over into an upper tributary of the Kemchik divided the Tannu-ola from the Saklia Range. The passage over the divide here was even easier than that of the Borashay Pass. A five-mile-wide break consisting of smooth, rounded, grassy hills lay between the two ranges. There were no natural difficulties on the south side; but we noted that the descent on the north was very much steeper and more sudden, and led into a wild-looking hill-country, which might prove difficult to negotiate with pack-animals. We climbed to 10,000 ft. on the west side of the pass, and noted that at its western end the Tannu-ola kept its typical character of flat-topped summits and terraced flanks; but the Saklia Range to our south was of great contrast, for its rough, jagged peaks and deep-cut valleys, proved it to be a range of very different formation and age.

Miller, who had gone off into the southern part of this range, afterwards claimed it to be the roughest country he had ever been in, and this,—after his previous experiences in the most difficult valleys of the Tian Shan Mountains,—shows that the Saklia Range is evidently geologically separate from the Tannu-ola. A change in the fauna was also recorded, for Miller saw herds of ibex and many snow-cock during his preliminary survey of the range,—two forms we had not hitherto come across. This region, too, is a former haunt of the Mongolian wild-sheep, but it is probable they do not exist here at the present day, having been driven out of the lower country by the innumerable domestic herds and their owners. We saw the first derelict horns of *Ovis ammon* near the base of the Borashay Pass,—that locality standing as their most north-easterly limit.

The upper half of the Saklia Valley belongs to Uriankhai of the Kemchik tribe, and about there we found them quite numerous. The grazing is good, and large flocks of sheep and goats, a few horses and cattle, but no camels, were herded by their owners, who appeared to differ in no way from the Mongols of the lower part of the valley. The Saklia Valley must always have been a desirable locality, judging by the abundance of old grave-mounds which adorned the whole length of the valley above the karaul. Some were of peculiar shape and remarkable size. Stone-circles, with a diameter of 60 yards, surrounded central mounds, cobbled with smooth round stones; others were square in shape, but these were rare, the most numerous being the ordinary cobbled mound of rather small dimensions. These, it will be noted, were of quite a different pattern to the giant earthen tumuli of the Minnusinsk steppe, with their addition of upright stone slabs, and belonged probably to a period when the Mongolians, and not the Uriankhai, held the upper Saklia Valley.

On August 10th we were all back at our camp near the karaul, and preparing our plans for the future. We had arranged our journey thus far with no other object than to accomplish our work of exploration and investigation in the country of the Uriankhai. Now that we were beyond the limits of their territory, we found ourselves faced by an altogether unexpected extent of Mongolia, which offered so much of interest, and so large a scope for useful work that we scarcely knew which way to turn. We had made no plans beyond that of our original itinerary, that we should traverse the north-western plateau of Outer Mongolia from the Upper Yenisei basin to the Great Altai, and should eventually cross that range of mountains into the lowlands of Dzungaria. We had but little knowledge of the region or its conditions; so we did not predetermine our line of march, and rather decided on taking action according to circumstances which might arise.

Miller arrived back from his excursion to the Saklia Range, with glowing accounts of a high snow-range far to the south, which he had caught sight of from the summit of a peak he had climbed. Later on, when we moved the entire caravan over the rolling uplands to the south, and crossed a ridge out of the Ubsa basin into that of Uriu Nor, we, too, saw this range; and the beauty of its pinnacles, its glaciers, and ice-capped summits, caused us to turn our Mongol horsemen, and head over the downlands in that direction. The first sight of those eternal snows stirred us to a pitch of enthusiasm never experienced before, and aroused in us that "swift home-sickness for the world above the snow-line," which forced us to put aside any other thought beyond the longing to stand aloft and overlook Mongolia. Thus, by chance, we made the acquaintance of the Turgun or Kundelun group,[1] a mountain-mass of peculiar charm, holding an unique position on the Mongo-

[1] The nomenclature of the Turgun group and its principal peaks is somewhat undecided. The Russian "40-verst" map—the standard map of the region up to the date of our surveys—gives Turgun as the name of the principal northern summit, and Kharkir for the southern, but no name for the mountain-group as a whole. The Durbets themselves call the locality in general "Tszouselan," which signifies summer-resort, and refer to the highlands as "Mengou-tsason," or Eternal Snows. The principal rivers are named after the highlands they drain, viz. Kharkir and Turgun. Turgun, however, is the name for only the highest tributary, the remainder of the drainage being called Kundelun, after the Kuria named "Kunde." This is probably the largest valley in the range, and one of the most important on account of it being the residence of the Dalai Khan and the religious community. We have therefore adopted the name Kundelun as a secondary title for the range, and given it to one of the previously unnamed peaks.

lian plateau, and of surpassing interest, principally on account of it being the summer home of the Durbets,[1] a typical Mongol tribe.

On August 11th we started to journey southwards across steppe-country, alternated by well-pastured hills, until, on the evening of the third day, our straggling caravan of horses and oxen descended into a rich, well-watered, and beautifully green valley, the Kundelun, which led up through the larch-forests to the glittering snow-fields and towering peaks of the Turgun Mountains. At the point where the river leaves a steep-sided, narrow mountain-valley, there was situated a large Kuria, called Kunde-Kuria, with its annexe of lamaseries. Below this, where the valley widened into a broad meadow-land, were pitched the great white-felt tents of the Dalai Khan, or "Great Chief," hereditary prince of the Durbet tribe. The large number of yurts, the herds of yaks, horses, and sheep denoted a considerable population. Also, as is generally the case where a large population exists to-day, there were to be seen the traces of ancient occupation. The presence of burial-mounds of most pretentious size and stone effigies of long-dead Mongol chiefs adorned this part of the Kundelun Valley, and showed that for many ages it had been an important summer-resort.

The surroundings were certainly of exceptional beauty and charm. Encampments of nomads dotted the grassy swards beside the clear white glacier-streams, which flowed fast over rocky beds. Hills of short-cropped sheep-pasture led up to forested slopes, broken and

[1] The name is spelt by different writers Darbet, Dorbot, or Durbets. They belong to the western branch of the Mongols, and originally formed a part of a single tribe which included the Dzungars and Khoits, for which confederation the collective name was Choros.

rent by narrow valleys giving the traveller enticing glimpses of regions of rock and snow beyond. Flocks and herds, hurrying horsemen, and lamas "on tour" gave an air of life and importance to the Kundelun Valley. The beauty of our surroundings, the air of 6,000 ft. above sea-level, the presence of a typical tribe of the once-powerful Mongols—the remnant of a race who once terrified the Western world—stimulated our imagination, and aroused in us an ambition to investigate the problems which our surroundings suggested.

The usual courtesies were exchanged with the Dalai Khan. Mounted messengers passed and repassed between our camp beside the river and the white-domed yurt of the chief. The first deputation brought blue silk handkerchiefs [1]—as a sign of esteem—with inquiries as to who we were and what we had to sell. The only strangers who visited these regions,—that they had knowledge of or dealings with,—were the Siberian traders, who annually make a circuit of the Mongol encampments to barter Russian goods for hides, wool, and furs. Their surprise was great when we told them that we were not Russian, and had nothing to sell. We "came from a land the other side of Siberia and beyond Russia, from an island in the sea," and this we could only explain to them by comparing our home to that of the Japanese, of whom they had knowledge. They grew doubtful, however, when we said we were not the subjects of the Czar; they could not believe this, for all men who were not Chinese—all men who were white—must be Russian.

[1] These finely woven pieces of blue silk, called "hattaks," are in use throughout Mongolia as value-units. They are used for presents and the decoration of holy pictures; it is also customary for a Mongol, when making a request to a high official, to present, first of all, one of these hattaks.

Turgun Peak.
Highest point of Range.

THE CENTRAL GROUP OF THE TURGUN ALPINE REGION.

Kundelun Peak (2).

Kundelun Peak.

268a]

Kuudelun Peak. SURVEYING AT 10,500 FT. IN THE TURGUN RANGE. Yamachu Range.

These Mongols never grasped who we were, but certain lamas farther west who knew of recent affairs in Lhasa and the flight of the Dalai Lama to India, recognized the "Inglis"—the rulers of Hindustan—and immediately besieged us with questions as to where the Dalai Lama actually was, and whether he was going to return to Tibet. Religion can have the very greatest influence in widening the ideas of men. The lamas alone were aware of the existence of any other countries besides Mongolia, and even their worldly knowledge extended no further than to Lhasa and Urga. In this connexion, when we first came across Mussulman nomad-tribes in North-west Mongolia, we found that most of the knowledge they possessed of the outside world was entirely owing to the spirit of zeal in which they undertook their pilgrimage to Mecca. The old "hadjis" whom we met had some knowledge of the English, but had no idea of the whereabouts of our native country, except that it was "beyond Stambul westwards"!

The Dalai Khan of the Durbets was ill during our stay near his abode. At first we thought this was merely an excuse to avoid the trouble of paying and receiving visits, but we soon found out it was only too true. The lamaseries turned out in full strength to try and charm away the sickness; lamas were coming and going all day long between the temples and the chief's tent, and the sound of their doleful chanting was wafted to us across the meadows. Thus, we never saw the Khan; and much to our regret, for he was a rare type of an hereditary prince of ancient stock, claiming direct descent from Jenghis Khan himself.

One evening two of his sons visited us, giving us thereby an idea of the appearance of a Mongol of good birth. After our dealings with the riff-raff of the herdsmen, with rough soldiers and with primitive hunters, we had grown accustomed to the idea that all Mongols were heavily built, rough, ill-mannered, ugly to look upon, and with leathery faces; but these two Mongol gentlemen astonished us by their indefinable look of breeding and by their charm of manner. Of average height, and lightly built, with clean, sharp-cut features, a soft, dark, olive skin and small hands, they showed a marked contrast to their retainers. They had the refined air, the politeness of manner, and courteous style, which belongs only to those Mongols who are accustomed to rule. They investigated our belongings, were most interested in our writings and in our cameras, and we parted the best of friends. There is still "spirit" left in the Mongols, judging by these two men of good birth; they, at any rate, gave us no impression of decay or deterioration. Turned into the right channels, the Mongol Khans could wield great power to good effect. Even now the tide is turning, and when the nomads have realized their strength and regained their self-reliance, they may also regain their independence.

We have before mentioned the Kuria and the population of lamas which helped to make the religious element so marked; in proportion to the population this element was very much more numerous and pronounced than amongst the Uriankhai of the Yenesei basin. Lamaism, with its accompanying evils, creates a problem of unusual interest in connexion with the Mongols; and the information given in the next chapter, as to the effect it has had upon the race in the past, will go far to explain the present state of the Mongols under its influence.

The Kuria was a large, gaudily painted, wooden building of partly Chinese, partly Russian design, surrounded by a high stockade of larch-poles. Around it were grouped six other temples, numerous buildings, and innumerable palisaded enclosures, within which were pitched ordinary yurts, as dwelling-places for the lamas; for the Mongol always prefers his felt tent, even when living a sedentary life in a settled abode. Besides these sacred precincts there were a few houses belonging to the Chinese merchants, who carried on a lively business amongst the tribesmen, in clothing, pipes, snuff, tea, tobacco, and ornaments for their women-folk. In close proximity was the palace of the Dalai Khan, a brick-built dwelling of Chinese architecture. The chief, however, never uses it, for he prefers tent-life; but it is said to be full of old books, armour, ointments, and *treasure!*

Well away from the unsavoury quarters belonging to the lamas,—for when nomads take to sedentary life, cleanliness does not exist, and ideas of sanitation are *nil*,—we found the yurts of a Russian trader. He and his wife lived a curious existence, moving about from encampment to encampment, but becoming resident during the summer months near to the main summer quarters of the tribe, and trading with all the Mongols with whom they came in contact. In winter they return to Biisk in the Siberian Altai, in order to replenish their supply of trade goods and to transport their gain, in the shape of hides, wool, and furs to the Siberian markets. We found their yurts to be half-full of marmot-skins, which seem to represent the chief prey of the Mongol hunters.

Although the Khan of the tribe was ill and could not entertain us, yet he set aside men for our service, and liberally provided us with all the transport we needed.

Numerous presents passed between us. Sheep were of no value here, and as they used to arrive daily as presents, we always had a few attached to our caravan awaiting their fate. A Mongol saddle was amongst the presents he sent to us, on which saddle I rode all the way to Kashmir; whilst details which figured largely amongst our gifts to him were rolls of silk, blue velvet, bottles of brandy, and coloured beads.

The region in which we now found ourselves, was characteristic of Northern Mongolia, while the Turgun highlands were a typical summer-resort of a Mongol tribe. North-western Mongolia, of which, politically, this district forms a part, is divided into tribal areas, of which there are about thirty-eight, all of which belong to, and are still under the direct rule of, independent hereditary Khans. China holds suzerainty over the whole,[1] and an especially appointed official of military rank, resident at Uliassutai acts as intermediary between the Khans and the Emperor of China.[2] The Durbet clan is one of the thirty-eight, they claim an important and rich area of considerable size, and their Khan has the prefix of Dalai, which denotes that the tribe is of greater importance than the usual run of Mongol tribes.

According to Vladimirtsoff,—a Russian traveller who visited the Durbets in 1908,—the Durbet tribe is divided

[1] All statements concerning the political and administrative affairs of Mongolia, in this chapter, can be taken as reliable only up till the end of 1911.

[2] Outer Mongolia is divided into two administrative divisions. At Urga there resides a Chinese Imperial Agent, who rules over the eastern division of the Kalkha tribes, whilst at Uliassutai a military Governor (or Tzian-tziun) controls the affairs of the western Kalkhas, which includes these thirty-eight tribal divisions of Mongols and the Uriankhai people. The entire administration of Outer Mongolia is under the supreme control of the Mongolian Superintendency at Pekin.

into six "Khosuns," or administrative divisions, each division being governed by an hereditary prince of different title and rank. The first in order is the Dalai Khan, who rules the whole of the western portion of the Durbet country. The second division is under the Wang, who controls the eastern portion. Below these are four other minor chiefs. The old reigning family is now extinct, the contemporary Khan being an adopted son of the last of the line of hereditary Dalai Khans. However, he possesses the full title and rights of precedence and has six sons to carry on the duties of ruling chiefs.

Roughly speaking, the Durbets own about 16,000 square miles of country, which composes a region particularly favourable to nomadic life, and is in consequence more than usually well populated. Their territory stretches from Lake Ubsa to the Little Altai Mountains and includes the whole of the Turgun group, together with the Barmen Mountains and southern edge of the Sailugem Range, besides the intervening plains and plateaux. On the north, the line of Mongol karauls denotes where their land marches with that of the Uriankhai, and on the south the Upper Kobdo River and Kirghiz Nor roughly define the limits of the Durbet tribe. The whole of Lake Ubsa is included within their boundaries, as well as Uriu and Achit Nor. Of this area one-third—the western portion—which includes the Achit Nor basin, and half the Turgun Mountain group, belongs to the Dalai Khan, whilst the remaining two-thirds—the eastern portion—including the eastern flanks of the Turgun and the Ubsa basin, is under the rule of the Wang. The Dalai Khan resides in the Kundelun Valley, his winter quarters being in the above-mentioned settlement of

Kunde-Kuria, and in summer he lives in the neighbouring valley. The Wang uses his residence in Ulankom during the winter and moves in summer up into the Kharkir Valley, the main drainage of the eastern side of the range.

Thus the country of the Durbets is divided into two main divisions. We ourselves only visited the territory of the Dalai Khan, and had no dealings whatever with the Wang. In order to make the description of the Durbet country complete, I have included details of the Wang's district, most of my information having been sought out of Potanin's works and from the recent observations of Vladimirtsoff.

The Durbets' territory shows much contrast both in climate and in physical conditions. The tribesmen enjoy, by their close proximity to the low-lying Ubsa and Kirghiz Nor basins, most favourably situated winter resorts. Ulankom, a small settlement on the south-west of the Ubsa Nor, is the main winter resort of subjects of the Wang, and, being on the direct route between Kobdo and the Yenisei region in Siberia, has additional importance due to the passing of a certain amount of traffic. Ulankom, according to all accounts—for we did not visit it—is an important centre of trade of the whole of the Ubsa basin, which includes the well-populated valley of the Tess, as well as the Durbet encampments. It lies in a region which supports a considerable nomadic population, and it has no rival trading-posts nearer than Kobdo or Uliassutai. Ulankom is therefore of economic importance, which importance might immeasurably increase, if the trade-route connecting it with the Yenisei province, by way of the Kemchik and Abakan Valleys, were improved and opened up for the use of enterprising traders. Potanin remarks that it possesses one of the

HERD OF YAKS IN THE TURGUN MOUNTAINS.

largest cemeteries of old tombs and burial-mounds in Mongolia, proving that this locality must always have been a centre of Mongol life.

At the present day Ulankom is the haunt of a few Chinese and Russian traders as well as of the Durbet population, which is larger in winter than it is in summer, for the nomads in winter concentrate on the low, and comparatively warm, shores of Lake Ubsa, where the saline pasture affords winter fodder for their herds. The presence of the houses belonging to these traders, and the residence of the Durbet Wang—a house built on Chinese lines—raises Ulankom to the station of a town in the eyes of the tent-dwelling nomads. There is plenty of water, for the drainage of the glaciers and snow-fields of the Turgun, which sinks below the surface of the ground on leaving the mountains, at this point oozes up and forms fine meadows and marsh-lands. A small amount of cultivation is practised, wheat and oats being grown; but the nomads find it more profitable, on account of the saline nature of the soil, to use the pastures for fattening their great flocks of sheep.

The Durbets are equally well off in regard to their summer pastures, their territory including the famous Turgun Mountains, whose thousands of square miles of grassy downs, forested valleys, and luxuriant alpine pastures form an ideal summer resort for the nomads and their flocks. The cool uplands are a refuge for their horses from the annoyance of fly-pests, while at the same time supplying the most nourishing grass; here wander the herds of yaks which cannot endure the heat, and from the appearance of which we judged the locality to be eminently suitable to these strange beasts, which in these mountains practically reach the extreme northern limit of their range.[1] Here, too, great flocks of sheep,—the main source of wealth to the Mongols,—thrive and produce excellent wool.

The Durbets should be well satisfied with the territory allotted to them. Plain and plateau were alike at their disposal. Beyond the Turgun Mountains to the west their territory stretches for a hundred miles, the greater part of this region being a nomads' land, suitable for pasturing unlimited herds. There are rivers, lakes, and sheltered valleys giving most welcome refuge from the bitter winds and driven snows. And last, but not least important, the Durbet territory lies on the main road between Mongolia and Siberia, and consequently the Durbets find an easier outlet for their wealth than do the tribes of more remote regions.

The Turgun Mountains, the real home of the tribe, are the principal feature of North-western Mongolia. With superb grandeur the snow pinnacles rise above the forested valleys and grassy plateaux. From every point of the compass, for many days' journey away, one can

[1] Yaks (*Bos grunniens*), according to Klementz, are the only domesticated animals owned by the Darkat tribe of the region of Lake Kossogol. This, then, would be actually the most northerly extent of their range. They are not found within the basin of the Upper Yenisei. Their habitat in these Mongolian mountains is quite isolated and cut off from other haunts of the yak throughout Central Asia. They are to be found in the Turgun group and in the Eastern Altai. We next come across them in the Karlik Tagh Mountains at the extreme eastern end of the Tian Shan system, a locality separated from the Turgun Mountains by five hundred miles of steppe and desert. Here there were only small numbers to be seen, and we did not notice them in any quantity until reaching their true home in Little Tibet. To our knowledge there are no wild yaks anywhere in Mongolia. It is of interest to note that the early travellers, Rubruck and Carpini, made no mention of the yak in Mongolia, but Rubruck described them, by hearsay, as existing in the Tangut country, to the north-east of Tibet, where the "Moul" (Mongols) used them for drawing their big dwellings on carts.

see the principal peak, a cone of ice, which rises to over 13,000 ft. in altitude. For several weeks of continuous surveying, I kept this peak as a fixed point on my plane-table sheets; it was nearly always within view, and never failed to help me over my difficulties. From the highlands one can gaze over illimitable spaces and hold within one's view three separate, self-contained basins—those represented by the lakes of Uriu, Achit and Ubsa. The Turgun Range, indeed, forms a part of the watershed between these three basins, and its snows drain, in even proportion, into the basins of Ubsa and Kobdo. Ubsa lies like a turquoise sea in an ochre-coloured steppe,—a typical desert lake,—yet supporting on its shores a considerable population at certain seasons of the year. Uriu Nor, a comparatively small basin, is tucked away under the rugged and steep slopes of the Saklia Range to the north-west, whilst Achit Nor is a plateau-lake at an altitude of 4,600 ft., and drains southwards by way of the Kobdo River to its last home in the Kirghiz Nor.

The Turgun group covers roughly 3,500 square miles, that is to say, about one-fifth of the territory of the Durbets. Orographically the mountain mass is connected with the Sailugem portion of the Altai system by a plateau-like range called the Barmen, and by a lower downland with the Saklia Range. To the southwards its foot-hills run out and merge into the featureless, rolling plateau-country which extends for some hundred miles to the Great Altai. As a snow-capped mountain of alpine character, the Turgun stands solitary, rising sharply above the steppes and the desert-ranges which surround it on all sides.

The importance of these mountains as being the home of the Durbet tribe, and also, no doubt, their attractiveness, have caused them to be visited by more than one explorer. No Englishman, except Atkinson,—who, by the way, never mentions them,—has even set eyes on these untrodden snow-fields, and none have ever peeped into the beautiful valleys which lie below. Russian travellers have reconnoitred this region and given us a general impression of the physiography of the Turgun Range, but only one, so far as I can ascertain, has made any attempt to scale its peaks, or even to penetrate into its upper valleys. This was Potanin, whose labours at exploration have already been noticed and commented on, in the Introduction to this work. Between the years 1876–9 Potanin seems to have repeatedly visited the Turgun Range or its neighbourhood. He gives most detailed descriptions of every day's work, but he fails to generalize or to describe the range and its inhabitants with any thoroughness. Potanin's labours lay entirely on the eastern flanks of the range in the valley of Kharkir; consequently the western and southern portions of the range remained unknown. Other travellers to the Turgun have merely followed in Potanin's footsteps, and our previous knowledge of this region resulted only from his work, or that of his subordinates. The west or south-west portion of this range doubly demanded our observation and attention, and in the pleasant valley of Kundelun, we prepared a plan of work which included an exploration of the highlands at the sources of the Kundelun and the Turgun Rivers, and of all the western side of the range which drains into Achit Nor.

Our request for transport was acknowledged by the Dalai Khan by the deputing of an official, specially authorized to look after us and to provide us with all

TRANSPORT BY OXEN.

A CHANGE OF TRANSPORT-ANIMALS

we needed. A demand for a dozen oxen was promptly answered by the arrival of the animals, as well as of several riding-horses and innumerable Mongol henchmen. The word of this "King's Messenger" was law throughout the land. He wore the hat of a Chinese official, as a mark of his rank, and to show that he was on his Khan's special business. If he needed to hand over the management of our affairs to another he merely exchanged hats! Whoever wore the hat was in command, and could demand food and lodging wherever he went. No doubt they made full use of the scope thus provided for making good any debts owed to them, and for having a good time in general!

This supply of free transport across Mongolia was quite unexpected, and we nearly gave ourselves away by trying to bargain for the cost of hire, thereby showing that we did not demand it as a right. We soon discovered that the custom of the country entitled us, as strangers, to full use of all beasts of burden. How else could travellers proceed at all in such a land of distance, where horses are more numerous than people, and where one asks for the loan of a horse as we, at home, would ask for a match? Moreover, the provision of transport is demanded as a tax from the natives by the Chinese rulers. Any man may be called upon to supply horses, oxen, or camels to help transport the officials and their retinues to the next encampment, where another change is made, or the animals belonging to that particular locality are again turned to account.

Our passports from Pekin entitled us to travel as Chinese officials, and we were treated with all respect. By the help of a few useful presents to the head-men, we had free service of innumerable men and horses. The

Dalai Khan ordered men to go with us as far as the limits of his territory, and these men, in turn, found other men and horses for us. We merely had to ask for so many horses, camels, or oxen, and they were immediately forthcoming. Two head-men usually accompanied us, who had six or eight men under them. The Khan's word was law, his messengers had precedence over all that came in their way. One head-man generally went in advance to arrange for the necessary number of men and animals to be ready for us at the next encampment; for the Mongol never passes an encampment without changing horses. By the use of innumerable horses he can make greater speed, and avoid tiring out any particular animal.

The one idea of the nomads was to convey us as quickly as possible to the next encampment, and thus get rid of us. We travelled almost too quickly at times, for we had scarcely time to rest. Relays of horses took us from place to place at the greatest possible speed. We never knew from whence our relays appeared. The lonely plateau would suddenly discover a group of camels and horses, our jaded caravan would stop and unload, and within half an hour the fresh lot would be on the move. We used to get into camp late in the evening, with a tired caravan; during the night fresh horses and men would arrive, and in the morning we trekked on again without delay. All appeared as if by magic; often for many days' journey we saw no yurts nor herds, nor any sign of habitation. We sometimes counted twenty or twenty-five Mongols around our camp; they came and went, there was never a request for money. It was the Khan's pleasure that we should see his country, and we traversed Mongolia like princes.

Nor, indeed, would these hardy nomads have appreciated money, nor troubled to supply transport for remuneration. They had no need of silver or gold, and scarcely knew the value of money. As serfs they lived their lives under a feudal system, without ambition or desire for gain. Silver roubles were nothing to them, except as ornaments for their wives, and the faces of these rough Mongol cavaliers only broadened into smiles of appreciation when we offered them chunks of brick-tea at the end of a long day's journey.

We set out from Kunde-Kuria on August 15th to explore the upper portions of the Kundelun Valley and the peaks at its head-waters. The lower foot-hills of the range were a beautiful contrast of grassy downs and forested slopes. Nomads "tented" here in good numbers, and their herds found the very best nourishment in the luxuriant valleys. The forest-belt was not wide, and existed only on the flanks facing north.

After making a base-camp at forest-limit, we loaded up horses with firewood, and, moving up still higher, camped at an altitude of 8,300 ft. at the base of the terminal moraine of the glaciers. This we considered to be the main source of the Kundelun River, as the valley corresponded to that named Turgun by the Russian explorer Potanin, and we imagined the Turgun peak, the culminating point of the range, to be at the head of the valley. There were so many peaks of apparently equal height at the head of the valley, that it was difficult to decide which deserved the name of Turgun. We afterwards found that the highest peak of the group was not by any means the most conspicuous, and that it did *not* drain into the Turgun Valley, so, as we presume the name of Turgun was applied to the culminating point, we leave it thus, in deference to that great explorer, and have named the other peaks independently. All the peaks at the head-waters of the Kundelun River were new to the maps; in fact, the whole alpine region of the Turgun needed remapping.

We spent the next three days exploring the glaciers and peaks at the sources of the Turgun. We found that we had steered a true course towards the most conspicuous, if not the highest, peak of the range,—a peak which had caught our eyes from afar, on account of its summit being almost the shape of a pyramid. A nearer view showed us that this peak was one of the highest in the range, and formed one end of a semicircle of snow-summits which surrounded the sources of the Turgun River. We had set our hearts on climbing this peak, but after three days in its vicinity and careful reconnoitring of all its flanks both from here and again from its south side, we found its ice-cap to be impregnable to any but the most skilful alpinists. Indeed, we think the most experienced climber would find his match in the wonderful ice-cap which covers the top of this peak, which we have called Kundelun, from the name of the main valley which drains from it.

We spent some days on the two glaciers which form the source of the Turgun, and from a point of vantage on the peak named Kundelun we gazed down on to the glacier at the source of a tributary of the Kharkir, which is probably the largest in the range. At the bend of this glacier is the highest peak, Turgun, and we named the glacier after it. The longest glacier we estimated as being about three miles in length. The two glaciers which formed the source of the Turgun River were respectively two miles and a mile and a half in length,

PEAK KUNDELUN IN THE TURGUN HIGHLANDS.

282]

and about half a mile in breadth. Both were in a process of retreat. The present snout of the one that descends from the Kundelun Peak was a mile above the end of its terminal moraine. In altitude the foot of this glacier was 9,758 ft. above the sea-level and descended about 1,000 ft. below snow-line. The surface of the glacier was mostly smooth, but that of the Eastern Kundelun glacier was broken up at its base into fantastic seracs.

During our excursion we reached the top of the Eastern Kundelun glacier, and found ourselves on a narrow, knife-like edge,—the watershed between the Kundelun, Kharkir, and Enderti river-systems. This was the very centre of the range. Here we were surrounded by a world of snow-peaks, of which six were remarkable for their height; but all were outrivalled by the special and peculiar beauty of the Kundelun Peak.

Many interesting but arduous days we spent in climbing and mapping in these alpine regions. From our camp at the foot of the moraine we made excursions in every direction. Generally we had to go alone, for our Mongol horsemen were not at all at home on the ice and snow, nor indeed could they go where their horses failed them, owing to their ungainly walk and their big, long boots. So with ruck-sack, food, cameras, and instruments, we covered as much of the high country as possible by the simple means of long days on foot, and in spite of bad weather we were well repaid for our labours. The great extent of country above snow-line and the very considerable glaciation of the range, misled us as to its altitude. After careful work and the taking of many hypsometric readings for altitude, and the clynometer readings of those peaks of which we could not reach the summit, we found that the culminating point of the group reached no more than 13,350 ft. above sea-level, whilst there were many peaks averaging 12,500 ft. Thus, in comparison to its height, the Turgun group presents a remarkable exhibition of alpine characteristics. At first we were at a loss to explain a cause, but after our experiences in the Turgun Valley it was made clear to us. The great precipitation of snow which makes the Turgun so fine a sight is due indirectly to the position of the range over the Ubsa basin. Peculiar climatic conditions result from this, which cause cloudy weather during the summer months, thus preserving the snow from melting.

During our residence in August on the Turgun Range we were repeatedly hampered in our work by bad weather. Many consecutive days were so overcast and cloudy that climbing was difficult, and photography was out of the question. August was evidently a month of very unsettled climatic conditions; rain fell occasionally, but dull, cloudy weather was more common, and this completely wrapt in mist the whole area above 8,000 ft. for days at a time. When reading up Potanin's accounts I found that he made special reference to the same phenomenon prevailing in June and July; thus it is reasonable to suppose that the same cloudy weather which we experienced continues throughout the summer months. Potanin was on the plain at the east side of the range, and in the Kharkir Valley, during June and July and for twenty-three days between June 27th and July 19th he recorded the meteorology. The result was that, out of these twenty-three days, seven were fine but cloudy, and sixteen were cloudy with rain, there were eleven thunderstorms, and twice it hailed. He remarked on the low temperatures. An average midday temperature was 74° Fahr., whilst at nine in the evening it dropped to 43° Fahr. No doubt, with this temperature, the hail and rain of the plain fell as snow at 12,000 to 14,000 ft. on the Turgun highlands. Clouds and mist are the greatest preservatives of snow and ice; a summer season, such as the Turgun experiences according to both Potanin's and our own records, is all that is needed to make the alpine zone of the range remarkable for its excessive quantity of snow and glaciation.

This is one direct cause for the preservation of the alpine character of the Turgun Mountains; but, on looking further, we find that the position of the mountain over the Ubsa basin is the true cause of this peculiar summer climate, and indirectly responsible for the precipitation and preservation of the snow. The Ubsa basin is the lowest part of North-west Mongolia, the lake stands at an altitude of 2,370 ft., and the basin presents the appearance of a low, hot depression in the high, cold plateau-land which surrounds it. The Turgun stands up, overlooking the depression, at a distance of about sixty miles from the lake-shore. The close proximity of the high, cool alpine region to the hot depression is a probable cause of the frequent storms and of the cloudy weather. There is a similar example in the case of the Bogdo-ola Mountains and of the low depression of Turgun, where the same peculiar climatic phenomenon has been noticed. The hot air of the Ubsa basin rises and condenses on the cool Turgun highlands, where consequently, throughout all summer, clouds and mist hang and drift, preserving the unrivalled snow-fields and ice-peaks, adding to the beauty of the land of the

Durbets, and indirectly giving them a more than usual abundance of pasture.[1]

After mapping all the country that we could reach from our camp in the Upper Turgun Valley, we travelled slowly round the range to the west, and finally to the south, until we reached the valleys which drain the western portion of the range into the Achit Nor basin. This took us over a pass of 8,700 ft., which divided the Turgun from the Enderti waters ; here we encamped for two days at a high altitude on the south side of the Barmen Range, to make more certain of our surveys, and to allow time for a hasty visit to the Uriu Nor. Price undertook this lateral expedition, and returned after a trying experience of two days in the open without shelter, during which time bitter cold and a blizzard from the north showed us what Mongolia can be like in August.

Price's visit to Uriu Nor was of value, and his observations on the levels of the lake coincided with those we had made at a little isolated lake-basin in the plateau-region to the east of that lake. Many old strands indicated previous water-levels up to thirty feet above the present level of the lakes, and showed that these basins in North-west Mongolia are in the same state of fluctuation as are all other self-contained inland drainages throughout Inner Asia. These are the rain-gauges which testify of days when a moister and cooler climate

[1] The whole of Northern Mongolia is subject to severe weather even in summer. The earliest travellers remarked on this. Carpini, who visited this region early in the thirteenth century, remarks : "The ayre also in that country is verie intemperate. For in the midst of sommer there be great thunders and lightnings, by the which many men be slaine and at the same time there talleth great abundance of snowe. There be also such mighty tempests of colde windes that sometimes men are not able to sitte on horsebacke."

filled the basins to a higher water-level and also covered the land with better and more reliable pastures. Around Uriu Nor Price found no nomads, no trace even of a present-day occupation, and little in the way of pasture to attract them in this direction. Yet old burial-mounds and monoliths proved, that once people must have been numerous enough in this locality. The water of Uriu Nor is fresh, and is inhabited by quantities of fish which attract innumerable birds, such as gulls, terns, and cormorants.

From our camp on the south side of the Barmen Range, we sent the main caravan to await our arrival on the shores of Achit Nor, whilst we, with a light caravan and a few Mongols, explored the western side of the Turgun. One valley alone gave us access to the highlands from the west, and this was Yamachu, a tributary of the Enderti, which eventually flows into Achit Nor. This was a fine, open valley, with wide, shingly river-bed, but without a great flow of water. Bare, grassy hills bordered it, and a narrow zone of larch forest clung to the side of the valley facing north. On the second day, reaching the limit of grass and fuel, we found ourselves beneath the inaccessible Kundelun Peak, and we encamped a mile below the moraine of the Yamachu glacier. We had half expected that the Kundelun would be accessible from the south, but found that its southern face was a steep wall of rock, which dropped sheer on to the glacier. The Yamachu glacier was about three-quarters of a mile long, and filled a narrow gorge between the Kundelun and Yamachu peaks; it ended in a steep rock-wall and ice-cliff, which joined the two peaks at the head of the glacier. The cliffs bordering the glacier were accountable for the enormous accumulation of rocks and rubble on the ice, and the very large terminal moraine at its snout.

On climbing over the ridge bordering the valley on its south, we discovered a beautiful contrast in the sight presented to our view by a rolling grassy plateau which lay beyond. Our work grew as we advanced; new geographical features rose before us, and demanded our attention, and long days with the plane-table had ample reward.

The exploration of the Turgun leaves in my mind the remembrance of some of the hardest work I have ever accomplished. The continual keeping up of a plane-table survey is no light labour in itself. So large an area of unknown country, presenting the explorer with a vaster area to map than he could possibly accomplish, bred in me an insatiable desire which, of course, could never be gratified and therefore intensified the strain of continuous labour. There was no end, no relief, no hope of achievement; no matter how much I did, there was still more to do. The extraordinary charm of plane-tabling in an open country, with immense views and the best of instruments, increased the already great desire to go on and on. The keeping up of a continuous survey as we moved was merely a detail of the day's work. There were altitudes to record, notes to write, photographs to be taken, besides the successful collecting of birds, the trapping of small mammals, all of which had to be skinned and preserved; after which I slept only if there were time left for such a luxury. Whilst working at high pressure on the Turgun, fifteen hours in the saddle or standing at the plane-table, seemed to be the ordinary day's work! With a mounted Mongol to carry the instruments, with a dog

ON THE YAMACHU PLATEAU.

and a collecting-gun, I made use of the precious moments, whilst moving from one plane-table station to another, by shooting all I saw in the bird-line.

On reaching camp there were all sorts of details concerning transport to be managed, and perhaps a Chief to be called upon, or servants to be despatched with presents. And then, after camp was quiet, and even the dogs were asleep, I used to start to prepare the results of my day's collecting, and, by the light of a flickering candle, birds and beasts were skinned, "made up," and packed away. All this would have been impossible, without the keenness of my companions to aid me in many branches of the work. For, although it is true that "if you give a man more work than he can do, he will do it," yet hard living, high altitude, and none too nourishing food, tell quickly when ambition drives one irresistibly forward. As it was, Miller kept up his survey with prismatic compass, took innumerable photographs, and hunted every beast he saw, whilst Price was continually employed at his botanical and geological work. I think we accomplished, whilst in the Turgun highlands, the maximum amount of work possible during the time at our disposal.

The Yamachu was one of the most beautiful spots we found in North-west Mongolia. Leagues of rolling country covered with rich, golden-yellow grass, dotted with blue patches denoting lakelets, lay untenanted and inviting around us. Beyond, to the southwards, was a new range, which we named after the plateau; to the east we had the background of the conical ice-capped Kundelun. The average height of the plateau was 8,200 ft., and it kept up its altitude until it suddenly dropped off in sharp escarpments to the Achit Nor plain.

Unnumbered lakes formed the homes of many wild-fowl, but the pastures still remained unused by man. So far as we could ascertain, the Yamachu plateau did not, for some unknown reason, attract the Durbet nomads, yet its pastures must be of the richest quality. The question naturally arises, Why are the Mongols decreasing when they own so good a land ? whatever the cause of Mongol decadence, it cannot be through lack of available territory.

From the Yamachu plateau we descended by steep and sudden declivities into the dry, barren plain of Achit Nor, and eventually arrived at the altitude where the water from the mountain percolates up through the ground, and marshes, meadows, and acacia-scrub make a suitable resort for the shepherds. We pitched our tents close to the lake. Within view was a scene characteristic of Northern Mongolia, the lake, teeming with bird-life, and alive with fish, was surrounded by marshy shores, where saline pastures afforded unlimited grazing for immense flocks of sheep and herds of two-humped Bactrian camels, there was a wealth of animal life as well as the presence of a numerous and hardy Mongol population. Beyond, was a zone of more barren steppe, leading up to the highlands where plateaux and valley-pastures abounded, where pleasant larch-forests gave protection from the cold in winter, and made a pleasing contrast of scenery in summer. Higher still were alpine pastures, and a world of rock and snow,—features in the scenery of Northern Mongolia which add to its beauty and mean much to the shepherds who are dependent on them for summer grazings.

There are great delusions about Mongolia. These descriptions of ours may seem exaggerated to the ordinary reader, whose idea of Mongolia is that of a hungry land, where men live in utmost poverty, and where camels and sand are the chief features of the landscape. We are not surprised if our impression of Mongolia seems optimistic, for the popular idea of this country is gained from the accounts of its southern borders, from descriptions of travellers who have only seen the barren frontiers which border on the Great Wall of China. Men who have crossed its inhospitable centre from Pekin to Urga have only seen a very small portion of the true Mongolia, where the ancient Mongols not only lived, and thrived, but increased in numbers and rose to power. Sir Francis Younghusband, who rode across a thousand miles of Mongolia, and traversed a region not very far south of the scene of our labours, was astonished at our descriptions of the pleasant regions of the north-west, with its mountains and forests and large tribes of nomads. Younghusband travelled only by camel through an almost unpopulated region, and never saw a tree during the course of his journey.

But ours is a new Mongolia. We present to our readers a land of wealth and beauty, a land occupied by great nomadic tribes, supporting immense herds, and peopled by a race who are still numerous, still have good qualities in spite of their decadence, and who may still some day become of account. Ours is a region of plain and plateau, mountain and lake, a pleasant country of pasture and forest, situated, not at the back of the world, as might be supposed, but in close proximity to Siberia, which is a land of growing importance, and one which will eventually affect the whole existence of Mongolia.

Mongolia is so vast in extent, and spreads over so many degrees of latitude, that its different portions come under many varied climatic conditions, and consequently its scenery is very contrastive. Broadly speaking, Mongolia can be divided into four zones. On the south is a zone which comes under the climatic influence of the Pacific, and in consequence is a pasture-land well named by the Chinese the "Land of high-grass." This zone was formerly Mongol, but is now rapidly becoming Chinese; instead of tenting nomads and innumerable flocks, there are now farmers and colonists, who are rapidly breaking the soil and building settlements, with the result that Southern Mongolia will soon be Chinese in all but name.

North of this zone is desert Mongolia,—the second zone generally called Gobi, or Shamo. The Chinese call this region Han-hai, which means "dry sea"; not a sea which has *dried up*, but a region as vast as the sea, which is rainless—desiccated. This barren, worthless region occupies only about one-quarter of the whole of Mongolia, yet its aridity and desert nature has often been applied to the land as a whole. The Gobi occupies the heart of Mongolia, and in character is a depression in the middle of the plateau. In its northern part it averages about 3,500 ft. in altitude, and is of a hard, strong surface; in the south it descends to its lowest altitude (2,400 ft.), and here there are large tracts of sands. The surrounding border-ranges intercept all rainfall, and the Gobi is left devoid of moisture and useless to man except in the spring months. Even in the driest localities pasture appears during the spring, and nomads may be found wandering over the worst zone of Mongolia and making good use of it.

The third zone of Mongolia lies along the northern edge of the Gobi, between the desert and the northern border-ranges. This is again a pasture-land, where the tribes find sufficient grazing to last all the year round, and this area merges imperceptibly into the fourth zone, that of Northern Mongolia, which borders on Siberia. Here the Mongolian plateau reaches its highest elevation, and here the land comes under the influence of the Siberian climate. The plateau is studded and broken by ranges of snow-capped mountains; in consequence summer rains are frequent, and there is no lack of pasture. Here are the forests of larch and spruce, the luxuriant meadows and the wealth of wild-flowers, the land of our descriptions. This is the true Mongolia, the primeval home of that race who, as nomad shepherds, left their native plateaux, rose to power, and eventually became a nation. It is here they built their capital, Karakorum, and it is in this zone that the only towns of Mongolia exist at the present day. Whatever the total population of Mongolia, it is probable that two-thirds of it reside in the northern zone, where the tribes live within their ancient boundaries, under the rule of their hereditary Khans, with ample good land at their disposal and ready markets at their doors. The importance of Siberia to Mongolia (and vice versa) is incalculable. Mongolia must have a future, must grow in importance as Siberia develops, and the Mongols may find themselves in a very much improved position.

This is the important zone of Mongolia, the zone which demands attention. For nearly eight hundred years it has been behind the scenes. The once-valiant Mongols have sunk from their high estate. Lama-ridden, and fleeced by the Chinese, the Mongols remain in a state of serfdom under their chiefs. But the tribes stir; there is discontent in the encampments; Mongolia has appeared again on the world's stage.

CHAPTER X

MONGOLIA, PAST AND PRESENT[1]

WE could not visit the ancient home of the great Mongol tribes, we could not ride all day in company with the rough Mongol cavaliers, and encamp at night in close proximity to the domed tents clustered like bee-hives on the open plateaux, without becoming intensely interested in all that concerned them. We saw them as they are, under the present conditions, we studied their character, their social conditions, their modes of government, and this study stirred the imagination and forced us to look far back into the past. We endeavoured to grasp a knowledge of their history, and, when a glimpse of their remarkable past was obtained, we could not refrain from trying to forecast the future of this mysterious race, for the whence and the whither of the Mongol peoples must be of absorbing interest to all students of Asiatic history and Eastern politics.

The story is concerned with a race of shepherd-warriors, who, suddenly realizing their power, " burst all link of habit," deserted their native steppes, and, conquering empire after empire, overran all Asia, then, with unsatisfied ambition, started to terrorize all Europe.

[1] This chapter has been added as a sequel to our experiences of Mongolia in 1910–11, before its severance from Manchu suzerainty. The subject is treated from a non-political aspect. I attempt to theorize only as to the effect this change may have on the Mongols themselves.

Such a story lives as a fact of unsurpassed and unparalleled achievement. Such an unaccountable migration is of the deepest significance. With what force were the nomads suddenly imbued? What strength of ambition compelled them to launch out into the world—the unknown world—which lay far beyond their desert fastnesses? Was it fanatical zeal, or discontent, lust of plunder, or a mere letting loose of a super-abundance of martial and adventurous spirit? Did the Mongols burst their boundaries because, owing to increase in population, they had to move forward and discover fresh lands; that is to say, did they desire more space, owing to excessive well-being and opulence? Or was the exact opposite the case? Were the Mongols driven to seek new lands through poverty and lack of substance? When the struggle for existence is severe, men become desperate, and, as poverty rather than plenty increases population, it is possible that the Mongols may have outstripped the means of subsistence and been forced to migrate. Such questions came to us as the red-coated Mongol horsemen rode near us during the day, and sat around the camp-fires with us at night. *They* could tell us nothing, they were unaware of their ancient greatness. Only the name Jenghis remained in their memory, and him they treated as a deity and spoke of with reverence.

The problem of the cause of the Mongol migrations claims close attention, and is in itself a subject demanding detailed and lengthened research. The exact cause of the eventual fall and decadence of the Mongols is, however, the special problem which, at this moment, chiefly influences us when we compare their past with their present. The same cause will, as far as can be judged, undoubtedly affect their future, and, in point of view of the recent disturbances amongst the Mongols and the possibility of a new autonomous Mongolia, the subject is of special interest.

We have only to judge of the condition of the Mongols at the zenith of their power, and to compare it with their present state, in order to bring forward a theory as to the cause of the change, and thereby to predict the effect on the future. By looking back into the past we shall see how greatly Mongolia impressed Europe in the thirteenth century, and we shall judge as to the extent of their downfall, by comparing with their greatness the condition in which we now find them. It is a knowledge of the past and the present that alone will aid us in arriving at some of the future possibilities of this remarkable race.

We, in Europe, scarcely realize the existence of the Mongols as a dominant factor in the world's history; it is difficult to believe that the Mongols once represented the greatest human force that Providence made use of, to kindle the dying West into new life. There is no doubt that such great movements, and the disturbances that follow in their wake, bring fresh virility and stimulus to countries sinking into a condition of lethargy, as instanced by China and Europe in those days. Nature realizes the necessity of periodically purifying the old, stagnant nations; and her plan is generally the same, namely, by war.

The thirteenth century stands out from the others as an epoch in the history of Europe and Asia. For the first time the two continents were brought into close contact. The pouring of the Mongols into Europe, and of the Crusaders into Asia, were comparatively small events when considering the immense influences brought

MONGOLS MOVING CAMP.

to bear on Europe by the sudden opening up of that vast world vaguely known as "The East." Yet the part the Mongols played in producing this Renaissance must be accounted to their credit. The Mongols may have been a scourge in appearance, but they were also a blessing in disguise. China's existence as an Empire for so much longer than any other nation, is entirely resultant from her record-history of changes of dynasty, revolutions and disasters. At the time of the Mongol invasion China was at its lowest ebb, but with the reign of Kublai Khan, her first Mongol Emperor, China sprang into new life, and this period is marked as an epoch of vigorous endeavour and rejuvenescence.

In the West it was the same. The influence of the feudal institutions and many intestinal wars had rendered Europe weak and inert; but the sudden appearance of innumerable hosts of Asiatics who threatened to eat up the whole continent, who forced Europe to take combined action, and who, incidentally, brought about a regular communication between Europe and Asia, was, no doubt, a great force in awakening Europe into new life. The Mongols did their service to mankind and then disappeared. The meteor-like career of the nomads seemed supernatural in its entirety from beginning to end. Their armies disappeared as suddenly as they had been called into being. Like the dying out of some plague, the Mongol Peril sank into nothingness. Yet in Mongolia, the old home of the race, there still remains the residue of the ancient clan who thus once disturbed the world.

We possess few records of the Mongols at their period of greatness, their actual character and habits at that time being only slightly known to us; for the Mongols, like other nomads, left no records of their achievements. Their Empire was entirely ephemeral, their far-reaching conquests had no lasting effect, and they disappeared as quietly and as quickly as they came into being. The existence, at the present day, of poor degenerate tribes of Mongols inhabiting isolated localities scattered across Asia, and even in Eastern Europe, shows roughly the extent of their ancient kingdom. Their amazing conquests and their extraordinary activity are brought strongly before us by the existence of the Great Wall of China—that tribute to their valour and strength. It is almost incredible, considering the present-day condition of the Mongols, that the stupendous labour which the building of the Great Wall entailed was undertaken simply in order to prevent the barbaric hordes of Mongols from overrunning China.

The existence of the Mogul Empire in India is another proof of the ambition of the Mongols and of their remarkable success in the days of their power. Yet nothing of this Empire remains in India, to show that its origin was Mongol; for there, as in other countries they conquered, their personalities have been entirely absorbed by local influences. Besides these few outward signs of Mongol power, we have some rough accounts handed down to us from the thirteenth century, in which we may read of the great days of the Mongols and of the manner in which these people impressed Europeans.

It was not until the early part of the thirteenth century that Mongolia began to thrust itself upon the attention of the Western peoples. Although the Mongols had already overrun Asia from the Pacific to the Black Sea, and although mighty upheavals had shaken the foundations of the Eastern kingdoms, Europe, in spite of these great movements, remained undisturbed and indifferent, apparently quite unaware of the great Mongol advance. Not until the eastern portions were assailed and the very heart of Europe threatened did the ruling Powers seem to realize the existence of the Mongol Peril. The ignorance which existed in Europe in those days as to the peoples of Asia is shown by the reports, stories, and legends which flew in advance of the onward-moving hosts of Tartars. For extravagance and romance these tales could scarcely be equalled. The sudden appearance of the Mongols on the edge of Europe awoke her to new life and created lively interest in these unwelcomed invaders. Who were these innumerable hosts of savage men who came from the uttermost East, and who were never sated with conquest?

The following is one of the earliest descriptions of the Mongols as given to Europe in the thirteenth century[1]:

"That the joys of men be not enduring, nor worldly happiness long lasting without lamentations," wrote Matthew Paris, "in this same year [*i.e.* 1240], a detestable native of Satan, to wit, the countless army of Tartars, broke loose from its mountain-environed home. . . . Swarming like locusts over the face of the earth, they have wrought terrible devastation to the eastern parts [of Europe], laying it waste with fire and carnage. They are inhuman and beastly, rather monsters than men, thirsting for and drinking blood, tearing and devouring the flesh of dogs and men, dressed in ox-hides, armed with plates of iron, short and stout, thick-set,

[1] Matthew Paris, as quoted in the Hakluyt Society's edition of *The Journey of William Rubruck*.

strong, invincible, indefatigable, their backs unprotected, their breasts covered with armour; drinking with delight the pure blood of their flocks, with big, strong horses, which eat branches and even trees, and which they have to mount by the help of three steps on account of the shortness of their thighs. They are without human laws, know no comforts, are more ferocious than lions or bears. . . . They spare neither age, sex, nor conditions. They know no other language than their own, which no one else knows; for until now there has been no access to them, nor did they go forth [from their own country]; so there could be no knowledge of their customs or persons through the common intercourse of men. They wander about with their flocks and their wives, who are taught to fight like men. And so they came with the swiftness of lightning to the confines of Christendom, ravaging and slaughtering, striking every one with terror and incomparable horror."

This was the reputation the Mongols enjoyed when their name first reached Europe, and created the terror which foreran their advance. The very name of the Tartars made men shudder. They were put down as a "scourge from God"; old writers refer to them as a "visitation from God, demons who had been sent to chastise mankind." Europe did not look on the Mongols as human enemies or as a common foe, but as something supernatural. Men then believed the Mongols had heads like dogs and fed on human flesh! Such wild terror spread through Europe in advance of the Tartars and the threatening danger was taken so seriously, that the Danish fishermen dared not put to sea for fear of the Mongols!

It was the same in the Farthest East as in the Farthest

MONGOL CAVALIERS

West—on the shores of the Pacific as on the North Sea. A Chinese historian of the period exclaims with disgust, that "since the commencement of the world no nation has ever been as powerful as the Mongols are at present. They annihilate empires as one tears up grass. Why does Heaven permit it?" Another writer describes the result of Mongol supremacy in significant terms when he remarks that "In Asia and eastern Europe scarcely a dog might bark without Mongol leave."

So overwhelming was the Mongol flood which, sweeping across Asia, arrived at the gates of Eastern Europe, that the rulers of Europe began at last to consult each other, as to what they should do. Combined action must be resorted to, to stay such a human flood, no single kingdom could resist by itself alone. Nothing so clearly shows the fear which the Mongol hordes inspired in the hearts of the greatest European kingdoms, as the appeal made by the Emperor Frederik II., the Holy Roman Emperor, to Christendom, in order to repel the invasion of the terrible Mongols. Imagine a letter being addressed "to Germany, ardent in battle; to France, who nurses in her bosom an intrepid soldiery; to warlike Spain; to England, powerful by its warriors and its ships; to Crete, to Sicily, to savage Hibernia, to frozen Norway," in order to raise an international crusade against the nomad invaders from Far Mongolia!

Extracts from this letter will give a fair idea of the Mongol terror as it appeared in 1240. "A people," the Emperor continued, "issuing from the uttermost parts of the world, where they had long been hidden under a frightful climate, has suddenly and violently seized on the countries of the north, and multiplied there like grasshoppers. One knows not whence this savage race derives the name of Tartar, but it is not without a manifest judgment of God that they have been reserved from these latter times, as a chastisement for the sins of men and, perhaps, for the destruction of Christendom. This ferocious and barbarous nation knows nothing of the laws of humanity. They have, however, a chief whom they venerate, and whose orders they blindly obey, calling him the God of earth. These men are short and thick-set, but strong, hardy, of immovable firmness, and, at the least sign from their chief, rushing with impetuous valour into the midst of perils of every kind. They have broad faces, eyes set obliquely, and they utter the most frightful cries and yells, which correspond but too well with the feelings of their hearts. They have no other clothing than the hides of oxen, asses, and horses, and, up to the present time, they have had no other armour than rough and ill-joined plates of iron. But already—and we cannot utter it without a groan—they are beginning to equip themselves better, from the spoils of Christians; and soon the wrath of God will perhaps permit us to be shamefully massacred with our own weapons. The Tartars are mounted on the finest horses, and they now feed on the most dainty viands, and dress richly and with care. They are incomparable archers. It is said that their horses, when they have no other forage, will feed on the leaves, bark, and roots of trees, and that they are, notwithstanding, full of spirit, strength, and agility."

The Mongols, at a distance of 4,000 miles from their native land, within thirty years after their first small, unambitious forays, had acquired this remarkable and, no doubt, deserving, reputation. They had stamped fear into the hearts of all men from China to Hungary,

A MONGOL GIRL.

they were ruthless in their dealings, they were born warriors, peculiarly suited to campaigning in open plain-lands; they were hardened to all privations, were in absolute obedience under their chiefs, and apparently no power could stop their advance or hinder the eventual subjugation of Europe. The rough, simple nomads of the far eastern steppes had grown during these few years of wandering and campaigning into a warrior race.

The Mongols were in those days the finest troops that could possibly be produced for Asiatic warfare. By birth they were wanderers, by nature the most mobile horsemen; they wanted little and lived on little, and were inured to hardship and fatigue. Carpini remarked: "They are also very hardie, and when they have fasted a day or two without any manner of subsistence, they sing and are merrie as if they had eaten their bellies full"! Every man was a warrior, and their number was great. They held manly virtues and martial valour in the highest esteem. The Mongol bards sang of the great bodily strength of Jenghis—their leader—rather than of his victories. They "vaunted in their songs the loudness of his voice, which sounded like thunder in the mountains, and the strength of his hands, like the paws of a bear, which could break a man in two as easily as an arrow." For sheer bravery, blind obedience, and physical endurance the Mongols have earned a recognition from all writers. In those days the race must have been virile, strong, and of good physique. The many different tribes must have been bound together by a common power, forming a great brotherhood of irresistible strength, with one aim and object, namely, to conquer, to slay, and to destroy all that came in their way.

As the hordes moved westwards and came in contact with civilized kingdoms, they began to ape the show and magnificence of the countries they conquered. Wealth, treasure, and luxury were suddenly placed within their grasp, and they scarcely knew what to do with it, the more recent accounts showing that the encampments of the Mongol chiefs led to a display and extravagance most unsuited to their rough nature. It is amusing to read Carpini's account of the splendour of the scene on the occasion of the election of the Grand Khan after the death of Jenghis. But it also proves once more the immense influence and far-reaching power of the Mongols at the height of their rule, and thus compares strangely with their latter decadence.

" This convocation," Huc relates, " had set in motion all the Tartar princes of Asia, and the roads that led from all parts of the continent to the centre of Tartary were covered with travellers." He then enumerates all the princes of blood that came with their military escorts, the governors of the Mongol possessions in China, the governor-generals of Persia, of Turkestan, and Trans-Oxiana, the Grand-duke of Russia, two contending Princes of Georgia, ambassadors from the Caliph of Bagdad—all bringing magnificent offerings, and rivalling one another in the richness and pomp of their equipments. " The merchants of Persia, India, and China flocked thither in great numbers, with the more precious productions of the various countries of the East." The Imperial tent of the great Khan was " crimson and gold, and had been made in China. On a circular divan was raised a throne of ivory, elaborately carved and enriched with gold and precious stones," and " it was a marvel to see the great quantity of presents given to the Khan by ambassadors; silks, samites, purples, balakins, silk girdles worked in gold, splendid furs, and other things." Here also it was that a kind of umbrella or awning that is carried over the Emperor's head was presented to him, and "it was all covered with precious stones." This took place at the Court of the Khan in Northern Mongolia in the wild nomad's land, where these same Mongols had, but a short time before, pastured their flocks in comparative poverty.

It is unnecessary to give further examples of the prowess, power, pride and might which the Mongols possessed seven hundred years ago. The Mongol Empire which stretched from Cathay to Central Europe was gigantic, the greatest ever built up by a single man, and in so short a period of time. Their amazing rise to power admits of no doubt, and was as unmistakable as the suddenness of their fall. The ephemeral Empire soon crumbled to pieces, and by slow degrees the Mongols, as a people, disappeared from all parts of Asia outside their own country of Mongolia.

If exaggerated, as no doubt these first accounts of the Mongols were, yet it is certain that these people not only held the uppermost hand in Asia, but even dictated terms to European princes. We wish to gauge the true value of the Mongol power in the thirteenth century, and the significance of these accounts surely proves our contention that the Western nations were compelled to join forces in order to expel the Mongols from Europe, and that the Mongol power was so great as to terrify the world, and to come near to conquering it. It is this fact that fills us with amazement at the sudden disappearance of those powerful nomad people. Where are now the Mongol armies? To what low number have their countless hosts dwindled? What remains to be seen of the widespread Empire of Jenghis? This race which, at one time, was said "to eat up Empires like grass," is now only to be found in the bleak and far-distant land of its birth, the warriors have returned to the simple life of a pastoral people, and there is no trace left of any desire to foster wars or to carry arms into a foreign land.

Let us now look at the Mongols of the present day. The traveller in Mongolia, alive to the history and former greatness of the people who dwell there, will recognize much at the present day that corresponds to those old accounts of the Mongols as here quoted. He will note that they are still hardy, still capable of enduring fatigue, cold, and hunger; so far, indeed, as physique goes, the Mongol of to-day is probably the equal of the men Jenghis Khan led to battle. They appear to live the same kind of life under the same physical conditions; but a most significant difference is to be noticed in the social and economic welfare of the people. Instead of being turbulent tribesmen held by military allegiance to their chieftains, instead of being a people who represented as a whole a great brotherhood with both ideas and wealth in common, they are now the serfs of their rulers, downtrodden, overtaxed, and bereft of that energy, fearlessness, and warlike spirit with which once they astonished the world.

Another fact of the greatest importance is that the Mongol has changed his religion, whilst the alteration which has taken place in the social conditions of the Mongols during the last six hundred years, has brought about a transformation which results in an economic exhaustion of the country. In studying these changes

A DURBET MONGOL.

which have taken place we are faced by the ever-recurring question as to the *cause* of the Mongol decadence. Several influences seem to be at work, such as a change for the worse in climate, the innovation of a new religion, and the burden of a foreign yoke. Each of these we will consider, for they best show the present state of the Mongols, in comparison with their past.

A deterioration in the pastoral wealth of Mongolia, owing to a change in its climatic conditions, is a possible reason for the exhaustion of the Mongol race. Judging from Professor Huntington's observations in Chinese Turkestan, which prove the greater aridity Central Asia experiences now, than in the past, it would be reasonable to suppose that the same conditions extend farther across Asia into Mongolia. We ourselves noted, in a significant manner, an obviously diminished rainfall as proved by the strands of ancient lake-beds. There is not the least doubt that a large area of Northern Mongolia, now very poor pasture-land, might, with a slightly greater summer rainfall, be greatly improved. A wide zone of country situated between the true Gobi and the mountain border-lands, has been affected by this decrease in rainfall. Rolling hill-country, rising out of the desert plains, extends over an immense area all along the southern borders of Outer Mongolia, all of which must have been utilized, in the old days, by the Mongol tribes. The addition of this hill-country, lying between the altitudes of 4,000 ft. and 6,000 ft., to the present available pasture-land, means almost doubling the area capable of supporting human beings, and yet this area is, at the present day, not looked upon as a grazing country.

That Mongolia has lost much good country does not

do away with the fact that the present population fails to fill the available lands. There is much unoccupied land in Mongolia. In making this statement I incur a responsibility, in that I am stating only the results of our own observations. The local conditions we experienced may not be universal in Mongolia. I only speak of the north-western portion; some further investigations are necessary before any definite conclusion can be reached. The case in point, namely, the Turgun highlands, and the extent of grazing those mountains afforded, supplemented by the proportion of land in occupation and of land untenanted, is worthy of record. We visited those regions towards the end of the summer, the season when Asiatic nomads are encamped at the highest altitude to which they ever ascend. Yet, in spite of this, and although this district was in the very heart of an area in the possession of a powerful and numerically superior tribe, we found a very large portion of the upland pastures unoccupied and apparently unused. Farther west we hunted for a week in the most magnificent grazing country, and never saw even a flock of sheep or a drove of horses. From this I argue that the poverty of the Mongols is not caused through lack of good country, for they could even increase and multiply, if they were able to do so, without having any occasion to enlarge their borders.

Turning to the question of the weight of a foreign yoke, which is often put forward as a reason for the retrogression of certain peoples, it is a fact of great significance that the Mongols have never been subject to great oppression on the part of their rulers, the Manchus, who preserved intact their rights, forbad the colonization and purchase of their lands by Chinamen, and kept the Mongols in quiet, untroubled peace. The Manchu yoke, up till quite recent times, has been a light one; the Mongols, as in the old days, have been left under the direct rule of their own chieftains, over the chieftains there being only an agent of the Chinese Government who acts as intermediary between the chiefs and the Pekin officials.

Of late years, however, with the denationalization of the Manchus, the Chinese have become more energetic and more eager to advance their interests in Mongolia. With an increasing population at home, and an ever-growing desire on the part of innumerable agriculturists to seek new homes beyond the Great Wall, there has begun a slow but sure colonization of all available land suitable for agriculture. Northwards creep the eager bands of tenacious Chinese colonists. They have passed the boundaries into Inner Mongolia, they have taken up land and pushed back the indigenous Mongols, they have even crossed the desert zone dividing Inner from Outer Mongolia, and started with eagerness on the most inviting lands lying along the Mongol frontiers of Siberia. These colonists are state-aided, they are forwarded to their destination by government help. They are not only farmers and agriculturists, but merchants with a keen eye to gain, and with intentions to dupe the unsophisticated Mongol herdsmen. Thus, all the wealth of Mongolia that does not go to Siberia is drained off by Chinese middlemen into Chinese markets; the sheep and cattle, for instance, which supply the markets of northern China, are bought up at small expense by the Chinese in Mongolia, and sold at immense profit in the home provinces. In spite of the opening up of Mongolia, the Mongols themselves profit nothing by it. It is said that the Chinese have even got hold of the small areas of cultivated lands in Mongolia, and are gradually dispossessing the princes of their property, by their iniquitous methods of money-lending.

China has undoubtedly become more prominent in Mongolia in recent years; the presence of a more virile and a more go-ahead people may have acted like a blight upon the Mongols. The decadence of the nomads, however, cannot be put down to a despotic and harsh foreign rule. Even the two years' conscription to which the Mongols are liable, the upkeep of the frontier guard-houses, the supply of transport for travellers and food for men on government service, as well as the tax demanded of them, would not in themelves cause excessive poverty, had they not other demands forced upon them, more. inexorable and continuous than these taxes due to their masters. It is, moreover, some cause deeper than that of mere poverty that we hope to discern, such as the cause for the decline of the birth-rate, or the mysterious influence which has been at work amongst the Mongols and changed them from proud, overbearing warriors to peace-loving, unambitious shepherds.

If a Mongol contemporary of Jenghis Khan came back to life he would find himself at home amongst the present-day Mongols. His clothes would be in fashion, the tent-life would appear the same, as also the herding of the beasts and the routine of everyday life. But, on the other hand, he would note one great change, which he would, at first, be altogether at a loss to understand. He would be surprised at the lack of young men working round the encampments, a lack of herdsmen tending the flocks; and in place of the noisy groups of hard-working men to whom he was accustomed, he would find a strange

YOUNG LAMAS.

MONGOLS LOADING UP OXEN.

but numerous element of men dressed in garments of a style unknown to him, lounging idly in yurts which did not belong to them, and in encampments where they apparently had no business. Our Mongol of the thirteenth century, visiting the Mongolia of to-day, would be also surprised at the numerous buildings which have sprung up since his day at every centre of Mongol life: buildings called lamaseries, where hosts of idle men live under the same roof. On inquiring, he would find that these buildings represented the temples of a new faith, and he would quickly realize that his Shamanistic ideas were ideas of the past, that this new faith had taken the place of the old. He would then understand why there existed no longer those bands of rough horsemen, exercising their prowess and keeping themselves fit for active service, for their places had been taken by these strange, yellow-robed priests, who were careful to preserve life, and who were advocates for peace, not war.

In short, the one supreme difference in the life of present-day Mongolia which has come about since the thirteenth century is the innovation of a powerful religious organization, which has made itself a power in the land equal to, or even greater, than that exercised formerly by the warrior chiefs. To the influence of this religious element, I feel I am right in attributing the great change in the Mongols of the present day. When we come to examine the doctrines advocated by the teachings of Lamaism, and when we realize the immense power which, by slow degrees, this organization has gained control of, until, as now, it represents the great social factor in the life of the Mongols, we shall not be surprised that the character of the Mongols has changed.

Lamaism in Mongolia has been countenanced, and in every way encouraged, by the Chinese, who were clever enough to realize the influence such an organization would exercise over the nomad people. The Chinese patronized and endowed the monasteries, and granted special privileges to the lamas, well knowing that, so long as they influenced the priests, neither the people nor the chiefs would give any trouble. This is the best proof as to what is the primary cause of the evolution in the character of the Mongols between the sixteenth century and the present day. From the earliest days of recorded history the Chinese have endeavoured to control the aggressive tribes along her Mongolian borderlands, but she had no success until this vital force—religion—came to her aid, and softened, in a few years, the vigorous warlike spirits and predatory habits of the Mongols. Never was there a more potent influence for peace introduced amongst a fighting race. The very essence of this religion is tranquillity. Where arms failed, Lamaism succeeded; a few years after the introduction of Buddhism the warriors turned priests, and the Mongols became subject to the Chinese.

The change is now complete. The men whose ancestors were the vilest butchers of their fellow-men in the history of the world, who were the most blood-thirsty of warriors, now, under the influence of Buddhism, scruple to take a human life, and even hold sacred the lives of animals and insects! Buddhism also teaches indifference to advance, learning, enterprise, and success; it has the effect of stifling ambition, and is, therefore, in a great measure, responsible for retrogression amongst a people.

Nor is the evil effect of Lamaism one which affects

the mental conditions only; it has even greater influence on physical conditions. Lamaism absorbs a large portion of the male population by inducing a vast majority of men, who under ordinary conditions of life would be the bread-winners and workers, to turn into a species of parasite. The boys, for instance, who in the earlier days devoted their time to martial and physical exercises, camp-work, or herding the flocks, are now entered at an early age as students in the lamaseries, and their lives are entirely sacrificed to the forms and services of religion; when grown up, this tends to make them lead idle, useless lives, wholly dependent on others, when they should be independent and self-supporting. This great army of lamas is the burden of Mongolia. There exists a constant struggle on the part of the laymen to provide their parasitic brethren with the best of the produce. The indolent life of the lamaseries becomes the life of the people as a whole, and inertia becomes their chief characteristic. The lama himself need never work, all his needs being provided for him; he is even exempt from military service, which is compulsory for the Mongols. This exemption may in itself be a great inducement for the Mongols to enter the religious profession, military service having become so distasteful to them that even those who are liable to be called upon often try to evade it through bribery. The observant Prjevalsky remarks that the Chinese officials are content that this should be so, for it proves that the martial spirit of the nomads, which once they stood in dread of, is year by year becoming extinct.

Another factor, which must not be overlooked in reviewing the influence of Lamaism over the Mongols, is that produced by the supposed celibacy of almost half of the male population. This may not, in itself, greatly lessen the birth-rate; but the fact, as mentioned above, of so many men being idle weakens the economic condition by limiting the increase of the herds and thereby decreasing the resources of the country. So great is this decrease that Mongolia shows an excess of population beyond its resources, resulting naturally in want, poverty, and perhaps an artificially reduced birth-rate.

From these arguments there seems to be no doubt that the influence of Lamaism has robbed the Mongols of their bravery, and has softened their character, and there exists equal proof that in Lamaism lies the chief cause of the present poverty-stricken state of the nomad tribes. As another and additional proof of this we have an example of a tribe living near by, who are neither Buddhists nor, by any means, decadent. Side by side with the Mongols, and living under the same environment, is the Turkish tribe of Kirei-Kirghiz, a nomad people whose mode of life exactly resembles that of the Mongols, but whose state of well-being and continued progress stands in direct contrast to that of the Mongols—these Kerei being *Mohammedans*.

We visited Mongolia before the Revolution of 1911; since that date surprising changes have taken place in the political situation of Outer Mongolia. At the present moment the future of this country appears to hang in the balance. During the present year, the power of the Manchu has fallen, the suzerainty of the new party has been questioned, and even repudiated. The Revolution in China has given the opportunity for the Mongol tribesmen to strike for independence;

MONGOL HAGS.

KIREI MATRONS.

for the Mongols argue that they are vassals of the Manchu Emperors, and if the Manchus are dethroned there is no reason why they should unconditionally accept Chinese rule instead. This step taken by the Mongols arouses the suspicion that these people are not so effete nor so incapable as might be supposed.

In spite of the fact that the authorities, both temporal and spiritual, were dependent upon Chinese support, both these powers have demanded independence from the Chinese. No doubt this is largely due to the recent high-handed action of the Government in dealing with the Mongols, which destroyed the loyalty of the Mongol Princes and drove them to seek outside help. Added to this grievance were the increased efforts China has made to establish herself more surely on her northern frontiers, the introduction of a Chinese garrison, the enlistment of Mongol troops, and especially the abolition of the law forbidding the colonization of Mongolia by Chinamen. No grievance so quickly stirs a nomad people into discontent and revolt as the slow enclosing of their prairies, and the transformation of pasture-lands into arable. The chiefs felt that their powers were not only decreasing, but were likely to altogether disappear, should the Chinese persist in their policy; the people, of course, upholding the views of the chiefs. The exact position of the Church is not so clear, for in time to come a Russianization of Mongolia would inevitably tend to weaken the powers of the spiritual authorities, and to an impoverishment of the lamaseries.

Taking for granted an autonomous Mongolia under the protection of Russia,[1] we can prophesy far-reaching and fundamental changes in the lives of the people and in

[1] For text of Russian-Mongol Protocol, see Appendix.

the future of the Mongol race. Mongolia will become—indeed, probably has already become—a land of activity and progress instead of, as formerly, a land of stagnation and suppression. Russian merchants will flock into the country, railways will be constructed, vacant land will be used for agricultural purposes, and waste-land reclaimed. There will be facilities for trade, which will prove advantageous to the Mongols as well as the Russians. In regard to the future of the Mongols, the impression we gained is an encouraging one. The bulk of the population is of fine material, and with fair dealing a future might be made for the Mongol herdsmen. No race could exist for any great length of time under such severe conditions of life as above described, joined to the continual demands on its resources made by the chiefs, the Government, and the Church.

The exploiting of the mineral wealth of Mongolia by Russia will, in itself, be an innovation of great moment, and will have an immense effect on the attitude of the people towards their rulers. It has been a divine law, since the days of Kublai Khan in the thirteenth century, that no man, under pain of death, should dig in the earth and extract treasure. China has upheld this law. Only the Government and the Princes of the Church—reincarnations of Buddha—have the right to deal with precious metals; for generations this monopoly has been meekly accepted by the Mongol races. But now this tradition will be broken through, and there will be a reversal of the divine law of the Tibetan Buddha. Foreigners will work gold-reefs, with the result that Chinese suzerainty and the Church will lose no small amount of prestige. With this new movement and activity the old lethargy will no doubt decrease, and, we hope, eventually disappear. The demands on the people will decrease, they will be free from Chinese tribute and from the extortionate demands of an overwhelming population of lamas. Lamaism must in itself be weakened, for under Russian rule only 20 per cent. of the male population are permitted to take up the religious profession.

In this connexion we have a precedent in the history of the Buriats, a Mongol people under Russian rule in Siberia, who are also Buddhists, and whose example, if followed, gives cause for hope as to the future of the Mongols. The Buriats, since their enrolment in the Russian Empire, cultivate the soil, engage in various trades, learn the Russian language, acquire positions in the Government service, occasionally embrace Christianity, and are remarkably prosperous and well off. The result of the new Russian-Mongolian Protocol will be the gaining by Russia of the use of a valuable land, while the Mongolians will have a near and certain market for their produce, and the friendship of traders and farmers who understand them and are far more in sympathy with them than are the Chinese.

The Russian influence has obviously an advantage over that of the Chinese. The Russians fraternize with the Mongol races, the race-barrier between them being much less marked than that between the Chinese and the Mongols. It is reasonable to hope that the Mongols may in time to come fall under this same influence, and by these means we may anticipate the lessening of the principal burden of Mongolia—the tyranny of the lamaseries,—which tyranny we have already proved to be the primary cause of the decadence of the Mongol race.

We can well imagine these people living under new conditions, coming back to new life, born again, as it were, as a respectable and well-to-do nomad people, and playing the part of a buffer-state between the two great Empires of Russia and China.

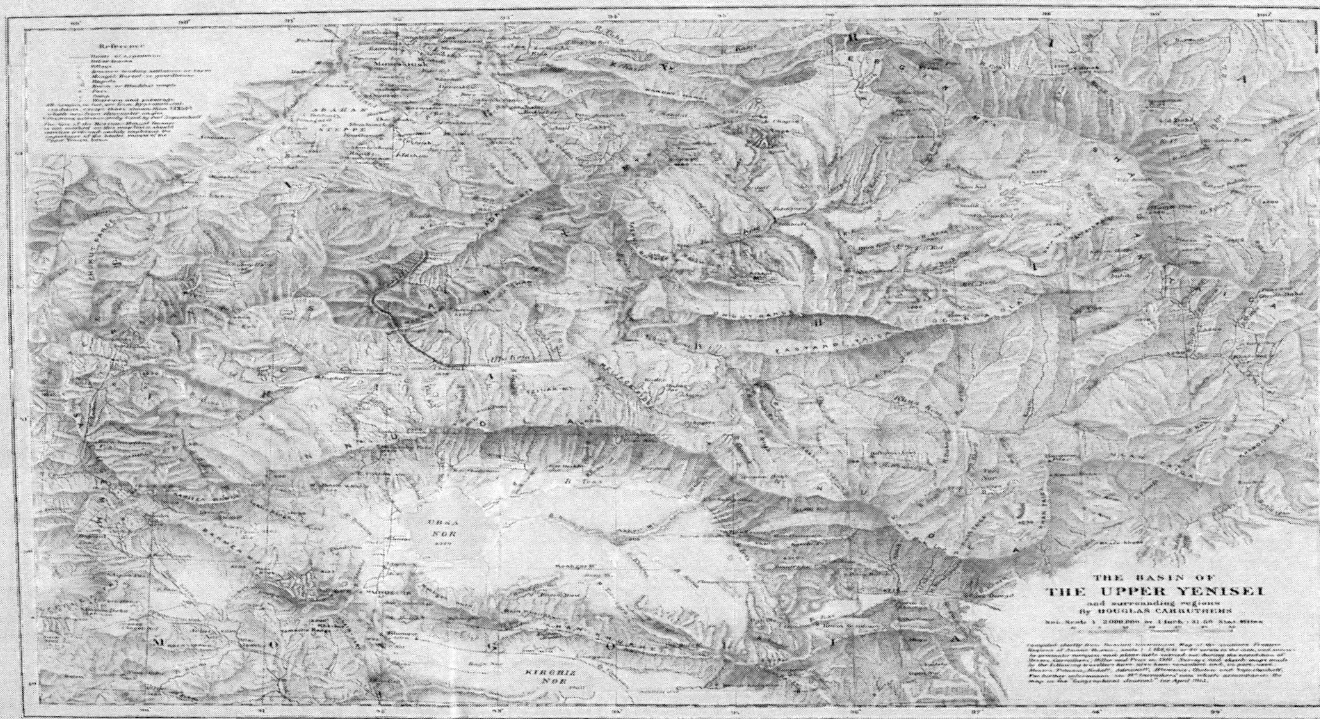

THE UPPER YENISEI
CARRUTHERS